Social History in Perspective
General Editor: Jeremy Black

Social History in Perspective is a series of in-depth studies of the many topics in social, cultural and religious history for students. They also give the student clear surveys of the subject and present the most recent research in the most accessible way.

John Belchem *... ntury Britain*
Simon Dentith *... entury England*
Harr... *...nce 1945*
...00–1800
...stuart Britain
He... *...rly Modern England*
Hugh M... *...ety in England, 1850–1914*
Donald M. M... *...nts in Modern Britain, 1750–1922*
Christopher ... *...ar Religion in the Sixteenth Century*
Michael A. Mu... *...nolics in Britain and Ireland, 1558–1829*
R. Malcolm Smu... *Culture and Power in England, 1585–1685*
John Spurr *English Puritanism, 1603–1689*
W.B. Stephens *Education in Britain, 1750–1914*
David Taylor *Crime, Policing and Punishment in England, 1750–1914*
N.L. Tranter *British Population in the Twentieth Century*
Ian D. Whyte *Scotland's Society and Economy in Transition, c.1500–c.1760*

FORTHCOMING

Eric Acheson *Late Medieval Economy and Society*
Ian Archer *Rebellion and Riot in England, 1360–1660*
Jonathan Barry *Religion and Society in England, 1603–1760*
A.L. Beier *Early Modern London*
Sue Bruley *Women's Century of Change*
Andrew Charlesworth *Popular Protest in Britain and Ireland, 1650–1870*
Richard Connors *The Growth of Welfare in Hanoverian England, 1723–1793*
Geoffrey Crossick *A History of London from 1800 to 1939*
Alistair Davies *Culture and Society, 1900–1995*
Martin Durham *The Permissive Society*
Peter Fleming *Medieval Family and Household England*
David Fowler *Youth Culture in the Twentieth Century*
Malcolm Gaskill *Witchcraft in England, 1560–1760*
Peter Gosden *Education in the Twentieth Century*
S.J.D. Green *Religion and the Decline of Christianity in Modern Britain, 1880–1980*

Titles continued overleaf

List continued from previous page

Paul Griffiths *English Social Structure and the Social Order, 1500–1750*
Anne Hardy *Health and Medicine since 1860*
Steve Hindle *The Poorer Sort of People in Seventeenth-Century England*
David Hirst *Welfare and Society, 1832–1939*
Anne Kettle *Social Structure in the Middle Ages*
Alan Kidd *The State and the Poor, 1834–1914*
Peter Kirby and S.A. King *British Living Standards, 1700–1870*
Arthur J. McIvor *Working in Britain 1880–1950*
Anthony Milton *Church and Religion in England, 1603–1642*
Christine Peters *Women in Early Modern Britain, 1450–1660*
Barry Reay *Rural Workers, 1830–1930*
Richard Rex *Heresy and Dissent in England, 1360–1560*
John Rule *Labour and the State, 1700–1875*
Pamela Sharpe *Population and Society in Britain, 1750–1900*
Heather Swanson *Medieval British Towns*
Benjamin Thompson *Feudalism or Lordship and Politics in Medieval England*
R.E. Tyson *Population in Pre-Industrial Britain, 1500–1750*
Garthine Walker *Crime, Law and Society in Early Modern England*
Andy Wood *The Crowd and Popular Politics in Early Modern England*

Please note that a sister series, *British History in Perspective*, is available which covers all the key topics in British political history.

CULTURE AND POWER IN ENGLAND, 1585–1685

R. Malcolm Smuts

Professor of History
University of Massachusetts at Boston

MACMILLAN

© R. Malcolm Smuts 1999

All rights reserved. No reproduction, copy or transmission of
this publication may be made without written permission.

No paragraph of this publication may be reproduced, copied or
transmitted save with written permission or in accordance with
the provisions of the Copyright, Designs and Patents Act 1988,
or under the terms of any licence permitting limited copying
issued by the Copyright Licensing Agency, 90 Tottenham Court
Road, London W1P 9HE.

Any person who does any unauthorised act in relation to this
publication may be liable to criminal prosecution and civil
claims for damages.

The author has asserted his right to be identified
as the author of this work in accordance with the
Copyright, Designs and Patents Act 1988.

First published 1999 by

MACMILLAN PRESS LTD
Houndmills, Basingstoke, Hampshire RG21 6XS
and London
Companies and representatives
throughout the world

ISBN 0–333–60629–9 hardcover
ISBN 0–333–60630–2 paperback

A catalogue record for this book is available
from the British Library.

This book is printed on paper suitable for recycling and
made from fully managed and sustained forest sources.

10 9 8 7 6 5 4 3 2 1
08 07 06 05 04 03 02 01 00 99

Typeset in Great Britain by
Aarontype Ltd, Easton, Bristol

Printed in Hong Kong

Published in the United States of America by
ST. MARTIN'S PRESS, INC.,
Scholarly and Reference Division
175 Fifth Avenue, New York, N.Y. 10010

ISBN 0–312–22327–7 (cloth)
ISBN 0–312–22328–5 (paper)

To my parents, Alice Boardman Smuts and
Robert W. Smuts,
who first gave me my love of history

Contents

List of illustrations	ix
Acknowledgements	xi
1 Frames of Reference	**1**
Cultural History and Seventeenth-century Politics	1
Honour	8
Law	17
Providentialism	27
Humanism and the Imitation of Antiquity	32
2 Political Imagination, *c.* 1585–1640	**41**
Religious Conflict and Invented Traditions	41
Cults of Authority, Royal and Otherwise	50
Faction, Rebellion and Violence	65
Court, Country and Town	78
Classicism, Nostalgia and Cultural Rhetoric	95
3 From Civil War to Tory Reaction	**99**
Civil War Cultural History after Revisionism	99
Print and the Dissemination of Controversy	106
Millenarianism, Republicanism and Cromwellianism	123
An Ambiguous Restoration	133
The Renewal of Partisanship	137
Society, Culture and Politics	139
The Crisis of 1679–81 and the Hardening of Partisan Cultures	150
Notes and References	156
Select Bibliography	185
Index	193

List of Illustrations

1. Jan Siberechts, *Wollaton Hall and Park, Nottinghamshire*, a great house of the 1580s as it appeared in 1697. Copyright Yale Center for British Art, Paul Mellon Collection. *page 9*
2. British School, sixteenth century, *Sir William Drury*. Copyright Yale Center for British Art, Paul Mellon Collection. *page 14*
3. Title page of Thomas Scott, *The Second Part of Vox Populi* (1624), showing the Spanish ambassador, Gondomar, as a Machiavel. Copyright the British Library. *page 49*
4. The funeral of Sir Philip Sidney, as depicted by Thomas Lant, *Sequitur celebritas et pompa funeris...Philippus Sidneis* (1587), plate 19. Copyright the British Library. *page 64*
5. *Heraclitus Dream* (1642), a satire of sectarian and anti-clerical agitation. Copyright the British Library. *page 112*
6. *The Sucklington Faction or Suckling's Roaring Boys* (1642), an early satire of the Cavalier. Copyright the British Library. *page 114*
7. Engraving of Sir John Hotham, commander of the garrison at Hull. A parliamentarian image of the virtuous gentleman soldier. Copyright the British Library. *page 115*

Acknowledgements

The author wishes to thank Jeremy Black for helpful comments on the text, Maureen Dwyer for assistance with some of the typing, and Arthur Kinney and his colleagues and students at the Massachusetts Center for Renaissance Studies, for providing a congenial interdisciplinary environment while this book was being written.

1
FRAMES OF REFERENCE

Cultural History and Seventeenth-century Politics

The culture and the politics of early modern England have both inspired prodigious quantities of scholarship. These subjects have normally been studied separately, however, by experts trained in different disciplines, employing different tools, asking different questions and often taking little notice of each other's preoccupations. The division partly reflects the specialization that always develops in densely populated fields of research. But it also stems from modern assumptions that the late Renaissance did not entirely share. Since the nineteenth century, Western society has associated culture with leisure, aesthetics and spiritual values, while regarding governance as practical work. Even when culture impinges upon politics, it is viewed as deriving from a different domain. Academic disciplines have reinforced this sense of separation by their distinctive methodologies, professional associations and journals.

Despite the obstacles, some interdisciplinary work has always been carried on, partly because the art and literature of the seventeenth century are so deeply enmeshed in its politics that a complete separation is impossible to maintain. In recent years developments in both history and literary studies have generated fresh interest in interdisciplinary perspectives. Debates over historical revisionism have ignited controversies over the role of principle and ideology, rejuvenating investigations of political ideas and culture. Meanwhile a reaction against the formalist methods of the New Criticism has led to a proliferation of historically oriented scholarship on literature. In some ways the current academic climate is unusually receptive to collaboration across disciplines.[1] Yet lack of agreement over fundamental assumptions and methodologies still impedes the emergence of a fully integrated approach.

The continued separation of seventeenth-century culture and politics will, however, only impoverish understanding of both. Governance always depends not only on administrative structures but systems of belief and cultural practices. This was arguably even more true in the seventeenth century, when the state's institutional machinery remained relatively weak and the need to maintain an aura of authority correspondingly great. In Elizabethan and Stuart England even brutally coercive acts of power, like the execution of felons, were highly theatrical events, conducted according to implicit cultural rules.[2] At all levels of society, power was supported by ceremonial, rhetorical and visual forms. The authority of householders over their wives, children and servants was reinforced not only by the arguments of moralists, but by communal sanctions like the ducking of female scolds and the ritualized shaming of henpecked husbands.[3] Gentry families asserted their pre-eminence through the splendour of their tombs and the architectural magnificence of their houses while, at the apex of the hierarchy, the royal court spent hundreds of thousands of pounds annually maintaining an apparatus of ceremonial and cultural display.

The point is not simply that cultural forms helped support political authority but that our ways of distinguishing between politics and culture do not correspond to early modern practices. In this period the pursuit of office still depended on royal favour and social alliances more than administrative competence or activity in Parliament. Such specialized political training as did exist was bound up with a humanist programme of linguistic and rhetorical education steeped in classical letters. Scholarship and literary skill were, therefore, often closely associated with political ambition, as any number of sixteenth- and seventeenth-century careers show.[4] Christopher Marlowe was a spy before he became a playwright, while Sidney, Spenser, Donne, Milton and Marvell all pursued governmental, rather than literary, careers. Conversely, monarchs and powerful courtiers had pronounced cultural interests that were much more than amusements. Elizabeth I's accomplishments as a linguist, James I's keen interest in theology and Charles I's habit of mixing diplomacy with art-collecting all provide examples. In this society the presentation of a poem or a painting was often a deeply political act, a way of soliciting patronage, cementing alliances, offering oblique advice or advertising one's talents.

Culture and politics need to be studied conjointly because they were both equally part of a single set of practices through which power operated. Separating them imposes anachronistic divisions upon the past. Linguistic usages demonstrate this clearly, especially for the earlier part of our period. The Elizabethans as yet had no word for either the later humanistic idea of culture (art, literature, music, aesthetic refinement), or the concept developed by modern anthropology (fundamental beliefs, myths and customs). Nor did they distinguish art from artisanship, which they normally valued for the ways it met specific social and ceremonial needs, rather than as a purely aesthetic pursuit. Literature meant literary and intellectual learning in general, rather than imaginative writing or a canon of especially esteemed texts, while politics usually referred to expertise in the mysterious arts of governance, rather than the pursuit of office or exercise of institutional authority. In that sense 'politics' was a subdivision of 'literature', a special kind of esoteric knowledge.[5]

The modern terminology in these areas is so deeply rooted that it would probably be futile to try to eliminate it from historical discourse, and no attempt has been made to do so here. But we need to recognize that a twentieth-century vocabulary can suggest sharp categorical distinctions that do not fit early modern patterns of thought and behaviour.[6]

The need for a new synthesis

This book represents one historian's attempt to explore the cultural dimensions of power and political dimensions of culture in England during the century separating the death of Sir Philip Sidney (1586) from that of Charles II (1685). Inevitably it presents a highly selective account of a vast subject. Culture and power operate and interpenetrate at all levels of society, from the international arena down to intimate relations between ordinary people. Examining their interactions thoroughly would mean including topics like the policing of morals in rural parishes and the theory and practice of marital relations. To impose some limitations on its material, this book will focus mainly on developments of national significance. At times more local and intimate perspectives will become necessary, however. Contemporaries were acutely aware that the power of kings and magistrates ultimately depended on practices and beliefs operating throughout society, among neighbours and family members. If only to understand their outlook, it is sometimes necessary to place 'high' culture and politics within broader contexts.

Because it lacks obvious boundaries our subject particularly requires disciplined efforts to map the terrain and establish methodological parameters. One way of achieving greater rigour is by focusing on specific topics. Many of the most successful recent essays in interdisciplinary cultural history have taken this approach and it is arguable that progress will be most readily achieved through case studies rather than attempts at generalization. Yet there are times when even a premature attempt at synthesis can be a useful way of posing questions and clarifying directions for future research. The history of Elizabethan and Stuart political culture has perhaps reached such a juncture. Old ways of unifying the subject, rooted in Whig, Marxist and other teleologies, no longer appear convincing, but adequate alternatives have not yet emerged to replace them. This situation has variously resulted in a tendency toward fragmentation or the stubborn persistence of outdated ideas that at least lend coherence to an unwieldy subject. The only way of moving beyond the impasse is to rethink our view of the period from the ground up, taking into account both current historiography and recent work in other disciplines. It is in the hope of stimulating such reconceptualization that this book has been written.

The conventional narrative of English culture in our period begins with a picture of an orthodox Elizabethan 'world picture' or ideology, which is progressively challenged by various forces of change, such as the spread of capitalism, constitutional conflict or the rise of secularism and modern science.[7] The climax to this contest arrives in a mid-seventeenth-century revolution, which brings about a fundamental and irreversible transformation to a more 'modern' environment, despite the persistence of some reactionary trends in the Restoration.

It will be argued here that such a view is fundamentally flawed for several reasons. It exaggerates certain kinds of change embedded in a retrospective account of the origins of modernity, while often minimizing other tensions, especially those deriving from religious conflicts ultimately rooted in a wider European situation. No sensible historian would seek to discount the effects of the Civil War and regicide in altering English culture in the later seventeenth century. Turning these events into the climactic moment of a much longer historical transition will, however, inevitably generate highly teleological interpretations or – if the teleology is removed – a static picture of the pre-war period, devoid of any real dynamic until political events intervene in the reign of Charles I. Both tendencies have appeared in recent historiography and both distort through a shared fixation on the mid-century political crisis. Rather than picturing Elizabethan and early Stuart cultural history as being pulled towards a revolutionary transformation, it is often more instructive to regard it as being pushed from behind by the unfinished business of the Reformation and European religious wars.

Another difficulty is that the enterprise of reconstructing a single dominant traditional ideology can easily impose more coherence than is warranted upon the historical evidence. Instead of a unified world picture, it is arguably more accurate to see Elizabethan culture as providing several alternative ways of thinking about power and authority, rooted in distinctive social, cultural and institutional traditions that had never been fully integrated. The nature of an Elizabethan's 'world picture' depended, to a considerable degree, on whether he was a lawyer, a theologian, an aristocratic soldier or a provincial gentleman. If we add the perspectives of poets, labourers and women, the situation becomes more complex still. The desire to define a single dominant orthodoxy – or a single dialectic between 'residual', 'dominant' and 'emergent' forms – reflects particular ways of seeing history, indebted to Hegelian and Marxist philosophy and, more generally, to a nineteenth-century fascination with contests between traditional and revolutionary ideals, after the great cataclysm of 1789. This is not the best lens through which to view the very different historical landscape of the period around 1600.

Languages and frames of reference

A useful starting point, in attempting to develop a less teleological cultural history, is the method of studying political languages developed by Quentin Skinner, J. G. A. Pocock and their followers. These historians attempt to reconstruct the vocabularies and implicit rules of usage determining how political problems were discussed within particular historical contexts. They normally distinguish between several systems of discourse operating in a given society, often associated with specific social or professional groups. Lawyers and theologians, for example, had different ways of discussing political obligations, each with its own terminology, methods of framing problems and normal range of applications.[8] Once we have identified these languages it also becomes possible to recognize instances when a writer combined them in unorthodox ways, or employed one vocabulary to explore issues normally discussed through another. For example, we may find a clergyman using theological language to make assertions about a legal issue. Both normal and anomalous usages therefore emerge with greater clarity.

This approach has the substantial advantage of situating specific works within larger systems of discourse possessing discernible social and institutional roots. It allows for the complex and pluralist nature of political culture; the capacity of people to think and act within alternative frames of reference, sometimes holding potentially contradictory beliefs without undue discomfort. It can also be broadened to accommodate concepts of genre and decorum prevalent in literary studies and art history.

The methodology also has certain limitations, however. Despite theoretical emphasis on historical contexts, the analysis of political languages has remained in practice essentially a form of textual analysis, usually biased toward printed sources produced by groups possessing highly developed intellectual subcultures. Cultural historians also need to take into account less formal kinds of discourse, together with visual imagery, ceremony and behavioural conventions. As art historians and anthropologists have shown, paintings and rituals can be analysed as non-verbal systems of communication analogous to language. But there is a danger of allowing the number of verbal and non-verbal 'languages' to proliferate to the point at which understanding is impeded rather than improved.

This difficulty is related to a deeper issue. Historians are usually better trained to deal with written words than with non-verbal evidence. In addition, written documents often provide our chief means of access to early modern history, even when we are dealing with ceremonial performances or visible objects. These facts inevitably shape our perspective. Not only may we overlook practices and beliefs, especially among the illiterate majority, that have left less evidence behind. In addition the textual character of our documents can subtly shape perceptions even of the things they do record. Since all historians are captives of their sources, we can never entirely eliminate these biases. But we can seek to control them.

The historiography of puritanism provides one example. Not many years ago historians liked to construct pictures of the Puritan Mind through synthetic analysis of theological tracts, sermons and spiritual diaries.[9] Although this work was enlightening in many respects, subsequent scholarship has shown that it produced an overly monolithic and static view of relationships among various shades of Protestant belief. It gave insufficient attention both to shifting polemical contexts and to the ways in which Protestantism functioned at a grass-roots level, by shaping social conduct as well as written discourse. Most historians have now abandoned a generalized concept of a Puritan Mind, perpetually disagreeing with its Anglican counterpart, as misleadingly simplistic. But one still encounters references to 'the common law mind' and to other entities like humanism that seem scarcely less monolithic. As we learn more about the period, these abstractions will likely be replaced by more nuanced descriptions of how legal and humanist thought functioned in various contexts, as flexible cultural practices rather than entirely consistent systems of belief.

Cultural, even more than religious and legal history has usually been written from the perspective of poets, artists and theorists whose views are most easily accessible and interesting to scholars. It is always tempting to allow exceptionally articulate writers to represent 'the period mind'. But doing so can beg numerous questions about how cultural meaning is actually constructed, transmitted and absorbed. What is especially needed at present is a widening of the range of documents and methodological approaches, to supplement and qualify traditional modes of textual, iconographic and intellectual analysis.

In attempting to map the main contours of English cultural landscape in the period around 1600, I have therefore begun not with political languages but with looser configurations of beliefs, rituals and social practices that provided alternative frames of reference within which contemporaries conceived of the operation of power. Four such configurations seem especially important: ideas of honour; the principles and procedures of the common law; religious ideas of providence; and humanist forms of political analysis. Each of these configurations gave rise to distinctive vocabularies and theories, and so might be analysed as a language in the Skinnerian sense. But they can also be approached through analysis of representational forms, social conventions, moral prejudices and institutional structures that supported them. By examining them in turn we may begin to form a preliminary sense of how early modern English political culture worked.[10]

Honour

From time immemorial local power in England had resided with landlords who regarded themselves as members of a warrior elite. This legacy left visible traces on the landscape, in castles and castle-like features, such as towers and massive gatehouses, incorporated into more modern country houses (*see* plate 1). Until the end of the sixteenth century English noblemen travelled about the country with cavalcades of armed retainers. Many still possessed armouries that had not entirely lost their military relevance. Chivalric values remained alive, sustained not only by hallowed native traditions but by modern European fashions, like the developing code of the duel.

At the heart of this cultural system lay a concept of honour that structured both patterns of behaviour and a distinctive vision of society.[11] In some senses honour mattered at all levels of society, among both women and men, but its richest meanings applied exclusively to peers and gentlemen.[12] For women honour consisted chiefly in the passive virtue of chastity, while for tradesmen and husbandmen it involved qualities of honesty and sobriety, appropriate to a middling station in life. A gentleman's honour, by contrast, comprised a much wider range of virtues, including prowess, courage, loyalty, liberality and magnanimity, along with a fierce pride and assertiveness associated with those born to command.

Somewhat paradoxically, these qualities were regarded simultaneously as inherited traits, passed through bloodlines and inhering in a man's innermost being, and characteristics requiring constant demonstration and acknowledgement from others.[13] Honourable birth was held to engender a nobility of spirit that inevitably manifested itself in outward behaviour, even under unfavourable circumstances:

> For a man by nothing is so well bewrayed
> As by his manners, in which plain is shown
> Of what degree and what race he is grown.
> For seldom seen, a trotting stallion get
> An ambling colt, that is his proper own:
> So seldom seen, that one in baseness set
> Doth noble courage show, with courteous manners met
>
> But evermore contrary hath been tried
> That gentle blood will gentle manners breed.[14]

1. Jan Siberechts, *Wollaton Hall and Park, Nottinghamshire*, a great house of the 1580s as it appeared in 1697. Copyright Yale Center for British Art, Paul Mellon Collection.

The obsession with lineage did meet with criticism from humanists, who stressed the rival claims of education and merit.[15] In Elizabeth's reign a plurality of the published literature stressed the superiority of virtue to birth in conferring honour.[16]

Many contemporaries, however, persisted in regarding honourable virtues as traits transmitted through biological inheritance. 'It is ordinary among men to observe the races of horses and breeds of other cattle,' wrote Fulke Greville:

> but few consider, that as diverse humours mixed in men's bodies make different complexions, so every family hath as it were diverse predominant qualities in it, which as they are tempered together in marriage give a certain tincture to all the descent.[17]

Although perhaps logically contradictory, chivalric emphasis on lineage and humanist stress on learning were in practice reconciled by stressing the complementary roles of birth, education and action in constituting the ideal gentleman.[18]

Belief in an intrinsic relation between honour and birth inspired not only exalted claims concerning noble virtues but degrading stereotypes of the low-born. 'There is a kind of leprosy, or at least of dross and contagious corruption in base descents,' asserted the Earl of Northampton, creating 'a bar which neither can education alter, nor instruction can qualify'. By granting coats of arms to the sons of yeomen and clergymen Tudor heralds threatened to swamp true nobility with 'base competitors invited or extracted *ex ipsa faece populi*', destroying the virtues that made England great by diluting the bloodlines in which they inhered.[19] Such prejudices became especially virulent when reinforced by political malice against families like the Cecils and Dudleys, who had risen to eminence through court service. A notorious Catholic libel of the 1580s, *Leicester's Commonwealth*, argued that as a Dudley – a descendant of a family that had risen from obscurity in two generations, by men who had ended their careers on the block – Leicester was congenitally prone to lying, lechery, conspiracy, murder and treason.[20] The abuse later hurled against Robert Cecil and James's upstart favourites, Somerset and Buckingham, was similarly coloured by social bias as well as political anger.[21]

Most gentry were intensely conscious of an obligation to uphold the reputation of their lineage.[22] The deeds of valorous ancestors provided both a stock of honour that every generation needed to replenish and a set of examples to emulate, an attitude that led to a preoccupation with family history and its symbols, such as the coat of arms and ancestral seat.[23] In the early seventeenth century Edward Lord Herbert of Cherbury recited anecdotes concerning the martial exploits of ancestors as far back as the Wars of the Roses, which inspired him in his career as a soldier of fortune and duellist.[24] In the same period the Earl of Arundel asked Robert Cotton to research the history of the Howard family, with particular attention to incidents that might provide subjects for paintings.[25] The Elizabethan and early Stuart vogue for local topographical histories, which traced the genealogies of gentry families, derived partly from similar preoccupations.

Defending a family's standing and reputation often required intensely competitive behaviour.[26] Involving as it did claims to innate superiority, the concept of honour encouraged efforts to triumph over others and compel recognition. In dealing with inferiors this meant asserting dominance, whether benignly through paternalism or coercively through physical intimidation. Among near equals it often entailed elaborate forms of courtesy and generosity, which reinforced elite solidarities while displaying virtues like liberality and magnanimity. As Felicity Heal has shown, the highly developed rituals of life in great households, especially those employed in the consumption of food, were a 'coded language' for articulating the honour of both lord and guests.[27]

The quest for reputation often involved less amicable interactions, however.[28] Emulation took any number of forms, from disputes over going first through a door or possessing the best pew in a local church, up to enormously costly forms of magnificence. It provoked duels and violent affrays but also spurred competition in the building of great country houses and other expenditures. In April 1603 an observer complained that 'many noblemen' were spending £4000 or £5000 each on clothes for James I's coronation, so that a poor lord determined to maintain his honour might 'so endanger his estate that he could hardly recover it in many years'.[29] In ways like this honour competition led not only to duels and feats of arms, but activities that might appear superficially unconnected to chivalric ideals.

This point becomes especially important in considering the evolution of honour culture during the Elizabethan and Stuart periods. Many historians have seen a gradual but ultimately decisive shift occurring during the sixteenth century, as the violent chivalric ethos of the Middle Ages was domesticated by Tudor monarchs and ultimately supplanted by newer humanist and Protestant values.[30] The Crown's increasing effectiveness in curtailing casual violence, the decline in noble retaining, the growth of religious deference to the monarch and the spread of humanist and Protestant attitudes have all been credited with contributing to this fundamental change.[31]

Although these arguments contain elements of truth, they need qualification. Even in the Middle Ages the King had stood at the apex of the honour system, and in the Tudor period court service became still more important.[32] Association with the ruler conferred honour in itself, while also affording opportunities to obtain patronage and titles.[33] Cultural values and skills linked to success at court were, therefore, frequently cultivated. But this did not result in a simple process of displacement, through which the attainments of the courtier and humanist scholar-statesman supplanted those of the chivalric warrior. Instead, much more complex interactions occurred between ancient honour ideals and newer values. Men like Sidney, Essex and Ralegh were, self-consciously, products of *both* humanist and chivalric traditions.

The symbiosis between medieval and modern aristocratic cultures was an international phenomenon. In parts of Europe wars of religion brought a resurgence of armed noble power and a concomitant development of honour concepts into a language of political resistance. In France, appeals to honour arguably became the chief means of justifying rebellion, subsuming earlier constitutional and religious arguments, though they also figured prominently in the rhetoric of royal authority.[34] This period also saw the beginnings of a science of strategy and tactics and a profession of arms, developments that added fresh dimensions to the ancient view of war as a nobleman's true vocation.[35]

Circumstances were different in England, where even great nobles lacked large military followings and secure regional power bases.[36] But English peers and gentlemen were certainly aware of continental concepts of honour, not least because many of them fought in European wars. When serving in Normandy in 1591 Essex invoked honour principles to justify disobeying a direct order from the Queen not to risk his forces in the siege of Rouen. 'This place, while these great armies are unbroken', he wrote to her, 'will be the only school of our age, and to go out of action when all other men come into action, were to wear a perpetual note of infamy', unworthy of 'my poor house'. Essex sought to improve the discipline of English land forces by using Roman military histories as models, and he employed counsellors versed in up-to-date humanist learning, like Francis and Anthony Bacon, Sir Henry Savile and Henry Cuffe.[37] Yet he also once described 'the upholding of nobility' as 'a most necessary and *religious* care', citing as evidence the fact that God provided Christ with a distinguished lineage.[38] Humanist scholarship and Protestantism complemented and reinforced his honour values.

Essex's associate, Northampton, the only peer in the sixteenth century to hold a faculty position at an English university, shared this eclecticism.[39] When Elizabeth appointed Essex Earl Marshal, giving him authority over questions of honour, Northampton canvassed historical evidence concerning the privileges and duties of the office and presented Essex with a book-length manuscript treatise on the subject.[40] Recent work on Sidney has similarly revealed him as a far less docile courtier than some older accounts suggest.[41] Like his uncle and patron, Leicester, he felt deeply frustrated by the Queen's reluctance to enter fully into European wars.[42] Court jousts and other neo-chivalric forms allowed him not only to voice his devotion but to hint at his impatience with her policies.[43]

A similar kind of multi-layered ambiguity has recently been revealed in an analysis of a portrait of Sir William Drury, painted in 1587 (*see* plate 2).[44] It shows him in elaborately decorated armour, with a tournament lance at his side, alluding to the chivalric panoply of the Elizabethan court Accession Day Jousts in which he was an active participant. But the landscape background is Flemish, suggesting Drury's recent participation in an actual military campaign in the Low Countries. The tiny Italian word *sconsolato* (disconsolate) above his left shoulder and the shadowed sun in the background refer both to the severe financial difficulties Drury faced because of debts to the Crown Elizabeth would not forgive, and his perception of neglect at her hands. A visual symbolism rooted in chivalric traditions has here been refashioned into a complex courtly idiom, in an attempt both to gain financial assistance and vindicate Drury's honour as a soldier, despite his fiscal embarrassment.

Honour violence, especially duelling, survived throughout the seventeenth century, manifesting a belief that gentlemen had a right to live by their own rules even when these contradicted those of religion and the state. 'Laws keep but the dregs of a commonwealth in obedience,' the Jacobean courtier, William Cornwallis, asserted: 'upwards it provokes them not nor anything but custom and the estimation of virtue'.[45] Royal officials might argue, as Secretary Windebanke did in

2. British School, sixteenth century, *Sir William Drury*. Copyright Yale Center for British Art, Paul Mellon Collection.

the Star Chamber in 1634, that whoever 'takes sword in...hand to revenge himself, doth as much as in him lieth depose the King, at whose dispose the sword of justice is'.[46] Some gentlemen continued to act, however, on principles closer to those expressed by Chapman's Bussy D'Ambois: 'When I am wronged that law fails to right me,/ Let me be King myself (as man was made)/ And do a justice that exceeds the law.'[47] This attitude produced some spectacular affronts to royal authority. In 1634 the Earl of Holland, a member of the Privy Council, challenged the son of Lord Treasurer Weston to a duel for revealing details of an intrigue against his father to Charles I. The fact that Holland kept the King's favour after this incident demonstrates the degree of tolerance accorded insubordination stemming from honour principles.[48] As John Adamson and Caroline Hibbard have shown, Charles did not attempt to suppress honour principles but instead sought to sublimate and contain them by stressing religious strains within the chivalric tradition, the ceremonies of the Order of the Garter and his own role in mediating relations and arranging dynastic marriages among the nobility.[49] Even this strategy failed to prevent peers like the Earls of Essex, Manchester and Warwick from assuming command of Parliament's armed forces in 1642.

It was not simply noblemen and gentry, moreover, for whom the concept of honour provided a lens through which to view contemporary events. Chivalric imagery and emphasis on military prowess pervaded the civic culture of London, contributing to the formation of militia companies in the early seventeenth century.[50] During Elizabeth's war with Spain the exploits of Sir Francis Drake and Martin Frobisher were celebrated in popular ballads saturated in chivalric imagery.[51] History plays from the late 1580s centred on medieval warfare and depicted contests over power partly in terms of honour imperatives. At the simplest level this meant bringing medieval English heroes onto the stage, as in the rousing portrayal of Lord Talbot in Shakespeare's *Henry VI* Part I.

Plays like Marlowe's *Edward II* and several Shakespearean histories, however, display a much more complex grasp of the role of honour imperatives in the political arena. The first two acts of Marlowe's play show the Mortimers and their allies provoked by a series of insults stemming from Edward's attachment to his favourite, Gaveston. The homosexual nature of this relationship, though abundantly clear, is never the central issue for the dissident peers, who will allow the King 'his minion', provided their own honour and the supports upon which it rests are preserved.[52] But Mortimer and other nobles have pledged publicly to prevent Gaveston from re-entering the realm after his banishment by Edward I, and so cannot accept his return without violating a central principle of the honour code.[53] This affront is compounded by Gaveston's monopoly of Edward's affections and counsels, which ousts peers from their traditional places around the King, his elevation into the peerage and the fact that Edward protects him from retaliation when he publicly insults his enemies. The peers therefore cannot defend their reputations without defying royal authority. The Mortimers' rebellion is portrayed by Marlowe as the outgrowth of a series of frontal collisions between allegiance and honour imperatives.

Nearly all of Shakespeare's histories also feature characters whose obsession with honour leads to violent acts of self-assertion and major conflicts. Honour takes on a different colouration depending on whether a play has a Roman or an English setting. Roman honour, for Shakespeare, is usually connected with public office and often with Stoic and republican philosophical values, as among the conspirators in *Julius Caesar*. In English settings it is bound up with chivalric prowess, loyalty to kin and a preoccupation with avenging slights to personal and family reputation. When challenged it inspires intemperate vituperation, like the insults Bolingbroke and Mowbray hurl at each other in the first scene of *Richard II* or the ranting of Hotspur in *Henry IV*, Part 1.[54] Only among the Trojans of *Troilus and Cressida* is honour mainly about rules of fair combat and other benign principles. Elsewhere it is connected to a thirst for glory, a preoccupation with redressing injuries, a desire to dominate and a propensity toward bloodshed. Honour can be a necessary quality when turned against external enemies, as in Coriolanus's campaigns against the Volsci or Henry V's conquest of France. When tempered by other personal virtues it can even become admirable. But it is always dangerous and often leads to disastrous cycles of violence, as in *Henry VI* Part 3, where Yorkist and Lancastrian leaders alternately butcher members of the opposing faction in retribution for the deaths of their own kin. It is not clear, on the other hand, that Shakespeare offers any real alternative. Leaders lacking the pride and assertiveness possessed by men of honour, like Henry VI or the tribunes in *Coriolanus*, invariably end up bringing destruction on themselves and others. The message may be that the aggressiveness that comes from the thirst for honour is a dangerous but ineradicable feature of political life.

Honour was, in short, a pervasive but protean element within English political culture. As Richard Cust has written, there was a 'simultaneous existence of a variety of concepts, or discourses, of honour', used to define both public and personal conduct.[55] It was, in fact, characteristic of such discourses that they blurred distinctions between the public and private, personal and political domains that twentieth-century minds instinctively want to draw. In an honour culture, questions relating to personal reputation can easily blend into larger political issues, as happened during attacks on the Duke of Buckingham in the Parliaments of 1625 and 1626.[56] 'The King is the fountain of honor, and yet that has been made a merchantable commodity to be obtained by money rather than desert,' Sir Francis Seymour complained in the first assembly. 'Who will bring up his son in learning when money is the way of preferment?'[57] To Seymour the corruption of honour threatened to subvert the operation of justice, the prowess of English arms and the virtue of the kingdom's natural rulers. It was hard to imagine a more fundamental grievance. Only by becoming attuned to this way of thinking can we begin to hear strains in the political culture of the period alien to modern ears.

Law

If Tudor England was governed by an elite imbued with honour ideals, it was ruled through a law whose operation increasingly penetrated all levels of society.[58] In 1957 J. G. A. Pocock argued that a distinctive 'common law mind' developed around the Inns of Court before 1600, spreading 'to become the general belief of the gentry'.[59] Its cardinal principle was a concept of an ancient constitution deriving from immemorial custom, a claim variously interpreted to mean either that English legal usages had gradually evolved over a very long period or that 'the common law, and with it the constitution, had always been exactly what they are now'.[60] In either case, the crucial point was that since no king had created the law, none had the right to alter it through unilateral action.

To sustain this belief, English legal scholarship had to avoid recognizing any profound discontinuities in legal history. Limited change presented no problem, since everyone realized that laws were sometimes altered. But if it could be shown either that the law had been radically refashioned by a particular ruler, such as William the

Conqueror, or that circumstances had changed so completely over time that ancient customs had become irrelevant to modern problems, the whole fabric of common law thought might collapse. When faced with evidence of either kind of discontinuity, 'constitutionalists were forced into a kind of historical obscurantism', of which the best example, Pocock argued, was their inability to recognize the roots of English property law in a system of obsolete feudal tenures. Since the most advanced European legal historians had achieved an understanding of feudalism, English lawyers were also forced to ignore their insights. In addition to being obscurantist they were deeply insular.

These arguments have been widely discussed since 1957 and subjected to a number of revisions but Pocock's basic thesis has become widely accepted and remains highly influential.[61] Until the 1970s common law thought was usually associated with opposition to the prerogative.[62] Some historians, notably J. P. Sommerville, continue to adhere to the essentials of this position.[63] Glenn Burgess has recently advanced a very different view, treating legal discourse as a widely shared orthodoxy that provided the basis for deep ideological consensus.[64] In this respect, he argues, English common lawyers differed from French and Scottish Calvinists who also developed constitutional theories. The latter wanted to restore ancient liberties that tyrannical kings had allegedly overthrown, whereas the former wished to uphold rules and procedures that remained in use. Instead of a form of protest, their arguments were a way of justifying the existing polity.

The central premise of this outlook, according to Burgess, was that the common law had developed through the gradual adaptation of natural principles of justice to peculiar English circumstances, evolving into a body of customs so complex as to be comprehensible only through the professional lawyers' 'artificial reason'. That reason worked by balancing and adjusting conflicting claims, both among individuals and between the King's prerogative and the subjects' liberties. Although people often disagreed about the resolution of specific cases, all but a few untypical thinkers believed that law was the ultimate arbiter of questions that fell within its sphere of competence. Only under Charles I, who failed to respect the conventions of English legal discourse, did deep polarization begin to develop.[65]

Burgess's subtle and elegant exposition has advanced understanding of this subject. Whether he has also succeeded in showing that legal discourse provided 'the shared language of an entire political nation' will likely remain controversial.[66] His discussion exemplifies the way in which some revisionist historians have replaced an old paradigm of an harmonious Elizabethan polity disrupted by Stuart misrule with a model of Jacobean consensus ended by the perversity of Charles I.[67] This picture arguably exaggerates both the level of agreement in the early seventeenth century and the novelty of disputes arising after 1625.

Pocock and Burgess both developed essentially synchronic analyses of the common law mind. Neither provided a detailed account of how that mind developed, although they seem to share a view that it originated among professional jurists before spreading fairly rapidly 'along the lines of communication linking the Inns of Court to the county communities and parliament'.[68] Detailed studies completed since the 1950s have not provided unequivocal support for this view. The chief historian of the Inns of Court, Wilfred Prest, has warned against assuming that gentry who attended these academies necessarily picked up a very sophisticated grasp of the law's 'artificial reason', while C. W. Brooks is equally sceptical of the theoretical prowess of Jacobean country attorneys, who handled the great mass of provincial legal business.[69] Most legal training and litigation concerned technical minutiae of tenurial rights rather than constitutional theory. Some gentry undoubtedly did develop a grasp of the law as an intellectual discipline and even 'a reverence for legal culture' while studying at the Inns of Court. But the diffusion of such attitudes is very difficult to measure and probably should not be overestimated, especially for the earlier part of James's reign.[70]

As Sommerville has pointed out, the evidence for a common law mind used by Pocock, Burgess and other scholars derives almost entirely from the writings of a few unusually articulate jurists.[71] Yet detailed work on these figures does not provide unproblematical support for belief in a wholly consistent legal orthodoxy. Edward Coke, regarded by Pocock as the quintessential early Stuart legal thinker, now appears much less representative. Burgess at times appears ready to dismiss Coke as so untypical that his views should be discounted.[72] The need to circumvent the most prolific and – in the long run – most influential lawyer of the period surely weakens the case for consensus, however.[73] Nor were individual jurists always entirely consistent over time. Selden, for example, was more ready to admit that the Conquest had introduced significant changes in the law in *Jani Anglorum Facies Altera* (1610), than during parliamentary debates over the Petition of Right in 1628.[74] Brooks and Kevin Sharpe have argued that a view of the law as insular and unchanging developed only in the seventeenth century, in response to actions by James I and Charles I that threatened traditional rights and procedures.[75] The enterprise of reconstructing a *single* 'common law mind' may have produced an overly monolithic picture.

Scholars need to pay more attention to how common law thought developed over time and to the range of social, political and cultural influences impinging on its evolution. Every investigator has agreed that an initial impetus was provided by the Elizabethan antiquarian movement, which itself had diverse roots.[76] Antiquarianism reflected a patriotic interest in the English past, which developed gradually during the sixteenth century and flowered during the Spanish war. The lawyer's preoccupation with custom was, on some deep level, related to impulses that gave rise to numerous topographical histories of English counties, to the Elizabethan history play and to other forms of historically oriented research, writing and visual culture.[77] As Richard Helgerson has argued, all these developments reflected a desire to show that England possessed traditions as rich and glorious as any other nation, and so had no need to defer to the Roman Church, Italian civilization, or Habsburg pretensions to universal monarchy. Some contemporaries deliberately employed legal terminology in advancing other kinds of cultural arguments. Samuel Daniel based his defence of rhymed poetry, in opposition to classical metre, on 'custom which nature hath...ratified, all nations received, time so long confirmed', and justified 'gothic' rhyme by associating it with the Germanic 'laws and customs' which formed 'the originals of most of the provincial constitutions of Christendom', including England.[78]

For both poets and lawyers, the study of ancient custom often meant using advanced methods of humanist scholarship to illuminate venerable English institutions and cultural traditions. Antiquarianism displayed a paradoxical fusion of intellectual cosmopolitanism and stubborn bias toward indigenous materials.[79] The much debated insularity of common law thought needs to be seen in this light. Even Edward Coke – whose mind Pocock described as being 'as nearly insular as a human being's could be' – possessed a library stocked with European books on history, civil law and other subjects.[80] Other legal antiquarians, especially John Selden, were highly cosmopolitan thinkers.[81] The study of ancient constitutions was a European-wide fashion, deriving not only from patriotic sentiment but a belief that nations, like people, possess unique personalities best appreciated through long temporal perspectives.

Antiquarian thought also served the professional needs of lawyers on another level. The Elizabethan period had seen a rapid growth, not only in barristers educated at the Inns of Court but in country attorneys trained by apprenticeship.[82] This latter group – 'pettyfoggers and vipers... that set dissension between man and man', as Queen Elizabeth rudely described them – mostly came from humble social backgrounds, earned modest incomes and suffered from a reputation for chicanery, greed and incompetence, which threatened to rub off on the legal profession's upper branch.[83] Spokesmen for barristers, serjeants and judges needed to counter this threat. The best way for an occupational group to elevate its status in the sixteenth century was by showing that it practised a theoretical discipline oriented towards pursuits gentlemen respected, rather than a craft based on narrow technical skills. Legal writers exalted the history and science of the law partly for reasons similar to those that led Vasari to write a history of painting and Ben Jonson to cite classical authorities on the political utility of poetry.[84] Jonson – who wrote verse epistles to Lord Chancellor Egerton, Coke and Selden – was acutely conscious of the affinities between legal scholarship and his own philological approach to literature. As common law thought developed the Inns of Court also developed into training grounds for aspiring courtiers and lively centres of literary culture. As the law became better defined as a distinct intellectual discipline its study was also becoming associated with other fashionable social and cultural skills.

Recognizing this wider context need not invalidate Burgess's argument that common law thought supported an essentially conservative and consensual outlook. On the contrary, the analysis presented thus far tends to strengthen the view that legal culture was naturally allied with patriotism and service to the Crown, rather than opposed to it. The point is reinforced by taking note of the unsettled circumstances of Elizabeth's last years: the strains of war; the court factionalism that culminated in Essex's rebellion; the prospect of a disputed succession after the Queen's death. In the 1590s arguments from precedent and immemorial custom provided a defence of continuity and stability in a world threatened by fierce dogmas, armed conflict and unpredictable events.[85] Burgess is undoubtedly right to see a parallel with Richard Hooker's defence of religious ceremony and tradition in *The Laws of Ecclesiastical Polity* (1594–7).

Indeed the parallel can probably be pushed further. As Peter Lake has shown, Hooker wrote *The Laws* to counter presbyterian arguments for radical ecclesiastical reforms based on central Protestant values of scriptural authority and hostility to 'popish' corruption.[87] He needed to justify ecclesiastical tradition precisely because there seemed excellent reasons for discarding it. Lawyers did not face any group as formidable as puritan critics of the Church but they did have to contend with demands for change that were in some ways comparable. Reverence for the common law and its practitioners was by no means universal in Elizabethan England. In addition to widespread complaints about lawyers fomenting litigation, there existed much more cynical views about the basic character of the law itself than those reconstructed by Pocock and Burgess. Some contemporaries were strikingly ready to discuss legal history as a process having less to do with the working out of natural principles of justice than with episodes of brute force and oppression. John Hayward regarded Law French as a language *intended* to confuse the populace and provide more room for 'arbitrary' power and 'the malice of some officers of justice, who are many times the instruments of secret and particular ends'.[88] The Elizabethan courtier Fulke Greville similarly argued that 'king's self-love' and 'corrupted might' will always find a way to pervert legal rules.[89] Samuel Daniel described the common law as inherently obscure and subject to misuse: 'what language soever it speaks, it never speaks plain, but is wrapped up in such difficulties and mysteries (as all professions of profit are) as it gives more affliction to the people than it doth remedy'.[90]

If Elizabethans believed in natural principles of justice, they also regarded all societies as inherently unstable and corrupt. Their attitudes towards the law reflected *both* attitudes, although a particular writer might emphasize one over the other. Alongside belief in the innate rationality and permanence of the law – 'a rock [that] stood firm against all storms and against the change of all nations here in England' – one can find writers describing it as variable and exploitative.[91] The very fact that law was deeply embedded in the fabric of society implied that it reflected prevalent social vices. Hence claims that 'the inward canker and rust in men's minds' had generated a rise in litigation and proliferation of superfluous statutes that badly needed pruning.[92]

In the legal, no less than the ecclesiastical sphere a plausible case therefore existed for fundamental change; and like its clerical counterpart, the legal profession was itself divided over this issue. Advocates of reform included the prominent Crown lawyers Francis Bacon and Lord Chancellor Egerton. In the hands of a conservative lawyer like Coke, antiquarian argument became a way of countering the threat by proving that the common law was not a disordered and virtually incomprehensible mass of arcane rules and precedents, but an exquisitely rational system. In making this case Coke had to contend with the problem that, as a customary system, the common law was deficient in general organizing principles. Richard Helgerson has argued that he solved the problem by adapting the traditional format of the legal Report, summarizing decisions in individual cases, to the task of building up a systematic body of rules and maxims.[93] From his *Second Report* of 1602 onwards, Coke used prefaces to enunciate a general defence and exposition of the law, while simultaneously developing a mass of particular rules and maxims while reporting individual cases. It is often difficult, as a result, to decide where his pronouncements leave off and the voices of other jurists begin.[94] This was intended: rather than an individual interpretation, *The Reports* try to speak with the majestic voice of the Law itself. Although Coke's contemporaries were not always fooled – Egerton accused him of 'scattering or sowing his own conceits almost in every case' – his method eventually turned him into the 'oracle of the common law' for more than a century after his death. Long-term success should not, however, lead us to exaggerate the ease with which a celebratory view of the law consolidated its hold in the early seventeenth century.[95]

In considering the role of the law in contemporary political culture we also need to distinguish between philosophical generalizations and the practical effects of legal antiquarianism as a working procedure. The pooling of expertise by the Society of Antiquaries and the assembling of antiquarian libraries, especially the great collection of Sir Robert Cotton, greatly facilitated applied research into precedents relevant to current policy issues.[96] Cotton's own papers contain numerous memoranda for members of the Council of precedents bearing on topics of interest to the Crown.[97] Others used his library for similar purposes. Francis Bacon wrote a note to himself in 1608: 'For precedents and antiquities to acquaint myself and take collection from Sir Robert Cotton'.[98] Younger men availed themselves of the same resource. 'For the remainder of the month,' Sir Simonds D'Ewes wrote concerning a period of study at the Inns of Court, 'I usually went to Westminster each morning the court sat, to report law cases at the Common Pleas; and when I found there was little there worth my attendance, I stepped aside into Sir Robert Cotton's, and transcribed what I thought good out of some of his manuscripts.'[99]

Arguments from custom and precedent were thus becoming more widely available in the political arena, often serving both sides in a policy debate. Meanwhile the supply of ancient and modern political manuscripts grew as scriveners who specialized in writing legal documents branched out into other kinds of work.[100] It consequently became easier to challenge political decisions by arguments from custom, a fact not lost on contemporaries. 'We have in this age so many Questionists', Egerton complained in 1604, '... that they leave neither religion, nor law, nor King nor council, nor policy, nor government out of the question. And the end they have in this question, What is the common law? is to shake and weaken the ground and principles of all government.' Concerns of this nature lay behind James I's decision to suppress the Society of Antiquaries in the early seventeenth century. If we think of legal culture as an activity rather than a system of ideas, it begins to take on more ambiguous characteristics. Appeals to the ancient constitution did provide a language of consensus, but they could also magnify disagreements by relating practical issues to deep and fundamental principles.

This ambiguity is especially important with respect to attitudes towards the prerogative. The common law mind was not intrinsically hostile to strong royal power. It often treated law as a constructive instrument of government: a set of customary principles and procedures that helped rulers preserve peace and order. This was especially true with respect to outlying areas of the British Isles, not yet fully assimilated within an English polity. Here the law became an agent of cultural, as well as political dominion. Bacon defended the jurisdiction of the Council of Wales, when it came under attack from Coke, by claiming that it had civilized the Welsh.[101] The same reasoning was used by Spenser in the sixteenth century and Sir William Davies in the early seventeenth, to justify the imposition of English law on Gaelic Ireland.[102] 'These civil assemblies at assizes and sessions', Davies wrote:

> have reclaimed the Irish from their wildness, caused them to cut off their glibs and long hair; to convert their mantles into cloaks; to conform themselves to the manner of England in all their behaviour and outward forms. And because they find a great disadvantage in moving their suits by an interpreter, they do for the most part send their children to schools, especially to learn the English language: so as we may conceive an hope, that the next generation will in tongue and ear and every way else become English.[103]

Antiquarians sometimes described the Norman Conquest in similar terms. Initially William's position had depended entirely on armed force and therefore remained insecure, but in the long run the Normans shrewdly established laws that the English themselves respected, and so came to enjoy a more secure power.[104]

However acceptable such ideas might seem when applied to the Welsh, the Irish or Anglo-Saxons, they raised very different issues when it came to a Scottish King of Great Britain. Even without the Union project, James's accession would probably have aroused concern over breaches of English legal rights by a foreign monarch. Highly critical remarks he let slip concerning purported defects in England's legal system cannot have helped matters. In 1604 he told the judges that 'the distribution of justice was better after the French manner... saying this course to draw all things to Westminster was to make him a King as it were of the Ile of France and not other provinces.'[105] But it was above all James's proposal for a formal union of his two kingdoms that set off alarm bells, by seeming to entail the abrogation of English common law. From a contemporary European perspective this was an odd view: France and Spain were obvious examples of large kingdoms ruled through a multiplicity of law codes. England's uniquely centralized legal system made it difficult for its inhabitants to conceive of political unification in terms that did not imply a uniformity of laws.

Since James soon abandoned efforts to consolidate English and Scots law into a single system, it might be thought that anxieties on this score quickly evaporated. Neal Cuddy has recently provided reason to think otherwise, however.[106] He has traced a protracted, three-sided contest between Robert Cecil, a 'high prerogative lobby' that included the English Earl of Northampton but depended chiefly on Scots in James's Bedchamber, and a vehemently anti-Scots group in Parliament, headed by the Earl of Southampton. Cuddy shows how attacks on the Union, and subsequently on alleged abuses of the prerogative, allowed Southampton's group to win popular support by opposing some of James's most cherished projects in the name of English laws and liberties.[107]

Some contemporaries regarded the relationship between royal prerogatives and popular liberties not as a delicate balance permanently fixed by law and custom, but as a dynamic relationship in which each tended to encroach upon the other. 'It is certain that all princes seek to stretch out their authority,' a discourse on the prerogative among the second Earl of Leicester's papers states: 'and as little as may be depend upon the will and content of the people, and the people on the other side, to draw to themselves as much power as they may'.[108] This statement may date from the 1630s and could therefore reflect the heightened tensions of Charles's reign. But Sir Thomas Smith, in the late sixteenth century, had also described all legal systems as subject to continuous alteration, caused by the inevitable tendency of liberty and power to encroach upon each other.[109] It was not only defenders of the subjects' rights who felt threatened. Some of James's servants believed his power was jeopardized by demagoguery dressed up in common law arguments. 'Monarchies in name do often degenerate into aristocracies or rather oligarchies,' Bacon wrote in 1607, '... when prerogatives are made envious or subject to the construction of the laws.'[110] Egerton made a similar complaint about Coke: 'It is to be observed throughout all his books, that he hath as it were purposely laboured to ... disesteem and weaken the power of the King in the ancient use of his prerogative.'[111] In 1611 Egerton complained that in 'the late parliament some breaches were made upon the regality and supreme prerogative of the Crown, under pretext of lawful liberty and ancient privileges'.[112] In 1627 James Bagg told Buckingham that Magna Carta itself had been 'wrung out' of medieval kings 'by the long, bloody and civil wars of those never to be honoured barons'.[113] Although Bagg was not typical even among Buckingham's supporters, his willingness to view Magna Carta as a document extorted at sword point represents an extreme version of a view that had long existed of legal history as a story involving considerable competition and conflict.

If the common law provided a set of rules for balancing and adjusting the competing claims of the prerogative and the subjects' liberties, it also furnished weapons of political combat. The expansion of legal antiquarianism strengthened both sides of the equation, generating more persuasive accounts of constitutional balance, while also furnishing an expanding array of precedents and arguments lying ready to hand when contention arose. In certain respects, moreover, this situation existed not only at the political centre but throughout English society. Custom, precedent and definitions of tenure were not only lawyers' terms of art. They were also concepts that affected vital interests even among quite humble people. When faced with an aggressive landlord whole villages occasionally found themselves locked into legal contests over definitions of custom, in which real or manufactured precedents could make a critical difference.[114]

It was not just the role of the Inns of Court as academies for the gentry that gave the language of the law wider currency. It was also the enormous growth of common law litigation, at the expense of local customary courts and informal arbitration, after Elizabeth's accession.[115] The law had always been the chief means by which royal authority penetrated the localities but its reach had expanded considerably in the late sixteenth century. This meant that local governors seeking to defend the interests of their community were increasingly likely to get drawn into legal disputes with national implications, as David Sacks has shown happened in Bristol in the 1620s. It also meant that, although complex legal theories were beyond the reach of all but a few, certain arguments made sense even to unsophisticated villagers. The idea that law is an artificial extension of natural principles of equity and justice resonated with the experience of a society in which people normally took legal action only after informal moral sanctions had broken down. Common experience taught the importance of law and custom in safeguarding security of property and civic peace.

But it also demonstrated that vexatious litigation might ruin the unwary. The image Holinshed and Shakespeare used in describing Richard II's tyranny, of a nation groaning under parchment bonds recording legal obligations extorted from the subject, spoke to a society in which many people felt victimized by mortgages, debts and other legal entailments. So did the cry of Cade in *Henry VI*, Part II:

> Is not this a lamentable thing, that of the skin of an innocent lamb should be made parchment? That parchment, being scribbled o'er, should undo a man? Some say the bee stings, but I say 'tis the bee's wax, for I did but seal once to a thing, and I was never mine own man since.[118]

As Tudor society became more settled, the English grew more adept at using the law both as an instrument of self-defence and an offensive weapon against each other. The experience taught them the importance of constant vigilance in securing their titles and customary rights against attack.[119] This lesson, in turn, shaped perceptions of larger issues relating to the King's powers over his subjects.

Providentialism

Concepts of law and custom provided one set of tools for understanding the operation of authority in everyday contexts. Religion furnished another. The argument that God had created the social order and appointed each individual his place within it was a thoroughly familiar commonplace. In the words of the Homily on Obedience (1547; reissued periodically):

> Every degree of people in their vocation, calling and office hath appointed to them their duty and order. Some are in high degree, some in low, some kings and princes, some inferiors and subjects, priests and laymen, masters and servants, fathers and children, husbands and wives, rich and poor, and everyone have need of other: so that in all things is to be lauded and praised the goodly order of God, without the which no house, no city, no commonwealth can continue and endure or last.[120]

If this appointed order is shaken, all manner of 'abuse, carnal liberty, enormity, sin and Babylonical confusion' will follow. 'Take away kings, princes, rulers, magistrates, judges and such estates of God's order, no man shall ride or go by the highway unrobbed, no man shall sleep in his own house or bed unkilled, no man shall keep his wife, children and possessions in quietness: all things shall be common, and there must needs follow all mischief and utter destruction.' The alternative to settled authority was already envisaged in essentially Hobbesian terms, as a condition in which unbounded liberty meant limitless destruction.

This reasoning linked the King's role at the political summit to a chain of rights and duties extending throughout society, especially the authority of husbands over wives, parents over children and employers over labourers and servants.[121] This argument worked with the grain of a society organized into patriarchal households whose heads oversaw the religious instruction and moral behaviour of their dependents.[122] Disordered households and masterless men and women were universally seen as threats to the community. Household governance depended on a delicate balance between subordination and cooperation, authoritarian coercion and unforced consent, which served as a model for larger political relationships. Ultimately the battle against disorder extended to the individual psyche, as people internalized moral values, checking passions that might otherwise threaten civic peace. Fear of the effects of disordered passions – especially among masterless vagrants, oversexed adolescents, habitually drunken and violent men or incurably quarrelsome women – was a constant feature of village and town life, which population growth and other economic strains of the period exacerbated.[123]

The rhetoric of the Homily on Obedience therefore corresponded to familiar experiences and habits people absorbed from childhood. Some historians have argued that this was especially true in traditional face-to-face villages with stable subsistence economies. More competitive and mobile economic arrangements, engendered by market forces and urbanization, arguably acted as solvents of deferential religious values, stimulating more individualist and secular attitudes. Economic change has been credited with eroding traditional belief in hierarchy and replacing it with puritan individualism and ultimately with modern rationalism.[124]

Historians are certainly justified in seeking connections between religious culture and changing social experiences. It is important, however, not to underestimate the flexibility and resiliency of the period's religious outlook by overly schematic distinctions between 'medieval' and modern attitudes. Providentialism should not be regarded as a single doctrine, inextricably wedded to inherited cosmologies, so much as a variety of thought capable of giving rise to numerous theoretical positions. Although virtually everyone believed that secular authority derived from God's will, the question of just how it did so could generate both fierce argument and fertile speculation. Belief in providence did not settle the question of whether God had appointed popes or kings as supreme rulers of Europe. Neither was it incompatible with strong interest in secular political causation, which might be regarded as showing the operation of forces God had implanted in human nature. Even Machiavelli's ideas were integrated, by sixteenth-century theorists, into systems of political theology.[125]

Very broadly speaking, two large families of providentialist ideas can be distinguished in this period. One comprised what historians sometimes call 'order theory', a belief that God created the cosmos as a chain of interlocking hierarchies, tying together metaphysical, physical, political, ethical and psychological realities. Analogous principles of order therefore operate throughout the natural and social worlds. Deriving ultimately from a synthesis of several Greek cosmologies with Christianity, order theory found support in pagan philosophers like Plato and Aristotle, as well as both scholastic and modern theologians.[126] In the sixteenth century it still represented the most coherent available basis for integrating all spheres of human knowledge, and thus grounding political thought in natural philosophy.

This would gradually become less true as new discoveries undermined ancient cosmology. Instead of discrediting belief in providential order, however, the 'new philosophy' stimulated efforts at bringing political theology into line with developments in natural philosophy. Hobbes, Locke and Newton are three prominent examples of thinkers who continued to see fundamental connections between politics, theology and physics towards the end of this period, even while discarding Aristotelian concepts of the Great Chain of Being.[127]

Conventional order theory fostered a habit of seeing the political world in terms of a basic opposition between form and chaos. Good government was that which restrained confusion by upholding proper boundaries and distinctions. This attitude often militated in favour of regulations favouring privileged corporate bodies, such as monopolistic trading companies, trade guilds, oligarchic town corporations and closed parish vestries.[128] The Stuarts, especially, tended to equate good order with a narrowing of political participation and tightening of regulation. The conviction that the King had a duty to promote good order also inspired rationalist schemes for improving social, economic and cultural life. An example is Stuart policy for London's growing suburbs, which exhibited many kinds of disorder. They housed a promiscuous assortment of rich and poor, living in non-uniform houses, built along irregular streets: conditions plausibly associated with a multitude of ills, from the danger of fire and the outbreak of contagious epidemics to the emergence of organized criminal activities in hidden alleys. The Crown responded by attempting to regulate new building through proclamations and royal licences, a policy that culminated in the planned development of Covent Garden in the 1630s. Here uniform and properly proportioned brick houses were built along rectilinear streets, without back alleys of mean tenements. Sewers, garbage disposal and even the number of taverns were all subjected to rules enforced by the Privy Council. Every feature of Covent Garden, from its architecture to its sanitary arrangements, was ordered to produce a neighbourhood at once more pleasing to the eye, more uniform in its social composition and healthier for its inhabitants.[129]

On an even more ambitious scale, Francis Bacon's schemes for promoting technological innovation derived equally from a religious belief in proper ordering. God intends us to seek out the hidden causes of phenomena and thus attain the power to reorder the world: 'For the command over things natural – over bodies, medicine, mechanical powers and infinite other of the kind – is the one proper and ultimate end of true natural philosophy.'[130] A king who encourages experimentation will contribute to the discovery of new tools for creating order that will enlarge the nation's wealth and power. It is a mistake to regard order theory as inextricably wedded to rigid conservative nostrums. In some cases it actually stimulated innovation.

A second family of providentialist ideas derived from scriptural concepts of history as sacred drama. It comprised various apocalyptic theories, which became particularly prevalent during the Civil War, as well as forms of prophetic discourse that did not necessarily imply the imminence of the millennium.[131] Although scriptural providentialism might be linked to order theory in various ways, it differed markedly in tone and emphasis. Whereas order theory stressed eternal hierarchical principles, biblical narratives portrayed world history as a dynamic struggle of good and evil, unfolding through cycles of sin, punishment, suffering and redemption. English Protestants like John Bale and his great Elizabethan successor, John Foxe, had quickly come to see their own Reformation in these terms.[132] Although neither regarded England as a uniquely chosen nation, both stressed parallels between modern England and ancient Israel. This equation was quickly picked up by others and persisted throughout the seventeenth century.[133]

A number of historians have seen scripturally based providentialism as a revolutionary ideology in the making, developed by puritans prepared to challenge royal authority whenever it failed in its sacred mission.[134] Without fully endorsing this view, Patrick Collinson has also recently argued that the scriptural paradigm encouraged certain kinds of dissidence. It fostered a view of the godly as a minority within a national population given over to sin, while encouraging suspicions of kings for being prone to flirtations with idolatry and ungodliness, like Saul, David and Solomon.[135] It needs to be emphasized, however, that the habit of viewing politics through a scriptural lens was never the monopoly of any one religious group. The Bible furnished Catholics, as well as Calvinists, with arguments for opposing 'ungodly' monarchs; but it was also used to support doctrines of non-resistance. Scriptural imagery figures very prominently in both Tudor and Stuart royal iconography.[136] Divine right arguments can legitimately be seen in the same light, as 'a polemical instrument forged in the age of regicide', designed to refute Catholic and Protestant resistance theorists through their own chosen methods of scriptural exegesis.[137]

Even more than common law arguments, providentialist beliefs generated a spectrum of discourses and ideas that both supported and subverted authority, often simultaneously. For in the sixteenth and seventeenth century there were always a number of overlapping and competing authorities, all claiming some kind of divine right. Examples included the King, the law, the nobility, the individual conscience, the Bible and both the English and Roman churches. Supporting one kind of authority meant limiting or rejecting the claims of others. The need to confront this problem, in the course of both domestic and international controversies, generated any number of interpretations of relationships between God's will and secular politics.

Humanism and the Imitation of Antiquity

Tudor humanism seems harder to describe today than it did twenty years ago. Until recently historians believed that the serious reception of the Renaissance began in England only around 1500 and rapidly accelerated under Henry VIII. His reign, it was thought, produced not only the first classics of English Renaissance literature but the beginnings of intellectual and educational revolutions that continued into the seventeenth century, transforming the outlook of the ruling elite.[138] The scholastic learning of the universities and the nobility's chivalric culture were challenged by an Erasmian programme of intensive training in classical languages and literature, combined with emphasis on preparation for practical service to the Crown. The influence of ancient philosophers and historians opened the way to more pragmatic and analytical treatment of social and political processes and an expanded concept of the role of the state as guardian of the 'common weale' – the whole range of material and spiritual needs of its people. Tudor humanism thus produced a sea change in political culture.[139]

This heroically whiggish picture, developed in the 1950s and 1960s by historians like Fritz Caspari, Arthur Ferguson, James McConica and Stone, has since been qualified in several ways. Some scholars, like David Starkey, would push the initial English reception of Renaissance political thought well back into the fifteenth century.[140] More important than chronological adjustments, the boundary between medieval and humanist culture is often difficult to delineate clearly. Humanism did not always entail a complete rejection of medieval culture but sometimes encouraged efforts to revivify native traditions by synthesizing them with classical ones. Medieval thinkers were not always as oblivious to practical concerns as some historians have suggested, while humanist learning was not necessarily as useful as its proponents claimed.[141] In any case scholastic teaching survived in the universities well into the seventeenth century, alongside humanist pedagogy. The educational 'revolution' described by Stone in the 1960s looks to some historians more like 'the intensification of an existing [medieval] trend'.[142]

No one denies, however, that humanism did ultimately have a profound impact. The challenge is to explain how its influence worked without falling into simplifications. Instead of concentrating on pronouncements by proponents of the new learning, which can exaggerate the scale of change, we need to examine the pedagogical methods and mental habits through which humanist attitudes penetrated society.

The broad base of classical education was provided by grammar schools rather than the universities. One hundred and thirty-six schools were founded under Elizabeth and another 83 in the reign of James I.[143] Although some quickly folded, educational facilities were undoubtedly expanding, especially in the towns. Curricula and teaching methods varied, with some schools emphasizing vernacular teaching and practical skills while others furnished academic instruction.[144] But many schools, including the most prestigious, such as St Paul's in London, and Eton, had been reformed along Erasmian lines early in the century. They provided not only instruction in Latin grammar but an intensive introduction to classical literature. Elementary skills were learned by rote, but more advanced students acquired proficiency through the method of double translation, by which they were required each day to turn an ancient text into English and, after an interval, retranslate it back into Latin for comparison with the original. This was accompanied by work in both Latin and English composition in imitation of classical models. Sir Simonds D'Ewes claimed to have composed 2850 verses in Greek and Latin, besides numerous prose passages, while a grammar school student.[145]

For the linguistically gifted this training produced not only a mastery of Latin but stylistic facility and considerable familiarity with the texts selected for school exercises. Shakespeare evidently internalized large parts of *The Aeneid* while at grammar school in Stratford-upon-Avon, enabling him to weave Virgilian images and phrases effortlessly into his own writing.[146] The greatest classicist poet of the early seventeenth century, Ben Jonson, had only a grammar school education under William Camden at Westminster, which he never finished. Although we should not draw too many conclusions from these obviously exceptional examples, they do show that it was possible to gain a solid grounding in classical literature without attending a university. The language of the English Renaissance was forged through the discipline grammar schools instilled by requiring students to translate Latin literature, with its rich vocabulary, grammatical complexities, fluid syntax and unfamiliar habits of mind. Although it is an exaggeration to say 'that the literary heritage of an Elizabethan writer was Latin rather than English',[147] since Chaucer, Skelton and other medieval writers were also admired, literary culture was always at least bilingual.

Access to grammar schools was confined to a minority of the population, though not entirely to the gentry, since yeomen's sons and boys from urban backgrounds frequently attended them.[148] For these pupils classical learning provided a badge of status and route to upward mobility. It is remarkable how many luminaries of what we call the English Renaissance were sons of townsmen of middling rank: examples include Shakespeare, Marlowe, Jonson, Thomas Middleton, John Webster, William Camden and Inigo Jones. We should not associate classical culture exclusively with the landed elite, except insofar as those who acquired it usually tried to claim gentry status.

Higher education was much more socially restricted, especially in the seventeenth century, when over half the students at Oxford and Cambridge were sons of gentlemen, professionals or clergy and most of the rest probably came from wealthy urban backgrounds.[149] Within the universities there was also an informal division between students studying for careers in the Church and young gentlemen who usually failed to finish a degree. The actual content of university education in the late sixteenth and early seventeenth centuries has been a subject of some dispute. A fairly traditional set of courses in logic and rhetoric remained the core of the formal curriculum, although new topics including Greek, Hebrew and mathematics were introduced in the sixteenth century. But this instruction was supplemented through tutorials that often stressed humanist material. Much depended on the aptitude of the student, the proclivities of the tutor and the orientation of a particular college. Puritans like John Preston at Emmanuel and Joseph Mead at Christ's worked hard to instil humanist and Protestant values, whereas others were more lackadaisical. Margo Todd's research on student commonplace books suggests, however, both a breadth of subjects covered and a continuing emphasis on humanist and classical authors throughout the Tudor and early Stuart periods.[150]

Humanism continued to shape not only the content of university education but an orientation towards moral instruction and public service.[151] Cicero's *De Officiis* and various works of Erasmus were particularly favoured texts stressing these values. In addition to logic and rhetoric – required for clear thinking and effective persuasion – students were encouraged to obtain a grounding in any and all disciplines that might contribute insights into problems of governance. These included philosophy, poetry, geography and especially history, regarded as a stockpile of human experience. What mattered was not just intellectual acquaintance with an encyclopedic range of knowledge, but the capacity to apply it flexibly in particular circumstances. It was therefore important to read analytically, with an eye towards issues of present concern. 'In reading of history,' the early Stuart diplomat, Henry Wotton, suggested:

> a soldier should draw the platform of battles he meets with, plant the squadrons and order the whole frame as he finds it written, so he shall print it firmly in his mind and apt his mind for actions. A politique should find the characters of personages and apply them to some of the court he lives in, which will likewise confirm his memory and give scope and matter for conjecture and invention.[152]

This method of extracting material from texts has recently become the focus of investigation by scholars such as Lisa Jardine, Anthony Grafton and William Sherman.[153]

Since knowledge needed to be 'applied' it was important to gather and organize information in ways that made it easily retrievable. Marginal annotations assisted this purpose but even more useful was the commonplace book, in which tags from classical authors and scraps of knowledge were catalogued under analytical headings. 'I hold collections under heads and common places to be of far more profit and use' than mere 'summaries', Bacon explained, 'because they have in them a kind of observation, without the which neither long life breeds experience, nor great reading knowledge'.[154] Whereas someone constructing 'an Epitome of Alexander' will merely observe details like 'the number of years he lived [and] the names of the places he conquered', the compiler of a commonplace book will concentrate on subjects like the methods through which Alexander achieved his conquests.

University students seem invariably to have kept commonplace books and some men continued to compile them long after graduation: the fourth Earl of Bedford left over 20 at his death in 1641.[155] Some specimens demonstrate remarkably thorough study of particular issues. The second Earl of Leicester kept a commonplace book in the early seventeenth century, containing voluminous historical and contemporary precedents regarding obedience to princes under problematical circumstances. There are separate headings dealing with obedience to rulers who are themselves under the power of a foreign king or domestic faction, as well as a section on 'different laws and customs in succession' broken down under 77 separate sub-headings.[156] Leicester had evidently set out to engage in exhaustive analysis of the nature and limitations of political allegiance.

Although it might be pursued by an individual working alone, the gathering of material through study was frequently undertaken by groups acting as teams. University students were encouraged to discuss their reading with each other. 'You shall find many learned men with whom [you should seek to] be acquainted,' John Holles's father admonished him as he went off to university, 'for reading without conferring is like eating without digesting, and one day's conference will more benefit your silent nature than five days studying.'[157] The Oxbridge tutorial was an outgrowth of this method.

Collaboration between amateur and professional scholars sometimes extended beyond the years at university, especially at court. Partly this was because the court was dominated by people who had themselves undergone a thorough humanist training. Elizabeth allegedly read Plato's Dialogues in Greek and amused herself by translating Latin works into English. She regarded learning and linguistic facility as recommendations for preferment and encouraged promising young men to acquire them. 'I cannot blot from my memory's table', John Harington wrote in 1602, 'her watchings over my youth...and admiration of my little learning and poesy, which I did so much cultivate on her commands.'[158] Lord Burghley shared Elizabeth's intellectual prejudices and used his authority as Master of Wards to promote them among young peers and gentlemen. Although less well educated Leicester was even more active as a patron, as was the Earl of Essex in the 1590s. Under such leaders court society acquired a learned tone. 'Truly it is a rare thing with us now', William Harrison observed in the 1570s, 'to hear of a courtier which hath but his own language. And to say how many gentlewomen and ladies there are, that besides sound knowledge of the Greek and Latin tongues are thereto no less skillful in the Spanish, Italian, French, or in some one of them, it resteth not in me.'[159] Even allowing for exaggeration, this suggests how far linguistic and rhetorical skills had become useful to English courtiers.

The orientation of the court helped sustain interest in humanist pursuits among the gentry, both by way of example and by offering incentives to the ambitious. It also led to more concrete links between the universities and the world of high politics, as academics were recruited to assist leading figures in government. At the outset of Elizabeth's reign Burghley had drawn upon a network of scholars grouped around his Cambridge tutor, John Cheke, to rebuild a Protestant Church.[160] In the 1590s Henry Savile simultaneously occupied the posts of Greek tutor to the Queen, warden of Merton College, Oxford, and provost of Eton, while serving as a policy adviser to the Earl of Essex. He counselled one generation of leaders while training another, including his future son-in-law, the Stuart diplomat Dudley Carleton. Savile's successor at Eton was another diplomat, Sir Henry Wotton.

Humanist intellectuals served the Crown in various ways, including the production of controversial literature. Leicester and Burghley both actively patronized Protestant controversialists, while in the early seventeenth century James I recruited the great French scholar Isaac Casaubon to write tracts defending the Oath of Allegiance. Scholars were also frequently called upon to engage in research and analysis of specific problems of concern to court patrons, an activity Jardine and Sherman have labelled 'knowledge transactions'.[161] In the late 1570s, for example, Gabriel Harvey guided Philip and Robert Sidney through a reading course in Livy and other classical texts, directed to furnishing insights relevant to the governance of Ireland, where their father had just been appointed Lord Deputy.[162]

In the dangerous environment of the late sixteenth century, some of the most useful knowledge transactions involved gathering material not from classical texts, but direct observation of contemporary affairs, especially abroad. During a period without newspapers or bureaucratized foreign offices, even leading statesmen had to keep informed through correspondence. Anyone engaged in diplomatic work or court politics was accustomed to sending and receiving streams of newsletters. Walsingham in the 1560s and 1570s and Anthony Bacon in the 1590s built up networks of 'intelligencers' to provide reliable information about international events.

Contemporaries distinguished between common intelligencers, who merely reported gossip, and observers trained to assess information analytically. 'For government your end must not be like an intelligencer, to spend all your time fishing after the present news, humours, graces or disgraces of the court,' Francis Bacon advised the Earl of Rutland as he departed on a tour of the continent in 1595:

> but your lordship's better and more constant ground will be to know the consanguinities, alliances and estates of their princes, the proportion betwixt the nobility and the magistracy, the constitution of the courts of justice, the state of their laws... how the sovereignty of the king infuseth itself into all acts and ordinances... what discipline and preparation for wars; what inventions for increase of traffic at home, for multiplying their commodities, encouraging arts or manufactures of worth of any kind; also what good establishments to prevent the necessities and discontents of the people, to cut off suits at law and quarrels, to suppress thieves and all disorders.[163]

This kind of analytic observation might extend to gathering pertinent books and documents, such as treatises on law and military strategy, political pamphlets, or diplomatic correspondence and policy memoranda. The young Henry Wotton tried to attract Lord Zouche's patronage in the early 1590s by furnishing him with this sort of material from the imperial archives in Vienna.[164]

Such activity required both fluency in foreign languages and powers of classification and analysis that humanist education sought to instil. Even more, it demanded that the observer develop a sense of how politics really worked and an ability to discriminate misleading appearances from meaningful information. A growing body of European theoretical literature arose around these issues, devoted to what Justus Lipsius called 'prudence' and Giovanni Botero 'reason of state'. Prudence, as Lipsius defined it, is the study of political contingencies, which by their nature can never be known with certitude, but which can be anticipated with some reliability through the systematic study of past experience. It involved efforts to distil the lessons of history into maxims useful for judging current affairs.[165]

This enterprise began with the recognition that the true nature of politics usually lies hidden from the casual observer, not only by the confusion of events but the dissimulation of rulers who do not want their intentions discovered. It is therefore necessary to penetrate disguises and anticipate events before they happen. Lipsius thought the best single guide to this enterprise was the Roman historian Tacitus, though other writers, including Guicciardini and Machiavelli, also provided useful insights.[166] Although it took longer to catch on in England than in France and Flanders, prudential thought influenced the Earl of Essex's circle from the late 1580s and soon gained wider currency.[167] The gathering of intelligence and probing of *arcana imperii* soon became a cultural fashion, giving rise, in the early seventeenth century, to the practice among gentlemen of gathering daily to exchange news in St Paul's Cathedral (Paul's Walk).

The new prudential literature conveyed a rather sinister vision of political life. Richard Tuck has argued that a sharp change in Europe's intellectual climate occurred around 1570, as an older humanism oriented around the positive values of Cicero's *De Officiis* gave way to a 'new humanism' marked by scepticism and Taciteanism.[168] This claim has rightly been criticized for ignoring the continuing influence of Cicero well into the seventeenth century, sometimes among the same people who were absorbing the fashion for Tacitus.[169] Ciceronian and Tacitean views might be made complementary, by associating the former with the virtues of a healthy commonwealth and the latter with vice and corruption. Tuck's discussion is useful, however, in pointing out the need to broaden our definition of humanism to accommodate different emphases, particularly as we move forward into the late Elizabethan and early Stuart periods.

In addition to Ciceronian and Tacitean concepts of political life, classical and humanist learning often served a variety of ornamental purposes, in fashioning a gentleman not just for active service but leisured pursuits. This was especially true at court, where the chief model was Castiglione's *Book of the Courtier*, a treatise warmly recommended by the Queen's former tutor, Roger Ascham, in 1570, and which enjoyed a tremendous vogue during Elizabeth's reign.[170] Castiglione and his numerous imitators promoted a synthesis of humanist learning with older courtly and gentlemanly accomplishments, such as riding, dancing and military prowess. The man who came to personify this ideal in England – though mostly after his death in 1586 – was Sir Philip Sidney.

Nevertheless it is a mistake to regard any one individual as having achieved a definitive and permanent synthesis of humanist, Protestant and chivalric ideals. What we find instead is a continuous interplay between classical forms, modern European fashions and inherited medieval values, taking place from the Tudor period onwards. The assimilation of classical and Italian Renaissance culture involved not only innovations in fields like poetry and architecture, but countless adjustments made by individuals in their daily lives. 'I am now setting forth into the country,' John Harington wrote to Lord Thomas Howard in 1603:

> where I will read Petrarch, Ariosto, Horace and such wise ones. I will make verses on the maidens, and give my wine to the masters; but it shall be such as I do love, and do love me. I do much delight to meet my good friends, and discourse of getting rid of our foes. Each night do I spend, or much the better part thereof, in council with ancient examples of learning; I con over their histories, their poetry, their instructions, and thence glean my own proper conduct in matters both of merriment and discretion.[171]

Here we again encounter the humanist technique of 'conning over' texts in search of material fit for application, though the goal is not to reform the commonwealth but to adorn a courtier's speech and behaviour.

The fact that the classical culture was itself mainly the product of aristocratic societies facilitated its assimilation into an English environment. For all the differences between Roman and Tudor social values, there were enough similarities to allow the imitation of antiquity to complement old English customs at least as often as it undermined them. Stoic ideas of virtue had affinities with Christian values,[172] just as the Ciceronian concept of *urbanitas* could to some extent be harmonized with chivalric notions of courtesy. Rather than supplanting older cultural attitudes humanism often added new inflections and layers of meaning to them.

2

POLITICAL IMAGINATION
c. 1585–1640

The political culture of early modern England, we have been arguing, was complex and pluralistic. This complexity did not prevent contemporaries from forming coherent views of the practical workings of power, however, and this chapter sets out to examine more closely some of the ways in which they did so. It will be concerned partly with images of authority but even more with representations of faction, instability and conflict. In pursuing these subjects we will draw upon an eclectic range of sources, including visual materials, works of imaginative literature and polemical tracts and libels. Such documents do not analyse government in the explicit manner of legal and theological discourse, which has traditionally provided the basis for histories of political thought. But when properly interrogated they often reveal a host of assumptions concerning political behaviour and causation.[1] Through them we can probe not only normative ideas about how power ought to work but assumptions about how it actually does, in a corrupt world where people often fail to play by the rules.

Religious Conflict and Invented Traditions

In late Tudor and early Stuart England political parties did not exist and electoral campaigns were infrequent and almost never involved national issues.[2] The absence of modern forms of partisanship does not mean, however, that political life was devoid of other kinds of tensions, although some accounts may give this impression. Elizabeth's reign, especially, has often been portrayed as a period of conservatism and unity in the face of external threats. This view has its deepest roots in panegyrics produced during the Queen's life, and even more in the golden legend that developed shortly after her death. Yet it is essentially a retrospective one that overlooks important features of the period.

The most important of these was deep fear of civil conflict engendered by confessional differences. 'Your subjects,' as Sir Philip Sidney warned the Queen in 1579, 'are divided into two mighty factions, and factions bound upon the never ending knot of religion'.[3] The presence until 1586 of a plausible Catholic claimant to the throne in Mary Stuart, the danger thereafter of Spanish invasion, and a run of bad harvests in 1594–7, which brought the real value of wages to their lowest level since the fourteenth century, all compounded the problem.[4] So did the nightmare of a disputed succession after Elizabeth's death. No sooner had this threat passed than the Gunpowder Plot of 1605 once more reminded the English of their vulnerability to popish conspiracy. If the subjects of Charles I were unable to foresee the Civil War, their grandparents had been equally incapable of knowing that they would permanently escape the religious violence that had erupted in so many other parts of the British Isles and Europe during their lifetimes. Understanding their outlook requires an effort to recapture the sense of impending danger that haunted their world.

Popish antagonists

Religious conflict not only posed immediate threats to the kingdom's peace. It also disrupted Elizabethans' relations to their own past and the moral authority that past conveyed. All across Europe the ideological underpinnings of political authority were being subjected to searching examination and polemical assault by confessional adversaries.[5] Appeals to history had become double-edged weapons, used to attack government as well as to defend it.

Protestants especially needed to reinvent the past, to justify what might otherwise appear an arrogant break with ancestral customs. The English Reformation devastated a liturgical culture that had previously given definition to social relationships at every level from the royal court down to the village.[6] Familiar objects of communal devotion were stripped away by officers acting under royal commissions, a process epitomized by the destruction of rood images of Christ, Mary and

St John in parish churches and their replacement by royal coats of arms. This act signalled the triumph of a Protestant royal supremacy over old and familiar images now branded as popish superstition.[7] Symbols that had once expressed Christian solidarity became partisan emblems, as when the northern rebels of 1569 adopted a banner bearing the five wounds of Christ. In several European cities liturgical objects provided flashpoints of riots and ugly violence, as Elizabethans knew.[8] Marlowe's *Massacre at Paris* (1592) – a melodrama stretching from the famous murders of St Bartholomew's Day, 1572, down to the assassination of Henry III in 1589 – accurately portrays Catholic assassins taunting their victims by making them kiss crucifixes before stabbing them to death.[9]

Reformers regarded the old liturgical forms not as an ancestral religion, but aspects of a clerical conspiracy directed by the Bishop of Rome, to promote clerical power by keeping the laity ignorant and superstitious. They depicted Catholic ceremony as an empty theatrical show, while contrasting the pride, wealth and duplicity of the 'popish' clergy with the simplicity of religious reformers. This message was spread not only through sermons and pamphlets but popular media like woodcuts, plays and ballads.[10] Ballads were printed as cheap broadsides, hawked by itinerant peddlers and performed to well-known tunes in alehouses and other public spaces. They recounted stories of heroes and heroines victimized by bloody-minded priests and furnished partisan accounts of events like the Northern Rising, the Spanish Armada, and the arrest and execution of Jesuit priests. Until the 1580s itinerant theatrical companies performed plays that adapted the emblematic conventions of the old morality tradition into reformist propaganda, for example by including vice figures dressed in priests' garments with names like Perverse Doctrine and Malicious Judgment.

Protestants also turned individuals and groups who had quarrelled with the medieval Church into precursors of the Reformation. Anticlerical satirists going back to Chaucer and the fifteenth-century *Piers Plowman* were inaccurately regarded as followers of Wycliffe.[11] Even John Skelton, who had attacked Lutherans in the 1520s, was pressed into service as an anti-popish poet.[12] Monarchs who had clashed with the Church – King John who had been forced to pay homage to the Pope; Henry II who had famously quarrelled with Thomas à Becket; and, of course, Henry VIII, Edward VI and Elizabeth – were integrated within this picture, as champions in a struggle also being waged by much humbler people.

Collinson has argued that around 1580 Protestant spokesmen rapidly began to abandon traditional popular forms of culture and protest, adopting a more rigorous and 'fastidious' approach.[13] The clergy turned against stage plays and ballads, even (indeed often especially) when they were used to convey religious doctrine. Other scholars have qualified this account, however. Watt found that while the proportion of Protestant ballads did fall off after 1580, the decline was protracted and interrupted by a brief resurgence in 1623–5.[14] The decline in religious woodcuts was even more gradual and ambiguous.[15] Among more respectable poets Spenser and his seventeenth-century imitators continued to build upon the work of Skelton and the *Piers Plowman* tradition, as did Milton during the Civil War.[16] Tragedies about Lollard and Protestant heroes based on Foxe, such as Thomas Dekker and John Webster's *Famous History of Sir Thomas Wyatt* (*c.* 1604) or the anonymous *Oldcastle* and *Thomas Cromwell*, enjoyed a vogue on the London stage in the early seventeenth century, around the time of James's accession.[17] As Margot Heinemann has written, they invariably centred around the story of 'an independent, literate, Bible-reading individual, standing up for conscience and personal interpretation of the Scriptures against bullying bishops or erring monarchs'.[18] In doing so they perpetuated a myth of God's protection of the English people who, in these dramas, begin genuinely to assume the status of an elect nation.[19]

The imagery of popish rapaciousness and duplicity was also fleshed out by references to more current historical events, especially incidents in the religious wars of France and the Netherlands and plots against the Queen by Mary Stuart. Many Dutch and French Protestant pamphlets, newsbooks and histories were translated and reprinted in Elizabethan England: the peak decade, 1585–95, saw the publication of 130 tracts on French affairs alone.[20] One printer, John Wolfe, built up a network of foreign correspondents and a stable of hack translators, while working with Burghley and Walsingham to issue anonymous propaganda pamphlets in English and foreign languages.[21] It has been estimated that nearly a fifth of all works printed in London in the early 1590s consisted of political news and polemics concerning European religious conflicts. Marlowe's *Massacre at Paris* brought the French wars of religion on to the London stage. The arch-conspirator in this play is the Duke of Guise, who boasts of the legions of 'fat Franciscan friars' and pensioned priests ready to promote his ambitions. He seduces the Queen Mother, Catherine de Medici, who happily murders her own children to promote his interests. The play ends with Guise dead but his allies still engaged in treasonous plots, opposed by a new alliance between Henry of Navarre and Elizabeth. This was a highly topical allusion, since at the time of the play's first performance the English had 3000 troops on French soil.

Marlowe's play illustrates the porous nature of the boundary separating news from imaginative literature in this period. In the absence of newspapers, plays, ballads, pamphlets and partisan histories all helped convey information about current events. Modern historians have most often studied anti-popery through the writings of the clergy, in which it is frequently associated with millenarian ideas. We also need to take into account more secular accounts of Catholic plots and conspiracies, however, which usually lacked explicit theological content. As Peter Lake has argued, although anti-popery ultimately derived from radical strains of Protestant thought, it gained currency even among people who were not particularly godly, in part by appealing to a desire to find scapegoats and an ingrained habit of seeing the world in dualistic terms.[22]

A view of politics as an unrelenting struggle against ruthless papist enemies was obviously calculated to rally the nation behind its Protestant rulers. It might also inspire criticism of Crown policies, however, for being insufficiently vigilant against the foe. Philip Sidney and others in his circle, for example, associated Protestantism with watchfulness, courage, exertion and other active virtues, while alluding to the inactive and cautious European policies of Lord Burghley and the Queen through an imagery of sleep, idleness and delusion.[23] In both *Old* and *New Arcadia* these latter vices repeatedly threaten to bring political disaster.

The cultural construction of puritanism

Anti-popish rhetoric was used even more frequently against the ceremonies and bishops of the Elizabethan Church. In the 1590s a reaction developed, associated with Archbishop John Whitgift's drive against presbyterianism and responses to the notorious anti-episcopal satires of Martin Marprelate. From a theological perspective the most impressive product of that reaction was Richard Hooker's *Laws of Ecclesiastical Polity*, which laid the foundations for a fundamental re-evaluation of the Church of England's relations to its medieval past, on which Lancelot Andrewes and Caroline divines, including

William Laud, John Cosin and Richard Montagu, continued to build in the next century.[24]

In the short run Hooker's book was less influential than a spate of anti-puritan satires, many initially subsidized by the bishops as counterattacks on the anti-episcopal satires of Martin Marprelate.[25] These associated puritanism with popular sedition in both Church and state. Richard Bancroft regarded puritanism as one manifestation of a dangerous cosmopolitan republicanism infecting England:

> The world now a days is set all upon liberty. Every man almost is of their humour which thought scorn that any should be lifted above the congregation. The cantoning of kingdoms is in many men's mouths. You shall find it a great matter among those that have been travellers, and it is their usual discourse, viz. what a notable thing it is to live in Venice. There (forsooth) every gentleman liveth with as great liberty as the Duke himself. They have no earls, no barons, no noblemen, of whom their gentlemen should stand in awe. What is a nobleman (say these discoursers) but a gentleman?[26]

The fact that Calvinism had so often developed in rebellious republics, such as Geneva and the Netherlands, made it immediately suspect.

In a more colloquial vein, John Lyly lampooned seditious puritans in *A Whip of an Ape*:

> Yes, he that now saith, Why should bishops be?
> Will next cry out, why Kings? The saints are free.
> The German bores with clergymen began
> But never left till Prince and peers were dead
> ...
> And Martin's mate, Jack Strawe, would always ring
> The clergy's faults, but sought to kill the king.[28]

Religious extremism derived from unstable temperaments, 'men whose minds are of themselves as dry fuel, apt beforehand unto tumults, seditions and broils', as Hooker put it.[29] Although ostensibly motivated by godliness, it actually reflected the arrogance of people who granted 'too much credit...to their own wits',[30] who can usually sway 'the rude multitude (by whom bold counsel is always accepted for noble and wise)'.[31] 'It is not unknown,' Bancroft complained, what the profession of any extraordinary zeal...doth work in the multitude. When they see men go simply in the streets, looking downward for the most part, wringing their necks awry, shaking their heads, as though they were in some present grief: lifting up the white of their eyes sometimes, at the sight of some vanity.[32]

Conformists regarded this intolerant and histrionic zeal as the opposite of Christian charity,[33] a spirit that inevitably led to division and strife.

Like popery, puritanism was therefore stigmatized as factionalism propagating itself through religious theatricality. As such it readily became associated with demagoguery and sedition. Just as anti-popery gave rise to hostile portrayals of medieval clergy, anti-puritanism inspired satiric accounts of Lollards and early Protestant reformers. The character Falstaff in Shakespeare's *Henry IV* is probably an example, originally patterned after the Lollard Martyr John Oldcastle but renamed following a protest by Oldcastle's descendant, Lord Cobham. Falstaff uses typical puritan catchphrases, and although his sloth and gluttony seem to us anything but puritanical, these vices were associated with Marprelate and other puritans in the 1590s.[34] Drayton and Munday's *The First Part of the True and Honourable History of the Life of Sir John Oldcastle, the Good Lord Cobham* (1600) may have been a reply to Shakespeare's play, intent on upholding a more favourable view of Lollardy.[35]

Already by the end of the sixteenth century, concepts of England's Reformation and pre-Reformation religious history had therefore become entwined with contemporary controversies. A hostile view of the Henrician reformation remained a minority position under James but became dominant among the Laudian clergy in Charles I's reign.[36] It was also embraced by lay antiquarians, beginning with Camden, who in the 1590s expressed regret over the plundering of the monasteries.[37] In 1604 his former student, the Catholic Ben Jonson, celebrated the opening of James's first Parliament with a panegyric that scathingly alluded to Henry VIII's break with Rome as an act motivated by lust and resulting in tyranny.[38] Later in the century, John Spelman and William Dugdale voiced even more stringent condemnations.[39] Spelman regarded the confiscation of monastic property as an act of sacrilege that had brought the curse of God upon owners of former Church lands, while in the 1650s Dugdale commemorated monasticism in terms that implicitly linked the spoliation of the 1530s to puritan assaults on the Church after 1642.

Anti-popery and anti-puritanism were not necessarily incompatible. It was possible to believe, as James I did, that 'Jesuits are nothing but puritan papists',[40] essentially similar breeds of fanatics threatening the Church and Crown. Yet the two stereotypes appealed at opposite ends of the religious spectrum and frequently became entangled in political disagreements. Attitudes towards Spain provided one litmus test. Although for most of the Elizabethan period Spaniards had been vilified less frequently than French Catholics, during the Armada war Spain became especially identified with the foreign Catholic enemy.[41] The conviction that the Spanish monarchy would always seek the destruction of England had virtually become an article of faith among some English Protestants, including members of the Privy Council like Archbishop Abbot. Fear of Spanish infiltration naturally extended to mistrust of anyone at court who appeared sympathetic to Madrid, such as the Earl of Northampton before his death in 1614 or the Chancellor of the Exchequer, Francis Cottington, in the 1630s.[42] Popish and Spanish influence was also frequently blamed for poisoning James's relations with Parliament, partly on the assumption that Catholics would naturally want to destroy the bonds between the King and his Protestant subjects but also because popery was regarded as a natural ally of tyranny.[43] When Prince Charles and Buckingham turned against Spain in 1624, their actions were widely interpreted as proof that they had seen through the Machiavellian stratagems of Spain's ambassador, Gondomar, and pro-Spanish English ministers like the Earls of Bristol and Middlesex. Thomas Scott's pamphlets, *Vox Dei*, *Vox Regis* and *Vox Populi* developed this interpretation at length, depicting James as a ruler systematically duped by Habsburg stratagems into betraying the interests of his kingdom (*see* plate 3). The most commercially successful play of the period, Thomas Middleton's *A Game at Chess*, also revolved around the theme of Spanish plots, uncovered at the last moment by the acuity of the Prince and Duke.[44]

Anti-popery frequently tended to foster pro-war sentiment, since fighting Catholic enemies was easily associated with the active virtues and discipline advanced Protestants favoured. As Collinson has pointed out, 'almost the only pastimes of which Puritans approved, the only truly lawful games, were archery and other martial arts'.[45] Conversely, peace seemed to encourage luxury, corruption and vanity. Spiritual and physical militancy were therefore connected: 'As the spiritual warfare of a Christian is the matter of greatest moment under heaven, so next unto it, in my judgment, is bodily war', one puritan proclaimed.[46] On the

or
Gondomar appearing in the likenes of
Matchiauell in a Spanish Parliament,
wherein are discouered his treacherous & subtile Practises
To the ruine as well of England, as the Netherlandes
Faithfully Translated out of the Spanish Coppie by a well-willer
to England and Holland.

The second Edition.

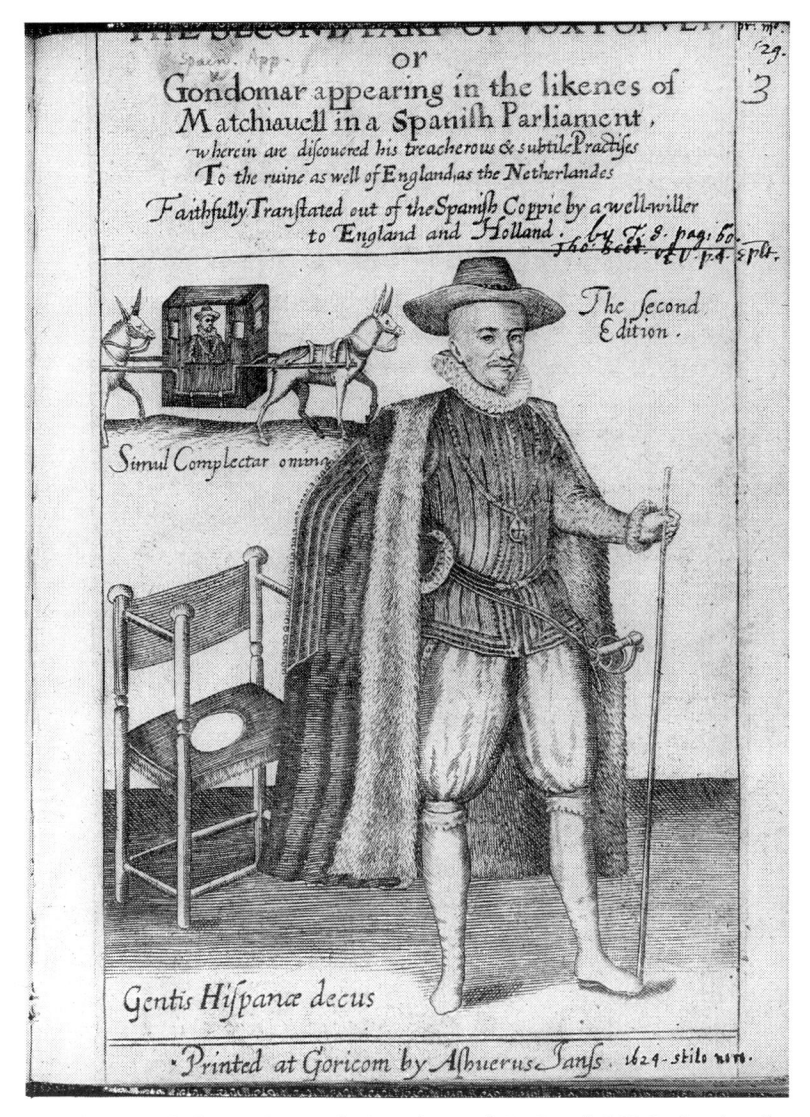

Simul Complectar omnia

Gentis Hispanæ decus

Printed at Goricom by Ashuerus Jansz. 1624.

3. Title page of Thomas Scott, *The Second Part of Vox Populi* (1624), showing the Spanish ambassador, Gondomar, as a Machiavel. Copyright the British Library.

other hand, many conformist clergy and laymen, remained deeply suspicious of the populist tendencies of puritanism.[47] Divergent views of the Reformation and its legacy had begun to sow division long before the 1640s.

Cults of Authority, Royal and Otherwise

Alongside the frequently polemical religious culture of this period, a large number of works were produced that attempted to buttress secular political authority. This kind of culture has attracted considerable attention from modern scholars, who have sometimes compared it to the mass propaganda of twentieth-century totalitarian regimes or the image-making campaigns of modern politicians.[48] This approach has generated important insights but has also encouraged some misconceptions.

The study of Tudor dynastic propaganda was pioneered in the 1950s and 1960s by scholars like Frances Yates and Roy Strong.[49] They sought to reconstruct an Elizabethan royal cult by searching for common themes among a wide variety of sources, including major classics like *The Faerie Queene* as well as largely forgotten occasional poems, pageants and paintings. Their research revealed surprising continuities, demonstrating that poets, artists and courtiers had drawn upon a common stock of symbols and tropes, with complex and varied roots in biblical, classical, chivalric and European sources, which gradually expanded over the course of the reign. In many cases Elizabethan royal imagery involved a deliberate reworking of Habsburg and Valois dynastic propaganda, itself often based on imagery originally associated with Augustus Caesar.[50] These were important and exciting discoveries that provided fresh insights into canonical writers like Spenser and Shakespeare, while at the same time uncovering a large number of previously neglected cultural documents. By amalgamating evidence from scattered sources produced over several decades, however, this scholarship sometimes made royal propaganda appear more imposing and systematic than was warranted. A good example is the way in which Strong assembled anecdotal accounts of celebrations on the anniversary of Elizabeth's accession (17 November) to argue that a new secular holiday had emerged in place of abandoned saints' days.[51] More systematic research by David Cressy and Ronald Hutton has now qualified this picture, showing that Accession Day celebrations spread only slowly, never became universal, and normally consisted of little more than the ringing of church bells in the evening, whereas saints' days had involved stoppage of work.[52] Strong exaggerated his findings, though his discovery remains important.

A second distortion was a tendency to 'read the reign backwards' by giving undue prominence to imagery created during the Queen's last years or even after her death.[53] Finally, earlier scholars sometimes read as simple adulation work conveying more ambiguous messages. Recent investigators have become more attuned to the ways in which, in this rhetorically sophisticated culture, praise could also imply criticism and dissent.[54] Rather than simple propaganda many forms of court culture served a process of veiled negotiation and argument, along the lines of Castiglione's precept that a courtier must guide his Prince while dissimulating his efforts to do so. Uncovering such indirect meanings often requires placing works within precise historical contexts, instead of reading them as expressions of generalized themes.[55]

The nature of the surviving evidence can also foster misunderstandings. For the modern student royal cults consist of printed texts and a few visual sources, especially court portraits. This material lends itself to systematic literary and iconographic analysis, encouraging an approach that treats cultural history essentially as an exercise in decoding poetry and painting. Contemporaries would normally have experienced the cultural apparatus of monarchy differently, however. They would have found it more difficult to assemble a large number of panegyrics than a modern student equipped with a good university library, but in compensation they might have witnessed displays we can no longer see. Interpretations based on readings of the surviving sources may, therefore, convey erroneous impressions. Even texts that purport to describe ceremonial occasions – for example, accounts of royal entries, Lord Mayors' pageants and court masques – are normally biased narratives.[56] They provide the illusion of plunging the reader into actual events but invariably leave some things out, while giving exaggerated prominence to others.

Ritual and the scenic apparatus of political authority

No sensible historian would want to dispense with the insights that textual and iconographic analysis can provide. The traditional materials and methods of literary criticism and art history need to be supplemented, however, by other kinds of analysis. To begin with, this means paying attention to ceremonial conventions and material objects that do not fit modern definitions of art and literature.[57]

The most impressive 'image' of royalty any Elizabethan could encounter was a sight of the Queen herself, whether at Whitehall or during a summer progress. The material culture and ceremonial routines of court life in this period continued to reflect essentially medieval conventions. The ruler was always surrounded by an impressive entourage and a profusion of luxurious objects, especially precious metals, jewels and expensive textiles. These materials were equally essential to the decor of royal palaces, the embellishment of the barges, chariots and coaches in which royalty travelled, the splendour of great public ceremonies, and the clothes courtiers wore. Royal and aristocratic portraits of the period normally depict costumes with meticulous care, while accounts of state ceremonies also tend to dwell on the splendour of jewels, gold and cloths. Such descriptions demonstrate not just a love of pomp but a habit of associating authority with particular forms of display. Further evidence is provided by the way in which certain words designating ceremonial actions or objects acquired more abstract political connotations. Examples include obeisance (the act of bowing, but also political submission) and 'the state' (the monarch's throne and canopy, but also government itself).[58]

The importance of ornate symbolic exchanges between ruler and subjects was never clearer than during the Queen's progresses. Cavalcades of liveried horsemen greeted Elizabeth whenever she entered a county, approached a major provincial city or returned to London, as in 1585, when a German tourist reported:

> The mayor with some hundred men met her on horseback – members of the town council, citizens, and tradesmen, especially many goldsmiths, clad in black velvet coats and wearing golden chains. Crowds of people came running after – men, women and young girls.[59]

Such events enacted hierarchical relationships as apparently spontaneous expressions of loyalty.

Much of the panoply of these displays was already ancient. Rather than being perceived as a sign of obsolescence, however, this old-fashioned quality stressed the monarchy's rootedness in the past and so was often deliberately emphasized. Before James I's coronation entry a special commission spent months investigating relevant precedents to assure the correctness of every detail. The feudal office of Constable of the Realm, vacant for nearly a century, was momentarily revived so that the order of march might conform to medieval precedents. Innovative rites like the Elizabethan Accession Day jousts, often assumed a spurious antiquarian aura. Even Stuart masques, for all their modernity, repeatedly displayed costumes and scenes purporting to represent British antiquity. Court ceremony provided another device for inventing tradition.

Analogous practices can be observed in London and several provincial cities.[60] In both cases older public rituals associated with Catholic feast days disappeared during Elizabeth's reign but civic pageants emphasizing secular history helped fill the gap.[61] In London the Lord Mayor's pageants incorporated mythical figures like the giants Gog and Magog – reputedly the last of the island's aboriginal inhabitants – and the founding kings Brute and Lud. They also represented legends about heroic medieval Londoners, like Dick Whittington, and flattering myths concerning specific trades.[62] Thus a 1605 pageant celebrated the seemingly unpromising theme of the martial heritage of London's tailors.[63] Many provincial towns initiated inaugurations during the latter half of Elizabeth's reign, in which the mayor and aldermen paraded in gowns and bore civic maces of traditional design, although in some cases they were actually newly invented. Robert Tittler has traced the emergence of a tradition of civic portraiture of mayors and other town dignitaries, including some spurious portraits of past mayors of great local repute. Although artistically crude, these images commemorated the regular succession of town magistrates, and hence the continuity and stability of the local corporation. Along with maces, robes of office, mayoral chairs and the new and grander town halls erected in many towns in the last half of the century, they gave civic authority tangible form.[64]

The rituals and paraphernalia of authority served both to establish and circumscribe contact between rulers and ruled. Events like mayoral processions and royal progresses enacted a medieval concept of princes and magistrates as guardians of the community, prepared to dispense justice and benevolence to all. Elizabeth emphasized these ideals by interacting with ordinary spectators along her route and using progresses to visit not only courtiers and great peers but middling gentry who were leaders within their own local neighbourhoods.[65] Exchanges of hospitality and gifts on these occasions established, however fleetingly, direct face-to-face contact between the sovereign and individual subjects. At the same time the opulence of the Queen's entourage and the formality with which she was treated established a kind of symbolic distance. The account of a German tourist who saw Elizabeth on her way to chapel in 1600 captures the paradoxical blend of grandeur and familiarity. Although she appeared 'glittering with the glory of majesty and adorned with jewelry and precious gems', when she 'entered into the view of the whole assembly [she] stretched her arms out wide as if to embrace everybody present'.[66]

A number of gradual cultural changes were beginning to place greater emphasis on separation rather than contact. These included architectural developments that created a much sharper differentiation between public spaces and more exclusive rooms inhabited by people of rank. Starkey and Simon Thurley have traced the process by which the royal Privy Chamber split off from the Chamber in the early Tudor period, creating a clear division between the apartments in which the ruler lived and rooms where he or she performed public functions. The guarded door between the Presence Chamber, with its royal throne and canopy, and the gallery leading into the Privy Chamber, marked a symbolic boundary between two sides of court life.[67]

Town halls evolved in somewhat analogous ways, though usually at a later date. Late medieval guildhalls with open timber ceilings provided a space in which the whole civic community assembled, whereas the town halls erected in the late Tudor and Stuart periods normally contained specialized court rooms and mayor's parlours, to which access was limited.[68] Even the interior spaces of parish churches were divided by private pews arranged to reflect the local pecking order. These developments exhibit an increasing tendency to mark social boundaries and limit contact between rulers and ruled. The decline under the early Stuarts of public rituals of kingship, such as royal entries, is another manifestation of this trend.[69] So is the development of the coach, which enclosed people even as they travelled along public highways. Similar changes occurred all over Europe, so we are dealing with an international movement. We also need to make allowances for survivals and revivals of old forms of public contact right through the seventeenth century. The Civil War convinced some members of the elite of the dangers of neglecting public rituals, and the coronation entry of Charles II was, accordingly, more ornate and expensive than any of the earlier period. In the long run, however, the trend toward greater segregation is unmistakable.

Can we also detect a movement toward symbolic deification of royalty, as some scholars have claimed? The answer is complex.

Elizabeth I and James I were certainly compared to biblical figures but this was not a new practice, since the use of Christian liturgical forms and symbolism in secular political culture was already commonplace in the Middle Ages.[70] The habit of treating monarchs as little kings set upon earthly thrones predates the early modern period and cannot accurately be regarded as a response to either the Reformation or modern ideas of absolutism. On the contrary, Protestantism tended for a time to inhibit many liturgical expressions of royal authority. The late Elizabethan period witnessed a revival of crypto-Catholic forms of queen worship discarded earlier in the reign, along with more novel images equating Elizabeth with pagan goddesses.

It has been suggested that this was made possible by the fact that Catholicism had declined to the point where it no longer posed a threat.[71] Although there may be something to this, a shift toward ceremonious imagery in royal panegyric also seems to have been connected to a reaction against puritanism. A pioneer of the new trend was the fiercely anti-puritan George Puttenham, though courtiers with more solid Protestant credentials, like Ralegh, soon followed. The rejection of rigorous reform allowed both the recovery of medieval forms of devotion that had become attenuated after the Reformation and the invention of new formulas treating the sovereign as a sacred figure. James's accession in 1603 slowed the process, since the new king was sufficiently Calvinist to share some puritan scruples about 'superstitious' practices like touching for the King's Evil. Pagan religious imagery remained common in court masques, however. Under Charles the habit of treating the King as a religious symbol expanded again, reinforced by baroque forms borrowed from the Continent. The deification of monarchs appears to have been less a substitute for Catholicism than something associated with revivals of religious traditionalism.[72] Civil War republicans like the poet John Milton had reason to regard royal ceremonies as a political counterpart to popery.[73]

Literary cults and the publicizing of court politics

Ceremonial events, especially involving the Queen, were frequently embellished with poetic speeches or theatrical pageants. This literature was generally occasional in the strict sense, intended to be performed in a specific setting and then forgotten. Especially during the last two decades of the reign, however, a substantial body of literary texts relating to Elizabeth began to circulate in printed or manuscript copies. They ranged from short poems and broadside ballads up to far more ambitious works, like Spenser's *Faerie Queen*e. Moreover, poets did not stop producing such work in 1603. Many continued to celebrate Gloriana up until the Civil War and beyond.[74] In that sense we can legitimately speak of a literary cult that helped create a posthumous legend, which sometimes provided a foil for the conduct of her successors.

Scholars have offered several explanations for this important development. E. C. Wilson, in the 1930s, regarded the Queen's literary cult as a spontaneous expression of national devotion.[75] Others have stressed the role of court patronage, the development of commercial markets for books and plays, and a growing sense of patriotism stemming from the Armada war.[76] No single explanation will cover all cases, since we are dealing with many kinds of literary artefacts that circulated by different methods.

In a 1951 article that has remained widely influential, J. W. Sanders drew attention to a basic distinction between court poets who shunned 'the stigma of print' as incompatible with gentility, and 'professional poets outside or only on the edge of Court circles' for whom 'the achievement of print became an *economic* necessity'.[77] The former wrote as an avocation, while the latter did so to attract attention from insiders who could provide cash rewards or jobs. To succeed, however, they had to emulate the court amateurs, rather than ballad-makers and playwrights whom no one respected. They consequently used print while pretending to disdain it.

This analysis has since been extended in several ways, especially through more intensive studies of Elizabethan courtier poetry and, more recently, forms of scribal publication.[78] It is tempting to construct a sociological map of Elizabethan and early Stuart literature by expanding Sanders's distinctions into wider dichotomies, between public and 'coterie' audiences, and a literature of patronage as opposed to one aimed at the market. Perhaps ultimately we might thereby locate the beginnings of a divergence between forms of discourse embedded within courtly and aristocratic affinities and an emerging 'public sphere' defined by print.[79]

Yet the moment we closely examine the subject, these binary opposites start to collapse into more complex and ambiguous patterns. Sanders's distinction between aristocratic amateurs and professionals works less well after 1603, partly because James I, who published a volume of poetry and a number of prose tracts, was himself a notable exception. Court poetry in the first quarter of the new century was mainly written by professionals, especially Jonson, who fashioned a public persona through both patronage and print.[80] A more fundamental problem is that simple distinctions between manuscript and print mask crucial variations within each media, as well as the ways in which work passed from one to the other. Penny broadsides cannot helpfully be lumped together with expensive folios, any more than unique private copies of court poems can be equated with manuscript libels tacked up in public places. Scribal publication could achieve a high degree of publicity, while print did not always guarantee a large audience. In any case, work written for an exclusive audience sometimes ended up being recopied or printed and thus disseminated widely. Not only individual poems but images, themes and styles travelled from one medium into another, gaining or losing shades of meaning in the process. The linkages between manuscript and print, as well as courtly and public audiences, can be as revealing as distinctions between them.

We can begin to illustrate these points through what at first seems the quintessential example of court 'insider' verse, namely love poetry written for the Queen by her favourites. Stephen May has shown that this genre was invented at Whitehall in the late 1570s, probably by the Earl of Oxford.[81] He employed Petrarchan formulas to produce sonnets voicing the complaints of a devastated lover, who has lost all reason for living because his mistress has abandoned him for a rival. These poems, which may have been read or sung to Elizabeth, would easily have been decoded as expressions of the Earl's fear of losing royal favour. Oxford was a highly cosmopolitan nobleman whose sonnets reintroduced a European courtly fashion into England.[82] His experiments soon found imitators, like Sir Arthur Gorges, Walter Ralegh and the Earl of Essex.[83] Ralegh added the refinement of addressing the Queen under the names of pagan goddesses, while alluding to himself through variations on the nickname 'Water', which she had bestowed upon him. The title of his longest poem, 'The Ocean to Cynthia', is an example.

Despite its intimacy this poetry did not always remain confined within the court. Some of Oxford's verse had already been anthologized in the 1570s. Ralegh's 'Farewell false love', composed around 1580, was set to music by William Byrd and published in 1588, while a lament of *c.* 1590 inspired by the rise of Essex, 'Fortune hath taken thee away my love', was quickly entered in the Stationers' Register as a ballad. It also circulated widely in manuscript alongside a number of answering poems – including one by Elizabeth that also seems to have been published as a ballad in the early seventeenth century – and a hostile reply, possibly by Essex, entitled 'Fortune's child, nature's defiler'.[84] This mocked Ralegh by referring to him as 'puddle'. The market value of these poems derived partly from their status as insider pieces.

The circulation of such verse contributed to a recognition that love might serve as a political metaphor. As Katherine Bates has shown, it was in the sixteenth century that the verb 'to court' and its noun form of 'courtship' entered the language. Initially terms describing the actions of a courtier, these words acquired their sexual meanings in Elizabeth's reign.[85] Whether in a political or amorous context, 'courting' had overtones of rhetorical contrivance and theatricality, suggesting the pursuit of favour through expressions of devotion that might or might not reflect true feeling.

Once established, the practice of using love conventions as political metaphors gave rise to several further developments. The image of Elizabeth as a beautiful but inaccessible virgin, inspiring men to feats of devotion, was picked up by writers of court entertainments as early as the late 1570s and by poets unconnected with the court. The theme seems initially to have been developed by writers opposed to negotiations for a marriage between the Queen and the Duke of Anjou in the years 1578–81, though it quickly became a standard trope, especially in poems extolling national unity during the Armada war.[86] The virginity topos even entered into jog-trot ballads celebrating privateering expeditions.[87] In *The Faerie Queene* Spenser took over and refined his patron Ralegh's method of celebrating Elizabeth under multiple allegorical guises, like Bellphoebe, Gloriana, Cynthia and Astraea. By the mid 1590s this technique had become an established fashion in royal panegyrics.

Meanwhile other courtiers – Sidney, Edmund Dyer and Fulke Greville – wrote sonnets to women aside from the Queen, which provided coded expressions of their political ambitions and frustrations. The posthumous publication of Sidney's *Astrophil and Stella* (1594) gave rise to a number of imitations by writers outside the court, including John Donne, whose verse recounting male sexual adventures and conquests, written as he embarked on a court career in the 1590s, has been convincingly analysed as an expression of political as well as sexual fantasy.[88]

The exaggerated language of courtly Petrarchanism also invited parody, while imagery devised to please and flatter the Queen might convey more critical undertones. Essex used Petrarchan poetry to complain of callous treatment at Elizabeth's hands:

> Her thoughts and mine such disproportion have:
> All strength of love is infinite in me;
> She useth the advantage time and fortune gave,
> Of worth and power to get the liberty;
> Earth, Sea, Heaven, Hell are subject unto laws,
> But I, poor I, must suffer and know no cause.

Some courtier poems and printed verse by writers enjoying court patronage voiced bitter factional attacks. Spenser's *Mother Hubberd's Tale* assailed Lord Burghley and Robert Cecil and was called in by the authorities in 1591, although the author had received a royal pension in that year.[89] The late Elizabethan fashion for allegory and elaborate metaphor facilitated political ambiguity, by allowing poets to deploy images that might be read in different ways.[90] Comparisons of the Queen to the moon-goddess Cynthia, for example, might imply either purity or inconstancy.

It would be naive to discount altogether the elements of personal flattery and political propaganda in poems about Elizabeth. The Queen's vanity, which expanded as she aged, and the government's desire for favourable publicity both exercised considerable influence over the period's literature. It is clear, even so, that we cannot regard all literary tributes as unalloyed expressions of devotion or propaganda. A number of converging trends were at least as important as court patronage and patriotism in generating a royal literary cult. One was the growth of a commercial printing industry and the emergence of a commercial stage in London after the late 1570s. Many occasional poems that might otherwise have remained known only to narrow coteries attained a second life through being printed years after their original composition. The drift towards war with Spain after about 1575 also seems to have resulted in an expansion of published tracts praising the Queen and other national heroes.[91] Intersecting with both phenomena was the premium that humanist culture placed on collecting documents relating to high politics. Court literary artefacts were copied and circulated in manuscript, often alongside other items, such as parliamentary speeches, tracts by leading courtiers and miscellaneous bits of gossip.[92] The Inns of Court were particularly important as centres for the production and dissemination of this material, although the royal court itself, the universities and independent efforts by some country gentlemen also generated manuscript collections.[93]

Humanism also heightened awareness of how literary forms had been used to comment upon politics in classical antiquity. Writers like Spenser and Jonson conceived an ambition to do for England what Virgil, Horace and Martial had done for Rome. This project required modern counterparts to Augustus and the imperial elite, to serve as subjects for English epics, odes and panegyrics.[94] Rather than seeing court poets as propagandists of the state, it is often at least as accurate to regard Elizabeth and James I as rulers co-opted by writers who needed royal patrons and heroes to fulfil their own aspirations. But if the classical tradition provided examples of panegyric and cults of authority, it also furnished models for more critical work. Virgil, Horace and Ovid had all displayed ambivalent or inconsistent attitudes towards the Imperial state. The enterprise of creating a national literature patterned after their examples implied a need both to glorify and find fault. This is precisely what all major poets associated with the Court – especially Jonson and Spenser – did.

We also need to take into account native traditions ranging from pageant skits during civic events, to carnivalesque celebrations of misrule and vernacular shaming rituals and satires. Pageants and lords of misrule had once been closely connected to seasonal festivals such as Christmas and the feast of Corpus Christi. They survived the Reformation by becoming secularized, through association with civic mayoral processions and festivities within the royal household. The Stuart court masque, for example, descended from carnivalesque antics by masked dancers during Christmas celebrations at court. Jonson's anti-masques reinterpreted this tradition in the light of antiquarian research on Greek and Roman satyr plays, which seemed fairly analogous in tone, content and purpose.[95] By an analogous process vernacular forms of satire and insult were skilfully adapted by Martin Marprelate and anti-Martinists like Nashe,[96] and then further reworked in the late 1590s by sophisticated Inns of Court poets imitating Juvenal, Martial and Horace.

In short, the decades on either side of the year 1600 saw a simultaneous expansion in the audience for political information, the use of both print and scribal copying to disseminate courtly material, and the sophistication of literary forms employed to comment on politics. The upshot was a significant growth in both quantity and quality of writing about monarchs and other leading personalities. Ralegh's career produced an especially large literary residue, consisting of his own poems, hostile pieces written by his enemies, and both real and suppositious prose works.[97] His great rival, Essex, provides an even better example. Essex deliberately tried to manage the dissemination of information about himself, as when he collaborated with his secretary, Henry Cuffe, to write an account of the Cadiz expedition of 1596 purporting to come from a disinterested eye-witness and slip it to a printer.[98] Like Ralegh, he encouraged the manuscript circulation of material casting him in a favourable light, such as the 'Apology' he wrote defending his opposition to Burghley's peace negotiations with Spain in 1598, of which many copies survive. But he sometimes proved unable to control the circulation of documents relating to his activities, and as his career neared its tragic close inopportune publicity contributed significantly to the Queen's resentment. Elizabeth reacted with fury in 1600 when 'some foolish idle ballad makers' printed an engraved equestrian portrait of Essex, since this was an iconographic formula traditionally reserved for royalty. A few months later she was again angered when his 'Apology' appeared in print, together with a letter by Essex's sister, Lady Rich, justifying his conduct.[99] About the same time London clergy were prohibited from praying publicly for the Earl during a period of illness. While imprisoned following his unauthorized return from Ireland in 1599, Essex himself complained bitterly of his public notoriety:

> I am gnawed at by the basest creatures on earth. The prating tavern haunter speaks of me what he list: the frantic libeller writes of me what he lists; already they print me and make me speak to the world, and shortly they shall play me in what forms they list upon the stage.[100]

His rebellion and execution in 1601 gave rise to a further spate of ballads, together with royal proclamations and officially inspired tracts and sermons that sought to blacken his reputation. These pieces were soon followed by the plays Essex had predicted, notably Samuel Daniel's *Philotas* and Shakespeare's *Coriolanus*. This publicity was not entirely unprecedented: Cardinal Wolsey, Thomas Cromwell and Protector Somerset had also attracted considerable notoriety. No earlier period, however, had produced as much written material on court politics.

All this justifies referring to the emergence of an embryonic public sphere of political discourse, a century before the date given by Jürgen Habermas in his classic discussion of the subject.[101] But the characteristics of political discourse in the late sixteenth century differed markedly from those Habermas identified in the early eighteenth century. Rather than being dependent on the circulation and discussion of print in public forums like the coffee house, sixteenth-century political culture depended on a combination of printed media, manuscripts, performances like plays and sermons, and gossip. Moreover, Elizabethan culture placed a premium on access to privileged news and the deciphering of secrets, rather than the free and open circulation of information. Unprinted material was valued for its rarity, while printed poems, like *The Faerie Queene*, often spoke a coded language of allegory and symbol that required inside knowledge to decipher. The codes sometimes helped to evade censorship,[102] but this was never their sole motivation. Encrypted messages were also valued because affairs of state were still regarded as mysteries.[103] The most valued forms of political discourse were, therefore, those which circulated within restricted networks or were far from transparent. The very emphasis on secrecy naturally had the effect of encouraging prying and speculation, thus broadening the audience for high politics.[104]

Habermas saw the 'public sphere' as sharply differentiated from court society, whereas in this earlier period public political discourse was continuously fed by gossip and representations emanating from Whitehall and allied environments like Essex House. It developed as court rivalries and aristocratic factionalism spilled over into wider arenas. For this reason political news and representations often centred around leading personalities more than abstract issues. Panegyric and satire were important forms of political discourse because affairs of state were so often imagined in terms of the actions of great men and women, idealized as personificatons of public aspirations or vilified as symbols of corruption.

Dead heroes and the fabrication of cultural memory

This mindset is well illustrated by the way in which certain figures acquired an almost iconic status after their deaths, as symbols for particular values and policies. Among the earliest was Sir Philip Sidney, who died fighting for Dutch independence in 1586 as a frustrated courtier who had failed to fulfil his political and military ambitions, and an amateur poet whose work remained unknown outside a small circle of intimates.[105] Nevertheless Sidney was given a massive heraldic funeral in London, which nearly ruined the finances of his father-in-law Francis Walsingham, who paid for it. A number of English peers and several prominent Dutch leaders attended and it was commemorated by a fine series of engravings, executed in a continental style normally reserved for the high nobility and royalty (*see* plate 4). Several volumes of elegies by English and continental poets soon followed.

These commemorative rites launched Sidney on a brilliant posthumous career as a paragon of Protestant chivalry embodying the aspirations behind the policy of active military intervention in Europe advocated by his uncle, Leicester. Essex, who inherited Sidney's sword and married his widow, saw himself as carrying on the dead hero's legacy. Despite official efforts to blacken his reputation after his execution, the Earl became a second icon of Protestant chivalry.[106] For a handful of English poets, especially Spenser, Sidney's memory meanwhile fulfilled another purpose, by raising the social pretensions of literature.[107] In the 1590s Sidney's poems and prose *Arcadia* were published, initially in a pirated edition but subsequently under the auspices of his sister and literary executor, the Countess of Pembroke. Her efforts culminated in a large folio edition of Sidney's *Works* in 1598, an unprecedented form of publication for a recently deceased English poet, which became the prototype for subsequent folios of the collected works of Samuel Daniel (1601), Spenser (1611, 1617), Jonson (1616), Michael Drayton (1619) and Shakespeare (1623). The Countess extended her patronage to all these poets except Shakespeare, whose folio was dedicated to her two sons. By doing so she provided a pattern of aristocratic literary patronage emulated by others in the early seventeenth century, while helping to define a canonical tradition of Elizabethan and Jacobean literature.[108] Sidney naturally assumed the place of honour at the font of that tradition, a man representing a combination of literary genius, enlightened patronage, Protestant rectitude and political virtue that was becoming associated with a vanished golden age.

The number of verse elegies commemorating Sidney actually exceeded those published for Elizabeth in 1603. His record remained unbroken until the death in 1612 of a royal paragon of Protestant chivalry: Henry, Prince of Wales. This event led to an even grander funeral than Sir Philip's and a huge outpouring of poetic lamentation.

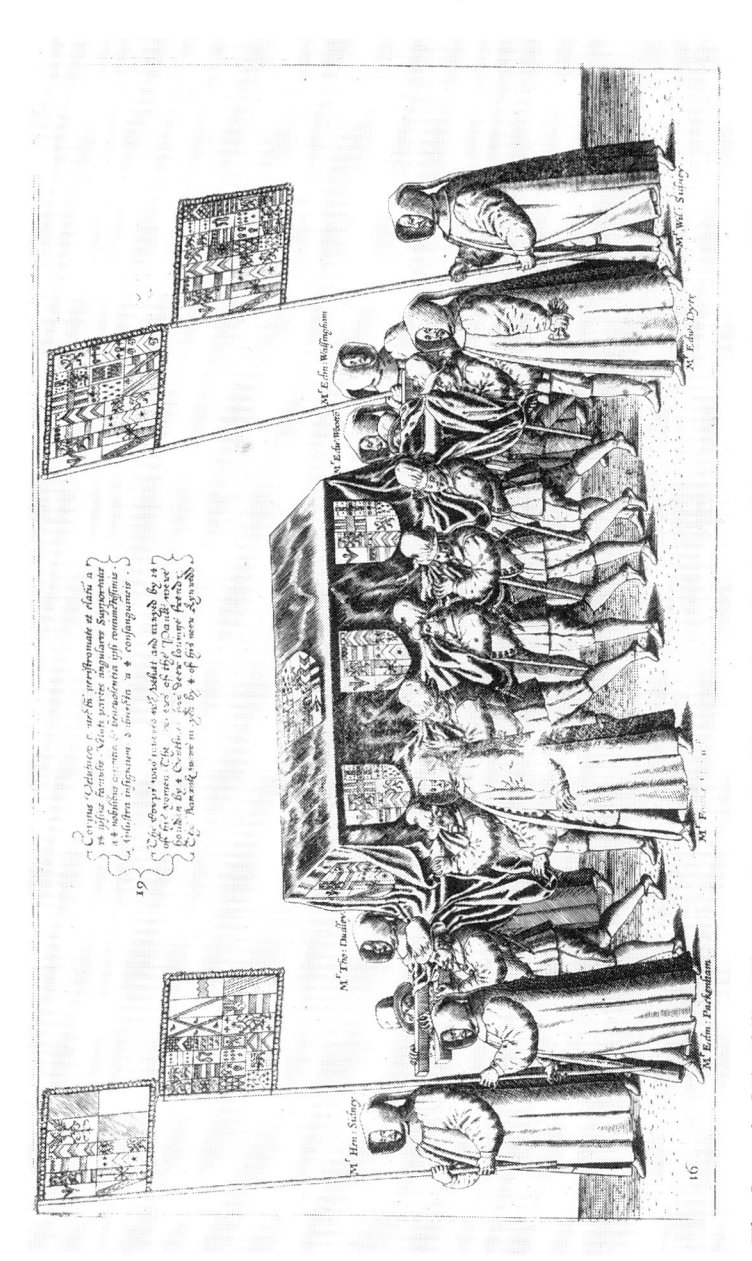

4. The funeral of Sir Philip Sidney, as depicted by Thomas Lant, *Sequitur celebritas et pompa funeris... Philippus Sidneis* (1587), plate 19. Copyright the British Library.

Like Sidney, Henry was remembered as both a discerning cultural patron – determined to advance English painting and architecture in the way that Sidney had advanced poetry – and a leader determined to defend international Protestantism through armed action.[109] In 1618 Ralegh joined the cohort of dead heroes after his execution at the behest of the Spanish ambassador. Ralegh manuscripts became much more popular following this event.

By the 1620s a pantheon of legendary figures therefore embodied values and accomplishments associated with the period of the Armada war. Historians have sometimes referred to this phenomenon as 'Elizabethan nostalgia' and William Hunt has gone so far as to discuss 'spectral origins of the Civil War', arguing that comparisons with dead heroes seriously diminished royal credibility.[110] To a greater extent than has sometimes been recognized, the nostalgia was deliberately shaped and nurtured by peers with personal or family connections to Sidney and Essex, and by poets like Michael Drayton, George Wither and Samuel Daniel, who in many cases enjoyed the patronage of the same aristocratic circle.[111] For these poets the glorification of Elizabeth's reign carried an implication that 'old English honour' and Protestant rectitude had since degenerated.[112] This attitude looked back to the ideal Queen Sidney and Essex would have liked to have served, rather than the actual ruler who had thwarted the ambitions of the first and executed the second. Moreover it was never the only view of the late sixteenth century available. In 'To Penshurst' Jonson associated Sidney's memory with an entirely different set of ideals, associated with the rites of hospitality and goodlordship rather than exploits in battle. *The Arcadia* became an important text within the Caroline court and was eventually quoted extensively by *Eikon Basilike*. No one group ever monopolized Elizabethan memories. But legends of her reign had become important components of Stuart political culture.

Faction, Rebellion and Violence

With the exception of the struggling Dutch provinces, western Europe in the sixteenth century was ruled by personal monarchies. But this did not necessarily mean that monarchs securely controlled the polity. Several states succumbed to conflicts engendered by deadly combinations of religious hatred, popular discontent and noble feuds. Until the 1580s resistance to royal authority was mainly associated with Calvinism but in France between 1584 and 1594 Catholics proved equally adept at fomenting and justifying rebellion. The period's religious wars gave rise to a very large body of controversial literature, ranging from tendentious pamphlets to major theoretical treatises.[113] Both varieties of commentary gave prominent attention to the problem of factionalism.

The cultural construction of faction

Because faction was universally deplored it was normally something associated with adversaries. English Protestants accused papists of forming a party or faction, while Huguenot writers depicted the French Catholic League as a faction constructed by the Guise family. The major early descriptions of Elizabethan court factionalism were Catholic pamphlets.[114] The most successful of these, written anonymously by men associated with exiled recusant nobles in Paris in the mid 1580s, is usually known as *Leicester's Commonwealth*.[115] Despite its Catholic provenance it circulated widely and, as Simon Adams has shown, later influenced Camden's great history and, through it, interpretations of Elizabethan court politics ever since.[116]

Much of *Leicester's Commonwealth* is occupied by a portrait of its protagonist as a moral monster, who ravishes the wives and daughters of men seeking his favour, poisons both enemies and servants who have come to know too much, and schemes to achieve absolute power. The pamphlet also provides a more sober analysis, however, of the mechanics of faction within a royal polity. The history 'of all nations, kingdoms, countries and states', shows that men who wish to gain supreme power always begin by trying 'to possess themselves of all such as were in place' around the prince or chief magistrates:

> This did all these in the Roman Empire who rose from subjects to be great princes and to put down emperors. This did all those in France and other kingdoms who at sundry times have tyrannized their princes. And in our own country the examples are manifest of Vortigen, Harold, Henry of Lancaster [Henry IV], Richard of Warwick, Richard of Gloucester [Richard III], John of Northumberland and diverse others who by this mean specially have pulled down their lawful sovereigns.[117]

Leicester was now pursuing this strategy, by stacking the Privy Chamber with 'his own creatures' to obtain 'a lock upon the ears of his prince' and control of her patronage. 'All the favors, graces, dignities, preferments, riches and rewards which her Majesty bestoweth... must serve to purchase this man private friends.'[118] By this means he had corrupted the legal profession and gained control of the kingdom's chief military strongholds.[119]

While consolidating his following, Leicester also deliberately fomented civil dissension by playing upon religious divisions and fear of Catholic plots.[120] Catiline once distracted Rome in much the same way. Puritans had been won over to his side, while Catholics were systematically persecuted and foreign princes antagonized. The nobility was divided into antagonistic parties, a situation that had presaged civil war throughout history. The story of Julius Caesar and the struggle between Octavian and Antony that followed his assassination, as well as the reigns of the English Kings Edward II, Richard II and Henry VI all provided illustrations. Once civil chaos broke out, Leicester planned to seize power from the Queen or her successor, just as his father, Northumberland, had attempted to do at the death of Edward VI.

For all its distortions, *Leicester's Commonwealth* developed its case around a highly plausible analysis of the operation of personal monarchy in early modern conditions. It rightly stressed the importance of controlling access to the prince and the information she received, the use of royal patronage to build court affinities and the dangers inherent in religious divisions and rivalries between great nobles. Anyone familiar with English or European high politics would have recognized the force of this discussion. It may, in fact, have been suggested by earlier Huguenot accounts of the Guise faction in Valois France.[121] If so, this illustrates how polemically constructed analyses might cross both national and confessional boundaries, becoming equally useful to partisans at opposite sides of the religious spectrum.

Malcontents and evil favourites

Leicester in this pamphlet illustrates both of the two main categories within which contemporaries normally conceived of great factional leaders: the malcontent and evil favourite. Normally the types were kept distinct. The malcontent was an overmighty subject of overweening pride and ambition, unwilling to submit to any authority, even God's. He might be imagined as a fundamentally corrupt figure, actuated by malice and cruelty as well as self-interest, or as an essentially good man led astray by the influence of corrupt dependents and an excess of noble qualities like pride and valour. The Earl of Essex was depicted in both ways after his execution. Officially sponsored accounts smeared him with accusations of atheism and treason, while his erstwhile followers portrayed him as a man destroyed by the plots of adversaries, the bad advice of his secretary, Henry Cuffe, and a nature incapable of adapting to a treacherous court environment.[122]

Whether regarded sympathetically or not, great noblemen pursuing their own political advantages, without due regard for royal authority, were all too familiar in the late sixteenth century. The term 'malcontent' had acquired its political overtones during the French wars of religion. Initially it referred to the attitude of a nobleman who had proclaimed himself dissatisfied (*mécontent* or *malcontent*) with a patron or superior. In the 1570s the word came to describe great lords who had withdrawn from the royal court and drawn their affinities into armed defiance.[123] By the 1580s it had passed into English, denoting either a feeling of being aggrieved or a disloyal subject. The two meanings were often associated in the figure of a leader driven by ambition and envy. The chorus of Samuel Daniel's *Philotas* summarized the type:

> See how these great men clothe their private hate
> In those fair colours of the public good;
> And to affect their ends, pretend the State,
> As if the State by their affections stood.[124]

Daniel here describes a politics of personal egotism, disguised by specious pretences of public service.

Because he intuitively understands feelings of envy and resentment, the malcontent is a natural demagogue. Frequently he also possesses a military following, as with Julius Caesar, who was often used as an archetype. Marlowe's Guise, for example, suggestively refers to himself as Caesar as he brushes aside warnings not to keep the fatal appointment with Henry III at which he is assassinated.[125] Recent European history furnished several additional examples of popular military leaders threatening legal authority. Great French malcontents especially intrigued English audiences: Marlowe's *Massacre at Paris* and Chapman's *Bussy D'Ambois* and *Tragedy of Byron* all deal with the subject.

English history plays are also full of malcontents, like York in Shakespeare's *Henry VI* Part II or the same playwright's Richard III. Both are soldiers driven by insatiable ambition, who deftly manipulate the discontents of others. Bolingbroke similarly arouses Richard's jealousy by wooing the multitude:

> Ourself and Bushy
> Observed his courtship to the common people,
> How he did seem to dive into their hearts
> With humble and familiar courtesy.[126]

Essex's career appeared to fit the same paradigm, as both he and the Queen recognized. John Hayward's dedication to Essex of a history of Richard II's deposition caused a furore in 1599, and the Earl paid Shakespeare's company to enact the same event on the eve of the ill-fated 1601 rebellion.[127] Essex was undoubtedly among those Sir Robert Cotton had in mind when he wrote of great men from 'our own times whose spirits [were] improved by military employments and made wanton by popular applause'.[128] The aristocratic leaders of the parliamentary movement of the early 1640s – among them Essex's son, who commanded Parliament's army – were portrayed by royalist pamphleteers in much the same light.

Whereas the malcontent built a popular and military following to overpower the state from without, the evil favourite sought to infiltrate it from within. Instead of playing upon popular grievances, he employed the courtier's techniques of artifice and dissimulation to enthral the prince and pervert his authority. Cultural forms like the masque might assist his endeavours. Although most often associated with the Stuart period, this last trope already existed in the sixteenth century. Marlowe's Gaveston in *Edward II* knew full well the uses of masques and court culture:

> I must have wanton poets, pleasant wits,
> Musicians, that with touching of a string
> May draw the pliant king which way I please.
> Music and poetry is his delight;
> Therefore I'll have Italian masks by night,
> Sweet speeches, comedies, and pleasing shows;
> And in the day, when he shall walk abroad,
> Like sylvan nymphs my pages shall be clad.[129]

Poetry, music and dance are associated with effeminacy and homoerotic passion, in implicit opposition to masculine pursuits like war, which Edward II neglects.

The problem posed by the evil favourite was at base an ethical one. He distorted the political system by pandering to the King's vices and excluding virtuous counsellors, with results that typically included distortions of the system of honour, defeat in foreign wars, the wasting of the King's resources and, in consequence, higher taxation. Holinshed and Hall described such problems in recounting the reigns of kings like Edward II and Richard II, while Marlowe and Shakespeare dramatized them on the stage. A similar range of abuses figured in parliamentary complaints against early Stuart favourites, especially Buckingham. The obvious remedy was the favourite's removal and replacement by wise and honest counsellors. Once this happened the polity was expected to heal itself. Political discourse couched in these terms allowed people to complain vehemently about grievances, while exonerating both the King and fundamental institutions from blame. The revival of impeachment in the Parliaments of the 1620s and attempts by the parliamentary leadership in 1641 to force Charles I to surround himself with counsellors in whom the political nation had confidence both reflected similar attitudes.

Weak kings and declining states

The problem obviously became more serious if the source of moral weakness lay partly or wholly in the King himself. A weak or depraved ruler could promote a whole series of evil favourites, as Richard II and Edward II had done. In the worst case, his misrule might produce a distemper in the commonwealth that threatened its very survival. The diagnosis of such political 'diseases' and the prescription of remedies for them was a major preoccupation of the European literature on reason of state, which frequently compared the statesman to a physician.[130] A number of Englishmen shared this interest, among them Hooker. 'Bodies politic being subject as much as natural to dissolution by diverse means', he wrote, 'there are undoubtedly more estates overthrown through disease bred within themselves than through violence from abroad.'[131] Foreign enemies inspired precautions, 'whereas...domestical dangers, for that we think we can master them at all times, are often permitted to run on forward till it be too late to recall them.'

Another Elizabethan interested in this problem was the anonymous author of the preface to Henry Savile's 1592 translation of *The Histories* of Tacitus, who may have been either Anthony Bacon or the Earl of Essex. He described the narrative that followed as the story of 'a torn and declining state...the people wavering; the soldiers tumultuous; nothing unlawful to him that hath power'. In his own preface Savile observed that such a commonwealth is like 'a body corrupt and full of ill humours' in which even a small pain 'discloseth old aches and strains, actuateth what else is unsound', so that the first 'disorder dissolveth the whole'.[132] Presented in this way, Tacitean history became something more than a grim record of evil under despotism. It provided insight into a problem that was effectively the reverse of that which Machiavelli had set out to analyse in *The Prince*. Machiavelli's goal was to explain how the ruler of a 'new state', lacking the stability and legitimacy conferred by ancient title, might establish his rule through the exercise of extraordinary *virtu*. Savile, by contrast, wanted to show how vice and incompetence could destroy a settled commonwealth that required only minimal ability to rule.

The two perspectives were essentially complementary but Savile's seemed more relevant to conditions in the late sixteenth century. The only new state in northern Europe was the embattled Netherlands, whereas several ancient polities, especially France, seemed on the verge of collapse. Established governments were assumed to possess reserves of strength because, as Samuel Daniel explained, 'there are so many ligaments in a state that tie it together as it is a hard thing to dissolve them altogether, unless it be by an universal concurrency of causes that produce a general alteration. And it is seldom seen of what temper soever kings are, but they find an eminent party in the greatest defection of their people.'[133] Yet at times the ligaments snapped and it seemed vitally important to understand how and why this happened.

Savile thought that the diseases afflicting the Roman empire on the eve of the civil wars related by Tacitus stemmed directly from its ruler. The basic problem with Nero was that he was not only vicious but 'contemptible'.[134] While his tyranny inspired hatred, his personal conduct dissolved the respect and fear that might have protected a more capable tyrant. He survived for a time because formidable military and political resources inherited from his predecessors deterred men from taking action. Once a sufficiently resolute opponent appeared, however, imperial power collapsed, since although people hesitated to oppose Nero they had no wish to support him.

Because Tacitus's narration of the rebellion that toppled Nero had been lost, Savile was able to replace it with a short work of his own that deserves to be regarded as the first of the new Tacitean or 'politic' histories written in English.[135] He portrayed the military officer

Vindex, who initiated the rebellion, as a man of great resourcefulness who unfortunately lacked an independent base of power from which to challenge Nero. Vindex therefore appealed to various provincial governors to lead his insurrection. All but one – the commander in Gaul, Galba – turned his letters over to the Emperor. Galba did nothing, since he wished to protect himself by remaining on the sidelines. A follower pointed out, however, that Nero would inevitably learn of Vindex's proposal, and this would seal Galba's fate. Emperors are always jealous of their authority and Nero, who was especially prone to fear and envy, would find a way to destroy any man with the ability to threaten him, regardless of actual guilt. Galba revolted to save his skin and succeeded in taking the throne, though he was soon deposed and murdered by another commander.

Savile's narration thus turned upon the jealousy that, in his estimation, must always exist between a weak ruler and his own subordinates. A few years later John Hayward effectively plagiarized this construction in his account of Bolingbroke's rebellion against Richard II.[136] In Hayward's treatise magnates headed by the Archbishop of Canterbury decide to topple Richard and invite the exiled Bolingbroke to lead their rebellion. Bolingbroke at first turns them down, saying he prefers an easy retirement abroad to involvement in a dangerous conspiracy. Canterbury convinces him, however, that he really has no choice, since Richard will learn that he has been approached and move to have him killed from royal 'jealousy'.

These histories invert the standard topos of the envious malcontent plotting against his King into a portrait of rulers who conspire against their greatest subjects. Savile elaborated on the point in a footnote to a passage in Tacitus's *Agricola*. Under a weak ruler men of pre-eminent virtue become the prince's rivals, since the people naturally honour them more than the ruler himself and often seek redress from oppression at their hands. Vicious courtiers who always surround a bad prince will eagerly fuel his envy. Virtue will therefore attract retribution while vice is rewarded. If the situation continues long enough, the whole population may lose its virtue so that the polity becomes incapable of reform. Such was the condition of Rome described by Tacitus at the outset of *The Annals*.

This analysis ultimately derives from classical republican ideas, whether Savile and Hayward appreciated the fact. It was also capable of linking up with chivalric themes of nobility and detraction, as seems to have happened in Essex's entourage. Bacon warned his patron as early as 1596 to beware of the jealousy his military reputation and popularity inspired in the Queen.[137] Essex rejected the advice because Bacon's remedies – seeking civilian rather than military offices, and offering the Queen counsel in which he did not believe, so he could respond gracefully when she rejected it – seemed inconsistent with this sense of honour. But he agreed that the detraction of malicious courtiers had damaged his relations with Elizabeth and his public reputation. 'I live in a place where I am hourly conspired against, and practiced upon,' he complained: 'What they cannot make the world believe they persuade themselves unto; and what they cannot make probable to the Queen, that they give out to the world.'[138] By the eve of his rebellion, he evidently viewed Elizabeth as a weak ruler whose mind had been poisoned against him by enemies like Ralegh, Cobham and Cecil. He may well have believed, as he claimed, that armed action offered his only hope of survival.

Some history plays reflect a similar analysis. A character in Jonson's *Sejanus* describes the destruction of Germanicus, Tiberius's popular heir:

> When men grow fast
> Honour'd and lov'd, there is a trick in state
> (Which jealous princes never fail to use)
> How to decline that growth, with fair pretext,
> And honourable colours of employment.[139]

Shakespeare is more circumspect but Bolingbroke's relation to the King in *Richard II* also seems shaped by royal jealousy and the detraction of courtiers like Aumerle.[140]

Emulation between princes and great subjects was ultimately only one possible source of unrest stemming from weak rule. Both Shakespearean tetralogies dealing with the Wars of the Roses can be read as dramatic portrayals of processes of unravelling brought about, at least partly, by ineffectual kingship. In the *Henry VI* plays of the first tetralogy the problem is not tyranny but weakness and naivety. Henry has all the right aspirations but he fails to arbitrate quarrels, punish lawless vendettas or even restrain the intrigues of his own wife. The result is a widening spiral of court faction and violence. From the outset of *Henry VI* Part I, rivalries among the nobility weaken English arms. This theme would have had a topical flavour at the time of the play's first performance in the early 1590s. Court politics had recently been unsettled by the deaths of several leading members of the Council –

Leicester (1589), Sir Walter Mildmay (1589), Francis Walsingham (1590) and Christopher Hatton (1591) – as well as competition among younger favourites, especially Essex and Ralegh. Although every member of the Council agreed on the need to fight Spain, strategy and the scale of military commitments remained issues. Essex and other commanders felt, with some reason, that their capacity to wage war was hampered by political indecision and infighting at home.[141] This is exactly the kind of situation Shakespeare dramatized:

> Amongst the soldiers this is muttered,
> That here you maintain several factions;
> And whilst a field should be dispatched and fought,
> You are disputing of your generals.[142]

The tragic fate of Lord Talbot, a heroic commander killed in battle because more powerful nobles are too busy quarrelling to send him timely aid, is one that some Elizabethan generals may also have feared.

In *Henry VI* Part II, more than any of Shakespeare's other English history plays, noble factionalism broadens out into popular insurrection in Cade's rebellion. As Annabel Patterson has shown, Shakespeare allows Cade and his followers to voice actual grievances or medieval modern popular rebellions. His extremism is likely to unsettle even modern audiences, however, and Helgerson is surely correct in arguing that most Elizabethan playgoers would have had little sympathy for it.[143] The blame is not cast entirely on the popular forces; instead the play shows the escalation of a savage mutual hatred between gentry and commons. Neatly symmetrical speeches by the leaders of the opposing forces just before the key battle encapsulate the cycle:

> *Sir Humphrey Stafford*: Herald away; and throughout every town
> Proclaim them traitors that are up with Cade;
> That those which fly before the battle ends
> May, even in their wives' and children's sight,
> Be hanged up for example at their doors... [*exeunt*]

> *Jack Cade*: And you that love the commons, follow me
> Now show yourselves men; tis for liberty.
> We will not leave one lord, one gentleman:
> Spare none but such as go in clouted shoon...

What stands out is the brutalizing and tragic effect of class hatred.

The opening scenes of *Richard II* – the first play of the second tetralogy – present a more complex picture of a King who is undermining his own authority. Richard weakens the law by turning it into an instrument of oppression, as Gaunt pointedly reminds him. His complicity in the murder of his uncle Gloucester – an event that looms ominously in the background throughout Act I – compromises the solidarity of the royal lineage, confusing the imperatives of honour. For the King's remaining uncles, York and Lancaster, and their sons, loyalty to Richard has been placed in conflict with the basic honour imperative to avenge a kinsman's blood, which Gloucester's widow eloquently evokes in Act I, scene ii. The opening feud between Bolingbroke and Mowbray is also connected to Gloucester's death.

Richard reveals himself as a King unwilling to accept counsel that conflicts with his own desires, as well as one who has squandered his revenues on court frivolities and therefore lacks the means to wage war without extorting money from his subjects. In all of these ways he has conspicuously failed to preserve the principles of order and justice that Kings, according to the conventional view, were appointed by God to uphold. Modern commentators have sometimes assumed that divine right principles are unambiguously aligned with Richard, so that anything in the play that casts doubt on his cause implicitly 'subverts' religious justifications for kingship. Richard has violated so many of his sacred duties, however, that he has come perilously close to unkinging himself by the conventional logic of royalist theology.[144]

The confiscation of the Lancastrian estates, which finally provokes the rebellion that topples Richard, therefore culminates a long series of acts that has already hollowed out his authority. Richard evokes the sanctity of kingship with magnificent rhetoric once he feels threatened, but it is already too late. Bolingbroke moves with brisk and taciturn efficiency to destroy the King's few remaining supporters and seize his throne. When the Bishop of Carlisle defends Richard's God-given legitimacy, he is simply thrown in prison. At least in the short run, divine right proves an empty rhetorical construct, incapable of affording serious resistance to an usurper who knows how to get things done.

In the long run things turn out differently, of course. Carlisle accurately predicts the future rebellions of Henry's own followers and the civil wars that will plague his reign, which the next two plays in the tetralogy dramatize, and which have already begun to erupt by the end of this one, in the conspiracy to murder Henry that Carlisle, Aumerle and others initiate in Act V. Nor is the curse of Gloucester's blood lifted. Instead

Shakespeare provides a grimly comic scene (IV,i), in which peers hurl accusations and gages at each other in mutual recrimination. Richard's overthrow *continues* the process his own tyranny began, stripping away the values and hollowing out the rituals that support royal power, leaving everything dependent on armed coalitions cemented by self-interest. As interests shift these coalitions will break up and regroup, leaving the new King to contend with a seemingly interminable series of conspiracies. Bolingbroke's usurpation also adds motives for vengeance to earlier crimes, a point reinforced, as Thomas Greene has shown, through images of blood spilled upon the ground, evoking a sense of physical pollution to be expiated through future sacrifices.[145]

Modern critics have variously interpreted *Richard II* as a defence of Tudor theories of legitimacy or a play about a tyrant who gets his just deserts. The fact that the text can support either view suggests that Shakespeare intended a more complex message. There seems no reason to doubt that, like nearly all his contemporaries, he disapproved of both despotism and rebellion. But he ultimately seems less interested in debating the relative merits of divine right and resistance theory than in exploring the processes through which polities disintegrate in violent conflict. Even more than Tacitean historians like Savile and Hayward, Shakespeare appears to have been fascinated by the complex causes and far-reaching ramifications of political upheaval. His history plays are not ideological statements so much as dramatic explorations of a central problem of prudential thought, namely how and why the moral values and institutional authority that normally preserve civic peace sometimes collapse in disastrous cycles of violence.

Fears of arbitrary government

The history play, centring on a story of civil war or rebellion, was a genre of the 1590s that declined in the new century, when relatively few examples were produced. One reason may be that James's peaceful accession and the winding down of Europe's religious wars created a more stable political climate. Anxiety over evil favourites persisted, however, frequently becoming linked to fears of arbitrary government.[146]

Early Stuart concepts of tyranny and constitutional subversion cannot be explained solely as responses to domestic events. Like so much else in the political culture of the period, they had important roots in a larger European polemical discourse spawned by wars of religion. Protestant writers accused both Philip II and the Valois in France of overturning ancient constitutional liberties and erecting tyrannical governments. Several had further associated tyranny with a secret lore of policy, associated with Machiavelli and the new concept of reason of state. Machiavelli's sinister reputation derived not only from the content of his writings but the ways in which he became polemically associated with unpopular figures in contemporary politics, such as Catherine de Medici and her Guise allies.[147] The most influential attack on Machiavellianism at the Valois court, Alberico Gentillet's *Anti-Machiavell* (1576), was translated into English in 1602.

Even before then stereotypes of Valois intrigues had become directly implicated in English politics through Elizabeth's marital diplomacy. In 1579, during negotiations for the Anjou match, both Philip Sidney and John Stubbes warned that if a Valois prince once became king consort of England he would place himself at the head of a subversive Catholic faction.[148] Although this particular danger soon vanished, fears persisted that a court faction with foreign popish ties might seek to destroy English liberties. So did the habit of picturing both unpopular English courtiers and foreign Catholic agents as Machiavels. Marlowe's stage Machiavel, in the prologue of *The Jew of Malta*, retained strong Valois connections, having been reincarnated as the Duke of Guise.[149] Ominously he states that he has just come from France 'to view this land and frolic with his friends'.[150] By the seventeenth century, Machiavelli in English literature is most often found consorting with Spaniards and Jesuits. He is the arch rival of Ignatius of Loyola in Donne's *Ignatius his Conclave* for the position of honour next to Satan's throne, while in Middleton's *A Game at Chess* and Thomas Scott's pamphlets Spain's ambassador Gondomar becomes the arch-Machiavel (*see* plate 3).

Roman historians, especially Tacitus, also contributed to an imagery of sinister court intrigues against liberty.[151] The 1620s saw a revival of Roman history plays based on Tacitus and Suetonius, depicting evil imperial favourites.[152] In Thomas May's *Agrippina* the villains are freedmen who have supplanted the Senatorial aristocracy, by knowing 'ways of power; that not the Senate,/ But Caesar's chamber did command the world'.[153] The parallel to Buckingham's relatively humble birth, hostile relations with ancient peers like Arundel, Bristol and Pembroke, and disregard for Parliament, was obvious.

In the parliamentary debates of 1626 even a court spokesman admitted: 'Men that love oppression and wrong love no parliament, and ever have been, are, and will be about kings.'[154] Sir John Eliot developed a picture of the Duke's power strikingly reminiscent of the image of Leicester's faction English Catholics had constructed forty years earlier. The Duke had:

> made a party, a party in the court, a party in the country, a party almost in all the parts of government both foreign and at home... And having thus drawn to himself... in effect, the powers of the whole kingdom either for peace or war... he made an alliance. He then sets upon the revenues of the crown, intercepts, exhausts, consumes that fountain of supply, breaks those nerves and sinews of the land, the stores and treasures of the King... and casts the whole body of the land unto a deep consumption.[155]

For Eliot, Buckingham's moral depravity had become the driving force within a vast engine of subversion.

These charges contained some elements of truth, mixed with considerable exaggeration and distortion.[156] What matters for our purposes, though, is not the objectivity of Eliot's speech but the degree to which it reproduced an imagery of court parties that long antedated Buckingham's rise to power. On the other side the Duke and his supporters dismissed popular and parliamentary hostility by invoking an equally well-established imagery of envy, malice and demagoguery. A contemporary newsletter reported that, just before his departure with the fleet in May of 1627, Buckingham presented the King and Queen with a masque, 'wherein first comes for the duke, after him Envy, with diverse open-mouthed dogs' heads, representing the people's barking; next came Fame, then Truth, etc'.[157] The images of Fame and Truth also figured prominently on Buckingham's tomb in Westminster Abbey.[158] Charles's great favourite was variously seen as a an evil favourite or a man of virtue wrongly maligned by factious popular spirits. Both interpretations were rooted in well established cultural typologies and cannot be understood purely as responses to short-term events.

Court, Country and Town

We have so far concentrated on views of politics pivoting around kings and others at the centre of the polity. Most political discourse of the period adopted this perspective, not without reason, since in a personal monarchy so much obviously depended on the quality of the ruler and his associates. But contemporaries did sometimes take a wider view, encompassing impersonal trends affecting both the centre and the provinces. Indeed the relationship between these poles was often a signifcant issue, which contemporaries tended to describe through the richly evocative terms of 'court' and 'country' – to which they sometimes added a third element, the 'town', or capital city.[159]

Although all three terms acquired both positive and negative connotations, the country was usually regarded as more virtuous than the town or court. The contrast between country simplicity and court corruption was, in fact, something of a seventeenth-century commonplace. Perez Zagorin first remarked upon this fact in 1962 and saw it as symptomatic of discontent with the Stuarts.[160] This argument was subsequently expanded, by Zagorin himself and historians like Lawrence Stone and P. W. Thomas, into an interpretation of the early Stuart period as one of growing court–country conflict, in culture and society as well as in politics.[161]

In the 1970s and 1980s several historians criticized this thesis. They pointed out that court and country could not become radically separate in England, since royal patronage and royal appointments of county magistrates mattered crucially in 'country' politics.[162] Gentry needed to worry simultaneously about their reputation among their neighbours and their standing at court, and when the two came into conflict they were caught in the middle. In the early seventeenth century, growing numbers of landed families travelled to London for the emerging winter season, visiting the court and participating in the culture that had grown around it.[163] Metropolitan cultural fashions, news and consumer goods therefore penetrated more readily into the countryside.[164] Rather than a widening gulf between the provinces and the court and metropolis, the period witnessed increased interaction between them.

Yet this very fact may explain why contrasting images developed. Contact had become sufficiently frequent to become unsettling, not least for gentry who divided their time between London and the provinces. Derek Hirst has rightly argued that conflicts between court and country were usually fought within the minds of individuals, rather than between opposing groups.[165] But this did not necessarily make the conflict any less intense.

The court: centre of civility, sink of corruption

The royal court was the epicentre of English politics, the ultimate source of power and patronage, towards which all politically ambitious men gravitated. In other European states, such as France and Spain, large bureaucracies of ennobled officeholders and expanding armies provided outlets for the energies of those eager to advance themselves while serving their king and country.[166] In England, with its tiny bureaucracy and modest military resources, court service provided almost the only opportunities outside the shires. By the late sixteenth century a surfeit of humanistically trained gentry sought to make careers there, in a period when the financial pressures of war and parsimony of the ageing Queen restricted opportunities. The resulting frustrations, combined with the factionalism of the 1590s, gave rise to highly critical views of the court, as a place of cut-throat ambition and vicious infighting, where deserving men rarely prospered.

Disgust found expression not only in private grumbling, of which surviving letters preserve many echoes, but anonymous squibs and libels. These proliferated in the 1590s, reaching a peak following Essex's execution, when a lawyer's clerk was hanged for copying them out.[167] Cecil, who was widely blamed for the Earl's downfall, was particularly vilified, but other prominent courtiers also became targets.[168] The increasing volume of such material, along with hostile oral comments on the Queen's government, worried some officials as a sign of impending disorder. 'Libels and licentious discourses against the state', warned Bacon, 'when they are frequent and open; and in like sort false news, often running up and down, to the disadvantage of the state, and hastily embraced, are amongst the signs of troubles.'[169] They betokened the growth of 'public envy', a disease that may begin as a localized infection but soon 'spreadeth upon that which is sound, and tainteth it', until 'it traduceth even the best actions...and turneth them into an ill odor'.[170] Lord Keeper Egerton similarly complained of men who sit 'at ordinary and common tables, where they have scarce money to pay for their dinner, [and] enter politique discourses of princes, kingdoms and estates, and of counsels and councillors, censuring every one according to their own discontented and malicious humours'.[171]

Although most libels were fairly crude, the example of Roman poets like Juvenal and Martial began to inspire more sophisticated satiric complaints from the late 1590s.[172] Along with the parallel influence of Tacitus, these models inspired a view of the political centre as a seductive but dangerous place that allured people by the promise of power and profit, only to destroy them once they came within its orbit. Donne expressed this idea through several vivid images. Power is a stream that nourishes plants near its 'calm head' but uproots those that come too close to its torrent, casting them over rocks and through mills before depositing them in the ocean. Alternatively the stream is Justice, pure and gentle at its royal source but soon converted by venal officers into a dangerous current that may 'suck thee in, to misery/ To fetters, halters'.[173] Great courtiers are compared to mills and suitors to the wind that drives them and the corn that is ground between their stones. In 'Metempsychosis', written in 1601 though published only in 1633, Donne traces the many reincarnations of the soul of the apple in the Garden of Eden, until it comes to dwell in the great man who 'moves that hand and tongue and brow/ Which, as the moon the sea, moves us': i.e. Robert Cecil.[174] Each incarnation becomes an image of the power to tempt, corrupt and destroy while remaining inactive. Thus the soul becomes a sea monster:

> He hunts not fish but, as an officer
> Stays in his court as his own net, and there
> All suitors of all sorts themselves enthrall,
> Soon on his back lies this whale wantoning,
> And in his gulf-like throat sucks everything
> That passeth near. Fish chaseth fish, and all,
> Flyer and follower, in this whirlpool fall.[175]

Joining the court thus meant sacrificing oneself to predatory leaders.[176]

Jonson's court poetry tempers this harsh vision without altogether displacing it. The Juvenalian voice of moral outrage gives way to an urbanely polished tone, modelled especially after Horace, while satiric volleys against court vices are balanced against praise for friends and patrons. Jonson's verse evokes values of discrimination and independence, suggesting an ability to live amidst corruption without becoming tainted.[177] This was a stance strongly indebted to Stoic ideas fashionable in the period, in several ways diametrically opposed to Castiglione's ideal of courtliness.[178] It valued constancy over adaptability, personal independence more than conformity to the Prince's pleasure, terseness instead of copiousness and intellectual discipline in preference to *sprezzatura* (nonchalance). Where Castiglione's followers had stressed artifice and dissimulation, Jacobean writers cared more about a capacity to see through appearances. 'The sinews of wisdom are slowness of belief and distrust,' Bacon advised.[179]

Even figures closely associated with Whitehall therefore adopted essentially negative views of the courtier's trade, especially as it had been defined a generation earlier. Rather than defending court life, they sought to distance themselves from it. The pendulum moved back slightly in the next reign, especially in circles around Henrietta Maria. The wit of Caroline poets like John Suckling and Richard Lovelace looked back to the cult of *sprezzatura* and the courtly love poetry of the sixteenth century, as well as to more recent French concepts of courtliness. But the courtiers' reputation never truly recovered. Thomas Carew's *Coelum Britannicum* (1634) portrays the court not as a centre of virtue but a place whose vices the King and Queen are reforming. The best way to praise a prince or courtier was by describing his lack of conformity to his surroundings. Satires by poets who failed to attract court patronage were sometimes even more biting. Several volumes of such verse – including Michael Drayton's *The Owle* and George Wither's *Abuses Stript and Whipped* – appeared in print in the 1610s and 1620s.[180] Anonymous manuscript libels also continued to circulate.[181] Marotti has identified several peaks coinciding with the trial and imprisonment of Ralegh in 1604; the death of Cecil, by then Earl of Salisbury, in 1612; the trial of Robert Carr, Earl of Somerset and his wife Frances Howard for the murder of Thomas Overbury in 1616; the impeachment of Bacon in 1621; Buckingham's career in the 1620s and the execution of Thomas Wentworth, Earl of Strafford, in 1641.[182] Some of this material certainly reached popular audiences. Whether it provided an 'adult education course in contemporary politics', as Cogswell has claimed, it surely indicates 'widespread and growing distaste for James's [and Charles's] court', as Croft has written.[183]

The country as refuge

An image of the court as a place of corruption and treachery often corresponds to a view of the country as a refuge from temptation and care, the setting for a purer life. At the most basic level, this imagery worked through contrasts between the simplicity and honesty of countrymen and the lying, hypocrisy and backbiting of courtiers. In the late sixteenth century some writers also began associating the countryside with Stoic concepts of self-sufficiency and Epicurean ideas of self-cultivation. The court threatened these values not only through its vices but because life there required subservience to others. Dissimulation, insincerity and ambition allegedly made it nearly impossible to form honest friendships at court or find opportunities for the contemplation essential to self-knowledge. Country life offered an escape from these evils. 'Give me leave to know and love the air of peace in the country,' wrote Thomas Roe: 'where there is no storm of humour, nor no great temptations to hinder us to serve God... He that is damned in the country is worthy of two hells.'[184]

This neo-classical cult of rural beatitude was first systematically studied by Maren Sophie Røstvig in the 1950s.[185] She saw the tradition as developing slowly in the early seventeenth century in the work of Jonson and his imitators, before flowering during and after the Interregnum. This is correct if we concentrate, as Røstvig did, on direct imitations of Latin poems and also leave aside a few early Tudor pieces by Thomas Wyatt and the Earl of Surrey. Many of the themes later voiced in neo-classical poetry were, however, anticipated in late sixteenth-century work. Images of country estates and landscapes as refuges from court politics appear in history plays, including the anonymous *Woodstock* and several by Shakespeare,[186] and in a poem by the Earl of Essex:

> Happy were he could finish forth his Fate
> In some unhaunted desert, most obscure;
> From all society, from love, from hate
> Of worldly folk! There should he sleep secure;
> Then wake again, and yield God ever praise,
> Content with hipps, and haws, and brambleberry
> In contemplation passing still his days
> And change of holy thoughts to make him merry
> Whom when he dies, his tomb may be a bush,
> Where harmless robin dwells with gentle thrush.

Here the country is seen as free from care because free of politics.

This was neither an accurate portrayal of the lives of large country landowners, who were actively involved in local government, nor an alternative that men like Essex can ever have taken very seriously. Such imagery represented a form of escapism and a means of dissimulating engagement in high politics, rather than a viable alternative system of values. At best country retirement might be regarded as prudent withdrawal from a world too corrupt for reformation.[187] Even this stance was usually a way of rationalizing failure to obtain employment. The real alternative to the court, for men like Sidney and Essex, was not life in the country but a wider field of action, especially international diplomacy and war.

Gentry culture and the political centre

What, then, of actual country gentry and their outlook? How did they view their relationship to the political centre? This question seems harder to answer now than thirty years ago. In the 1960s and 1970s a 'county community' school of historians constructed a picture of provincial gentlemen as deeply insular figures, absorbed in the petty quarrels and concerns of their localities.[188] Suspicious of the court and its leaders and hostile to outside interference, 'they almost always put concern for their counties above any concept of national interest'.[189] Clive Holmes vigorously questioned over-reliance on these assumptions in an article of 1980.[190] He pointed to the circulation of metropolitan news in the provinces, growing resort to London, and the fact that even local government needed to be conducted within a framework of national institutions and with some reference to national issues. Although most gentry felt strongly attached to their localities, their insularity had its limits. Subsequent work has largely confirmed and extended Holmes's arguments, while also making it apparent that provincial gentry did not respond to political issues or cultural influences in a uniform way.[191] Sweeping generalizations need to be treated with caution, although some broad trends can be identified.

The culture of English gentry had always involved an ethos of service to the Crown and the realm, chiefly in the two major spheres of local governance and war. Until well into the sixteenth century both functions often demanded physical exertion and courage, especially in regions like the northern marches and Wales. Lord Herbert of Cherbury, in the early seventeenth century, proudly recorded family folklore concerning adventures of Yorkist and early Tudor ancestors chasing outlaws through the Montgomeryshire hills and suffering ambushes in the county court itself. As lawlessness receded in the sixteenth century, however, deeds of courage came to matter less than administrative skills and a man's standing among his gentry neighbours. In describing his Elizabethan grandfather, Herbert reported not only feats of valour but legendary hospitality and the reliance of other gentlemen upon his patronage.[192] Local governance was coming to depend on collective leadership more than armed peace-keeping.[193] A relative decline in the importance of great magnate anities further enhanced the importance of gentry communities in many, though not all shires.[194] These developments fostered intense competition over local offices, but also reinforced emphasis on co-operation and the preservation of consensus among a county's leading families.[195]

None of this meant that skill at arms and concern for affairs beyond the shire ceased to matter. On the contrary, increasing levels of education and strong religious commitments generated more complex understandings of the gentleman's political role. The tarnished moral reputation of the court did nothing to diminish gentry interest in national and international affairs. But it did sometimes require adjustments in outlook. One response was to define service to the commonwealth in terms of county institutions like quarter sessions and participation in Parliament, rather than activity at Whitehall. In some contexts devotion to 'the country' came to imply independence from the court, viewed as a source of corruption rather than the healthy centre of the commonwealth.[196] This attitude rarely implied a desire for institutional change, beyond the paring back of abuses like monopolies and bribery. It did, however, reflect a perception that sound governance was more likely to result from local initiative than direction from above. In places strongly influenced by puritanism the commitment of local elites to rigorous disciplinary campaigns discountenanced by the official Church might reinforce such attitudes.[197] Not all country gentlemen were puritans, though; there was no single 'country' attitude on such issues.

War and peace

England's long domestic peace provided a different challenge by reducing demand for the landed elite's traditional military vocation. Responses varied widely. Some panegyrists hailed peace as a blessing conferred by the Crown, which permitted subjects to relinquish public burdens in favour of private pleasures. This message is already present in the concluding tribute to Elizabeth in Robert Greene's *Friar Bacon and Friar Bungay* (1587):

> ...here where Brute did build his Troynovant,
> From forth the royal garden of a king
> Shall flourish out so rich and fair a bud
> Whose brightness shall deface proud Phoebus' flower,
> And over-shadow Albion with her leaves.
> Till then Mars shall be master of the field,
> But then the stormy threats of wars shall cease:
> The horse shall stamp as careless of the pike,
> Drums shall be turn'd to timbrels of delight;
> ...
> And peace from heaven shall harbour in these leaves.[198]

This theme remained a staple of Stuart court literature, down to celebrations of Charles I's 'halcyon reign', as in Carew's often quoted lines justifying England's withdrawal from the Thirty Years War.[199] It was often developed through parallels to the reign of Augustus and images of a flourishing pacified empire derived from Roman poetry. It was also expressed visually, through scenes of gardens and rustic environments in court masques, symbolic putti carrying fruits and other agricultural produce in Rubens's Whitehall Banqueting House Ceiling, and the landscape backdrops to several Van Dyck portraits.[200] In work of this sort the country becomes linked to an ideal of innocent recreation and gentlemanly civility, rather than active service and chivalric virtue.

Peace and tranquillity were not universally welcomed, however. Besides concern over military threats, many contemporaries worried that prolonged peace would produce diseases in the body politic. Just as the human body needs exercise to remain healthy, Bacon argued, so states need wars, 'for in a slothful peace, both courages will effeminate and manners corrupt'.[201] Sir William Cornwallis agreed: 'War is the remedy for a state surfeited with peace...it is a medicine for commonwealths sick of too much ease and tranquility...it carrieth a reforming nature, and is part of justice.'[202] Historical precedents were cited to support this view. Henry V, the only king in Shakespeare's tetralogies to unite the nation, does so by embarking on a campaign of conquest, 'to busy giddy minds/ With foreign quarrels'.[203] In Samuel Daniel's epic account of England's fifteenth-century civil wars, domestic peace becomes a prelude to internal division.[204] Rome under the early emperors arguably provided another example. Tacitus had characterized the period as a 'peace worse than any war', portraying a society enervated by security, luxury and excessive refinement.

Some contemporaries associated the Stuart peace with other symptoms of decline blamed on the court, such as the inflation of honours[205] and the tendency of nobles and gentry to waste money on luxuries in London that should have been recycled back into the rural economy. 'The pride in court doth make the country lean,' Michael Drayton complained: 'The abject rich hold ancient honour mean.'[206] Early in Charles's reign, George Wither blamed the court's enormous extravagance for the King's inability to wage war without raising taxes:

> Hence comes it that rents and royalties
> Of kings and princes, which did well suffice
> In former times to keep in comely port
> An honour'd, and an hospitable court,
> (Yea and an army if occasion were)
> Can hardly now the charge of household bear,
> For they must either in their large expense
> Come short of that profuse magnificence
> Among their vassals: or else waste away
> The price of many lordships to defray
> The cost of one vain supper...[207]

Cultural fashions were occasionally added to the list of abuses, as in a ballad of the 1620s contrasting an 'old courtier of the Queen's' who lived in the country and cared for his tenants, with his heir, who followed the latest styles:

> With a new fashion'd hall, built where the old one stood
> Hung round with pictures, that do the poor no good,
> With a fine marble chimney, wherein burns neither coal nor wood
> And a new smooth shovelboard, whereon no victuals ne'er stood;
> Like a young courtier of the king's
> And the king's young courtier.[208]

Paintings and innovative architecture here become emblems of social irresponsibility.

The court and city as sources of cultural change

In ways like this the rhetorical opposition of court to country allowed contemporaries to simplify complex issues into easily grasped contrasts.

The court and city were blamed for a whole series of unhealthy social, economic, cultural and moral trends, while the country symbolized a conservative ideal. Obviously we need to make substantial allowances for exaggeration in dealing with such stereotypes, but can we dismiss them entirely? Was there any truth to the perception that courtly and metropolitan influences were slowly destroying an older and healthier provincial culture?

In answering this question it is vital to distinguish between deliberate royal policies and the unintended consequences of developments over which kings had little direct control. Some scholars have failed to do this, treating the growth of the court and London as intrinsically connected to Stuart absolutism.[209] In actuality James and Charles both deplored the increasing resort of peers and gentry to their capital. They exhorted landowners to stay in the country and tried to drive them away from London by proclamations, while also attempting to limit the capital's growth by curtailing its housing stock.[210]

Unfortunately these policies had only limited effect. One reason was sporadic enforcement: relatively energetic attempts to crack down on illegal building and gentry wintering in London during the early 1620s and mid 1630s alternated with periods of laxity.[211] The basic problem was that monarchs had only limited control over their own massive households and even less over the behaviour of people attracted to their palaces. Court life had its own inner dynamic, driven partly by ancient routines that were very difficult to change and even more by the remorseless efforts of courtiers and suitors to outshine each other in splendour as they competed for favour and patronage. The King's household alone employed over 1500 people and spent about £250,000 a year by the late 1630s, while great royal ministers also maintained substantial London households. Stone has estimated that Salisbury spent nearly £7000 annually at his Strand Palace in the early seventeenth century and about £20,000 building his country seat at Hatfield.[212] In the late 1620s Peter Paul Rubens, who was thoroughly familiar with European courts, commented pointedly on the ruinously opulent expenditures of the great nobles at the court of Charles I.[213]

Complaints about court extravagance did, therefore, have substance. The most expensive forms of opulence were, however, traditional ones like building, banqueting, clothing and jewels, rather than things like masques and paintings.[214] The basic problem was not cultural innovation but lingering attachment to inherited forms of magnificence, especially large retinues and prodigious entertainment. By the early seventeenth century most great country households had begun to retrench on such items, whereas at the centre expenditures on them continued to grow.[215] The problem, ironically, was that the fabled decline in hospitality had no impact on food allowances at Whitehall or the entertaining of courtiers like the Earl of Carlisle, who was rumoured to have spent £3300 on a single banquet.[216]

Great courtiers with their profuse lifestyles are fairly easy to trace; less prominent gentry visitors to London are more elusive, since many stayed for short periods in rented lodgings and left few traces behind.[217] Their numbers are attested, however, not only by contemporary complaints but the overseers' accounts of parishes adjacent to Whitehall, which show substantial increases in the number of peers and gentlemen paying poor rates, the returns produced in the 1630s when the Crown tried to enforce its proclamations against country landowners staying in London, and the development of blocks of town houses intended for gentry and tenants of quality in St Martin's Lane in the 1610s, Covent Garden from the early 1630s, and Lincoln's Inn Fields and Great Queen Street after 1639.[218] The resort of gentry to London also spurred an expansion of retail trades and service industries catering for wealthy consumers, which provided an increasingly varied and sophisticated material culture.[219] This economic activity accounts for most population growth even in fashionable districts like Covent Garden.[220]

For those who did not become caught up in court life, a visit to London might actually be cheaper than old-fashioned country living. On his own lands a gentleman needed to maintain a household commensurate with his standing and local ambitions. In London it was acceptable for all but great peers to live in a compact town house with a handful of servants, or even in rented lodgings. Services like the cooking of food and provision of transport could be procured as needed on the urban market, allowing much greater flexibility. Even though London prices were higher, it was possible to save on expenses. The density of the city's gentry population allowed for a much greater choice of social companions, while amenities like theatres and bookshops, along with the greater availability of news, permitted a more varied and sophisticated lifestyle. A growing number of great landowners clearly found these attractions hard to resist.

Few gentry families, however, permanently deserted the provinces for London. Far more typical were occasional or periodic visits. The real significance of London was not that it emptied the country of its natural elite, as moralists charged, but that the experience of urban life must frequently have left a permanent imprint on the tastes, manners and material culture of gentlemen and women even after they returned home.

Foreign travel and cosmopolitanism

Foreign travel provided another stimulus to cultural change, especially among the nobility and wealthier gentry.[221] Under Elizabeth and well into James's reign, trips to the Continent mostly served practical purposes. Some Englishmen went abroad as soldiers, diplomats or spies; others travelled to gain fluency in foreign languages, useful contacts and a deeper grasp of European affairs, to enhance their prospects of winning court patronage.[222] Cultural activities unrelated to politics, war and diplomacy were not generally stressed. Even during the Armada war, however, travel and contact with foreign nobilities inevitably had some broader cultural effects. European architectural 'plots', for example, circulated fairly widely in England and were often consulted in building country houses, although they were invariably adapted to suit English conventions.[223]

In the seventeenth century foreign tours became more common and cultural and social fashions gradually received more emphasis, as signs of proper breeding. John Holles's father advised him that each of the nations of Europe 'have their virtues, which are with study and due endeavor to be compassed, and as in times past, eloquence and philosophy were only to be had in Athens and magic arts among the Egyptians and Chaledeans, so in Italy riding, weapons and the mathematics, in France an assured, free and civil conversation, running at the ring, dancing, *viz*, qualities in these times most respected in our court'.[224] The requisite accomplishments included fencing, dancing, riding the great horse, fluency in languages and a wide acquaintance with the world. In France this kind of training was coming to be provided by specialized academies, in which Englishmen sometimes enrolled.[225] Sir Francis Kynaston founded an English academy, the Museum Minervae, in Covent Garden in the 1630s but it never eclipsed the grand tour as an essential stage in the complete gentleman's education.[226]

One fashion that spread to England in the early seventeenth century, although it remained a minority interest, was the collecting of paintings and sculpture. Systematic collecting had developed in Italy only during the sixteenth century.[227] Although a few Englishmen took a precocious interest in European visual culture even before 1600, it was the expansion of the grand tour in the early seventeenth century that first truly established an English fashion for art.[228] The pioneers were mostly younger nobles and Stuart diplomats like Dudley Carleton and Henry Wotton, who acted as advisers and art brokers for court patrons. Carleton presented Robert Cecil with the gift of a picture as early as 1602 and later assembled a large collection for the rising favourite, Somerset.[229] Prince Henry's appreciation for art was nurtured by young members of his household who had toured Europe, such as Sir Robert Dallington, who had already published two books on foreign travel in the 1590s, Sir John Danvers, whose special expertise was Italian gardens, and William Cecil, Lord Cranbourne, Salisbury's son and heir.[230] The influence of these young peers was further reinforced by European artists recruited into the Prince's service, especially Saloman de Caus.[231]

The Jacobean nobleman who best exemplifies this new cosmopolitanism was Thomas Howard, Earl of Arundel.[232] His great collection of paintings and antiquities, installed in a two-storey Italianate gallery Inigo Jones designed for Arundel House on the Strand, was a monument to much more than aesthetic taste. It was a visual parallel to the collection of antiquarian manuscripts of Robert Cotton, a man Arundel befriended and patronized. The Earl gathered a sampling of pieces of the highest quality available, representing the visual cultures of both modern and classical Europe. Like Cotton's library, his galleries were a resource open to 'ingenious spirits' interested in their contents. Just as Cotton was in contact with scholars throughout England and Europe, Arundel was acquainted with collectors and artists. He also patronized Henry Peacham and Francis Junius, whose published writings helped disseminate Italian concepts of painting in England. Arundel was important, not simply for the works he collected, but for the way he introduced European attitudes towards visual culture into England.

By the 1620s London boasted a number of additional sophisticated experts in the visual arts. Several lived in the new houses Salisbury had built in St Martin's Lane including, at one time or another, the Dutch artist Paul van Somer, the painter John Belcamp, the keeper of Charles I's collection Abraham Vanderdoort, the royal physician, Theodore Mayerne, and diplomats like Thomas Rowe and the secretary of state, Thomas Lake.[233] Although such expertise was much less common away from London, some interest in painting and sculpture did penetrate provincial culture. A few country landowners, like Arundel's father-in-law, the Earl of Shrewsbury, assembled collections in James's reign.[234] Courtiers sometimes decorated their country houses with art, while Van Dyck painted a number of country squires who sat for him on trips to London, including several who later fought for Parliament.[235] When a French painter passed through Dorchester in the 1630s the local puritan notable, William Whiteway, eagerly interrogated him about technical aspects of his art. Although we should not exaggerate the visual sophistication of most provincial gentry, historians have found little evidence of hostility to secular art, and some squires had plainly taken notice of the new aesthetic fashions.

Agricultural improvement and country living

Art collecting absorbed less energy than pursuits associated with the gentleman's traditional rustic lifestyle, like building and gardening, to say nothing of the demands of managing a country estate. Even these activities were being reshaped by metropolitan and cosmopolitan influences, however. A growing minority of landowners developed an interest in natural philosophy and experimentation, which sometimes connected up with practical schemes for agricultural 'improvements'. The agricultural revolution of the seventeenth century was primarily motivated by economic incentives but there was also an important and complex cultural dimension to it.[236] Attitudes were shaped by classical and European agricultural manuals, as well as poems devoted to farming, notably Hesiod's *Works and Days* and Virgil's *Georgics*. Joan Thirsk regards Xenophon, Cato, Varro and especially Columella as the most important of the classical texts, while literary scholars have argued for a diffuse Georgic influence.[237] All these sources praised a life devoted to agriculture, sometimes contrasting it favourably with existence in the city or court. The Huguenot poet Du Bartas produced a massive poem in the 1580s that integrated these themes within a Protestant discourse stressing the Christian's duty to discover and put to use the beneficial properties God had embedded within his Creation. Through hundreds of stanzas of florid verse, he celebrated the usefulness of both familiar and exotic plants and the joys of a life spent in their cultivation. His poem became an international bestseller, translated into English by Joshua Sylvester in 1605 as *The Divine Weeks*, a favourite book of the young Dryden that Milton admired throughout his life.[238]

An allied influence were the agricultural manuals that began to appear from the mid-sixteenth century, becoming far more common in the seventeenth, when Gervase Markham emerged as the most prolific writer in the genre.[239] These quickly moved beyond classical formulas to take a more 'experimental' approach. The manuals contributed to the rise of a concept of 'improvement', possessing both moral and practical connotations, which appears with increasing frequency after the late sixteenth century. Improving an estate might mean simply increasing the rents; but it could also involve experimenting with new crops and farming methods that benefited the commonwealth as well as the landlord. Networks of correspondence and the proselytizing activities of a few devoted proponents of change helped spread this ideal.[240] Those involved varied widely in their religious and political outlooks, from radical Protestants like the Dutch writer, Samuel Hartlib, to the Catholic country gentleman, Sir Richard Weston. What united them was a desire to apply knowledge of agricultural methods gathered through Europeanwide contacts to improve local farming practices.

In ways like this, the growing sophistication and diversity of gentry culture might actually deepen attachment to the land. The country house, the gardens and parks around it and the agricultural estate all provided opportunities to display new interests and accomplishments, including those acquired in London or on a grand tour. Dedication to an estate did not always bring a sense of devotion to its tenantry, however. In the seventeenth century the gulf that separated peers and gentry from the lower and middling strata of rural society began to widen, under the influence of a growing emphasis on good manners and new concepts of cultural refinement.[241]

This trend is clearly registered by changes in domestic architecture. At the end of Elizabeth's reign the great house remained a gathering place for an affinity that cut vertically across social ranks.[242] It was invariably divided into a household of service, consisting of kitchens, larders and cellars, and a household of magnificence centred around an open hall with a dais at one end used for communal dining. By the turn of the century this had begun to change, though at an uneven pace.[243] Households tended to diminish in size as landlords coped with inflation by retrenching. Servants were less frequently recruited from landed families, as the medieval practice of sending young gentlemen and ladies to be bred up in great households all but died out. The social distance between a lord's biological family and the rest of his household therefore widened. Some landowners eliminated the provision of food to the poor at the household gates and curtailed the right of entry into the hall by tenants and others of low rank. As Hutton has argued, the spread of poverty and establishment of mandatory poor rates probably helps to explain the first change.[244] The second was connected to a shift towards more professional estate management and less paternalistic attitudes.[245]

In seventeenth-century houses the hall ceased to be a communal gathering place and gradually declined into a vestibule, where humbler visitors waited as servants conveyed their messages within, while guests of rank quickly passed through to more important rooms above the stairs.[246] The trend was further reinforced after about 1630 by the development of compact double pile houses with symmetrical classical façades, which could not easily accommodate large halls with open ceilings.[247] The old courtyard house, developed in the late Middle Ages but persisting into the early seventeenth century, allowed for rooms built to different scales, since small chambers could be placed in low wings while a large central block accommodated a grand hall. Double pile houses required that all rooms conform to a single proportional scale.

As the hall declined the private suites behind it developed in elegance and complexity. Service rooms and servants' chambers were removed further from these private suites, eventually being relegated to basements or outbuildings, although this did not usually happen in the countryside until after mid-century. The grounds around the house were also more likely to be enclosed and devoted to lawns and gardens, which grew larger and more complex under the influence of Italian and French models. The house and its immediate surroundings thus became more clearly differentiated from the agricultural estate. Social segregation permitted greater informality in elite manners, since people no longer needed to be quite so concerned with asserting superiority through ceremony and display.

As these changes occurred the ancient forms of hospitality, where they survived, became more conspicuous as symbols of a vanishing ideal. Heal found that from the late sixteenth century funeral epitaphs of country gentry began to emphasize country hospitality as a virtue.[248] Some conduct books, such as Brathwaite's *English Gentleman* (1630), castigated the new 'humourous' gentlemen who abandoned the customs of their ancestors, 'whose chiefest glory it was to relieve the hungry, refresh the thirsty, and give quiet repose to the weary'.[249] Courtly and urban influences were often blamed for this trend but the impetus for change came mostly from within provincial society itself.

Classicism, Nostalgia and Cultural Rhetoric

From this perspective the cult of country virtue seems to betoken little more than nostalgic attachment to a vanishing world. It would be too simple to leave matters at that, however. For in describing and defending ancestral customs Stuart writers also reinterpreted them, in ways shaped by contemporary attitudes as well as by simple nostalgia. Once again we are dealing as much with the invention of tradition as simple resistance to change. The process worked by different rules depending on which artists and writers we examine.

One might naturally expect to find old country virtues celebrated through cultural styles that were themselves reminiscent of medieval or early Tudor traditions. This did often happen, especially in the late sixteenth century, as in the antiquated language and conventions of Spenser's pastoral verse or the towers and crenellations of the façades of some Elizabethan great houses. While not truly medieval, such culture was infused with an antiquarian spirit that shaped its aesthetic form as well as its content. This attachment to old native forms sometimes survived well into the seventeenth century, often becoming further associated with Elizabethan nostalgia.[250] In the Stuart period, however, more rigorous classical styles developed in both literature and the visual arts, increasingly overshadowing Elizabethan traditions. As this happened even old country customs came to be reconceived in ways deeply shaped by Latin cultural models.

Classical influence and imitation was, in itself, hardly new.[251] Even the most outspoken Elizabethan proponents of native traditions, like Spenser, never attempted to escape the influence of antiquity. On the contrary, they regarded the attainments of Greece and Rome as models for what they hoped to achieve using English materials, and drew eclectically on both ancient and medieval traditions. Spenser set out to be both a Virgilian and a Chaucerian poet, just as builders of country houses saw nothing odd about using columns and pediments to decorate façades that were anything but classical in overall design. The more rigorous Stuart classicists, such as Jonson and Inigo Jones, broke from these practices through a much greater concern for rigour in following ancient models. They engaged in careful antiquarian research into the minutiae of classical culture, while also paying careful attention to structural principles that determined how individual elements should be combined. Jonson proudly paraded his humanist scholarship in textual notes that accompanied some of his published work, especially court entertainments. Jones's philological research has been less obvious because he never paraded it in a theoretical treatise. Recent work by scholars like David Cast, Gordon Higgot and Christie Anderson has fully demonstrated, however, the degree to which Jones's architecture is rooted in careful and systematic research in both published treatises and actual buildings, including Roman ruins.[252]

The new classical idioms did not – indeed could not – eliminate all native features. Jonesian buildings and Jonsonian poems necessarily remained English interpretations of classical forms, rather than archaeological facsimiles. But in a number of ways, native elements were subtly reinterpreted to fit within classical frameworks. Roman styles evoked a very different range of historical connotations from native ones, while classical principles of regularity and proportion underlay an ideal of dignified restraint developed in reaction against the flamboyance and theatricality of an older courtly and aristocratic culture. Jones made the connection explicit when commenting upon architectural decorum:

> For as outwardly every wise man carrieth a gravity in public places, where there is nothing else looked for, yet inwardly hath his imaginacy [imagination] set on fire... so in architecture the outward ornaments ought to be solid, proportionable, according to the rules, masculine and unaffected.[253]

In architecture as in life the face of authority should be characterized by *gravitas*, while qualities of imagination and wit are revealed only in more intimate settings. This principle would have prevented the development of the Accession Day Jousts and the prodigy house, to say nothing of the histrionic careers of Ralegh and Essex. It was, however, congenial to Jones's patron, the Earl of Arundel, who was famous for his subdued black garments and outward formality.

The ways in which Roman models reshaped understandings of English traditions is nowhere more apparent than in certain literary descriptions of ancestral rural customs. Roman poets including Horace, Virgil and Martial had also celebrated the virtues of an older agrarian society, which they contrasted with the wealth and moral degeneration of the imperial city. They linked the rugged simplicity of subsistence agriculture to Stoic and Epicurean concepts of discipline, self-reliance and conformity to nature. Early Stuart poets adapted this model to seventeenth-century circumstances. If Roman poets had complained of exotic luxuries imported from the east, Drayton castigated the 'upstart gentry' who spent the nation's gold on things:

> Which our plain fathers erst would have accounted sin,
> Before the costly coach, and silken stock came in;
> Before the Indian weed so strongly was embrac'd
> Wherein such mighty sums we prodigally waste,
> That merchants long trained up in gain's deceitful school,
> And subtly having learn'd to sooth the humorous fool,
> Present their painted toys unto this frantic gull,
> Disparaging our tine, our leather, corn and wool.[254]

As in Roman poetry, attachment to new and foreign consumer goods becomes a sign not only of waste, but of a thoughtless addiction to luxury and fashion that destroys moral judgement. The symbiotic relation between the merchant and the humorous gull epitomizes a society built on the exploitation of false appetites.

Jonson's 'To Penshurst', and later country-house poems patterned after it, attempt to define a healthy society by evoking ancient rituals of communal life within medieval houses. Since the Romans had no comparable traditions of hospitality, there were no direct Latin models for this form. But it was developed in ways consciously patterned after classical values of moderation, balance and restraint, which differed markedly from the ethos of magnificence that dominated the great households of the medieval and Tudor periods. Jonson's poem is built around a basic dichotomy between vainglorious novelties and older customs that are simple and functional. Penshurst is defined as much by what it is not – a house 'built to ostentatious show' with pillars, a gilt roof, a fancy staircase and lanterns – as by what it is – an 'ancient pile' lying in the midst of an abundant estate, in which the lord, his tenants and guests share ample quantities of food around a common table. The contrasts finally culminate in a distinction between men who build 'proud ambitious heaps' and Penshurst's owner, Robert Sidney, who 'dwells' in a house that functions as the centre of a local community. The house and its great hall symbolize a society based on the natural fertility of the soil and a system of reciprocal exchanges between lord, tenant and guests, rather than one in which economic exploitation supports empty ostentation.

Jonson has, however, omitted to describe features of life in a great house that do not fit the values he is evoking. These include the more elaborate rituals surrounding the serving of food in the hall, the presence of liveried servants and, above all, the competition over local standing that motivated great displays of hospitality. Although the memory of Penshurst's Elizabethan owner, Philip Sidney, is a constant presence in the poem, Jonson avoids references to his political and military ambitions. The actual history of the house and the family it shelters has been carefully edited to fit an Augustan ideal alien to the Middle Ages and Sidney's own outlook.

An analogous process shaped the ways in which some Stuart poets celebrated traditional popular customs like May dances and village sports, which had come under attack from godly reformers. Leah Marcus has described this sort of verse as defining a 'politics of mirth'.[255] It was deliberately sensual, tolerant of eroticism, friendly towards practices associated with popish or pagan worship and, as a result of all this, defiantly anti-puritan. It assimilated folk rituals and English peasant customs within descriptions that were also thoroughly infused with themes deriving from Latin models.

In the early seventeenth century rural England and its traditions had thus acquired a variety of connotations, some of them implicitly contradictory. The country could be hailed as a locus of virtue by men of divergent outlooks because it was capable of being represented in so many different ways. Life in the provinces, no less than at the centre, had given rise to a variety of images and stereotypes that lay ready to hand when fierce political controversy erupted in the 1640s, for use in the construction of partisan political cultures.

3

FROM CIVIL WAR TO TORY REACTION

The upheavals of the 1640s transformed England's cultural no less than its political landscape. The theatres closed and court patronage disappeared but there was an explosion of controversy in the pulpit, the press and other media. The legacy of argument and invective remained long after the Restoration; for the rest of the century memories of the Great Rebellion overshadowed the nation.

Civil War Cultural History after Revisionism

Although a large amount of work on the Civil War has appeared recently, by historians and scholars in other disciplines, it has not resulted in an entirely coherent picture.[1] Part of the difficulty lies in the character of the period itself, which produced fewer dominant writers and artists than either the preceding or subsequent decades but far more aggregate material, notably the 22,000 tracts collected between 1640 and 1660 by George Thomason.[2] Scholars must therefore contend with what Nigel Smith has called the 'Babel effect': thousands of writers of uneven quality, articulating an enormous range of ideas in highly varied styles and formats. The formidable labour of sorting through this material remains only partially accomplished.

Major historiographical issues also complicate the picture, however. Until the advent of revisionism the Civil War was generally interpreted as the climax of fundamental and longstanding conflicts in society, possessing both cultural and political dimensions. In the early 1970s culture was often treated as a connecting link between socio-economic causes of the 'English Revolution' and the events through which it had transpired. Social tensions allegedly gave rise to attitudes and mentalities that subsequently shaped political behaviour. Thus puritanism became a religious ideology of the 'middling sorts', while royalism was associated with the brittle culture of the Caroline court and parliamentary opposition with the conservative outlook of provincial squires.[3] The collision of these cultures produced civil war.

The most prolific and influential among the historians investigating the cultural dimensions of the 'Revolution', in the 1960s and 1970s, was Christopher Hill.[4] He displayed an unrivalled command of the period's printed sources, a passionate commitment to recovering the voices of popular radical groups neglected by traditional historiography, and a talent for generating provocative ideas. His work also exhibited certain limitations, however, that made it vulnerable to criticism.[5] As a Marxist, Hill believed that social and economic conditions shape history, but he did not engage in archival research, so that his sociological analysis inevitably derived from printed sources or research by other scholars, rather than case studies based on local records. As he was writing, the opening of county record offices, the expansion of history Ph.D. programmes in Britain, and the resulting proliferation of focused research projects slowly altered the historiographical terrain. The decline of radicalism in the 1980s reinforced a reaction against Hill's work that would probably have occurred even in a more favourable political climate.[6]

Ultimately it was not simply an individual historian or school that suffered a reverse, so much as an expansive style of synthesis common in the decades following the Second World War. Other historians of Hill's generation who did not share his Marxism, such as Lawrence Stone and H. R. Trevor Roper, also enjoyed working on large historical canvases and constructing arguments that frequently owed more to intuitive leaps of imagination than painstaking empirical research. Above all, the grand interpretations of the English Revolution advanced in the early 1970s were rarely based on close analysis of events. The basic course of the political Revolution was assumed to have been established by S. R. Gardiner in the nineteenth century, leaving historians free to direct their attention to deeper issues.

The revisionist scholarship of the late 1970s and 1980s undercut this whole approach by demonstrating embarrassing discrepancies between the 'Revolution' that historians were trying to explain and the actual events of the early 1640s.[7] The claim that the Revolution pitted the court against the country was weakened by the finding that six members of the Privy Council, including two successive Lord Chamberlains and the Groom of the Stole, ended up on Parliament's side.[8] The picture of a parliamentary movement directed against a 'feudal' aristocratic order was difficult to reconcile with the discovery that, in the first battle at Edgehill, the parliamentary army contained a higher proportion of officers from titled families than its royalist opponent.[9] The concept of a 'country' revolt against the centre ran counter to substantial evidence of widespread neutralism in the counties in 1642 and the considerable appeal of royalism thereafter.[10] Even the middling sort of people proved to be more divided than the dominant models predicted.[11] Conrad Russell appeared to be on solid ground in arguing that, before engaging in the search for causes, historians needed first to discover just what they had to explain.[12]

Although revisionism did not convince all historians, it did have a pronounced effect on the kind of history written after 1980 about a conflict now less frequently called a revolution. Expansive syntheses integrating social, cultural and political trends became uncommon, while detailed narratives returned to fashion.[13] Scrutiny of short-term events largely replaced emphasis on long-term explanations. As Jonathan Scott has complained, the change at times produced a fragmented historical landscape, in which an ever-growing mass of detail obscured unifying themes.[14] But it would be wrong to suggest that this was either the intention or the necessary outcome of revisionism.[15] The goal of the return to narrative was not to foreclose but to reformulate larger questions, by replacing a nebulous concept of revolution with a more exact understanding of what had happened in the 1640s.

There is no reason why a cultural history of the Civil War cannot be reconstructed on the basis of such an approach, and some recent work suggests that this may be starting to happen. Revisionist studies have, if anything, placed even more emphasis on religious issues than older Whig narratives. Puritanism has retained its significance even as its definition has become more complex, while new work has revealed surprisingly widespread attachment to the established Church and its rituals.[16] Religious rhetoric and myth have received fresh attention.[17] The role of secular political ideas has come to seem more problematical but this has merely underlined the need for further work. Recent studies by Michael Mendle, David Smith, Richard Tuck, David Wootton and others have significantly extended our understanding of how debates over 'constitutional' issues developed.[18] Meanwhile studies of

Civil War newsbooks and their relation to earlier forms of scribal publication has generated a richer view of the cultural terrain.[19] The fragmentation of which some scholars have complained may simply indicate that we are moving through a transition, between now-discredited older syntheses and a new view that will gradually emerge as fresh research is assimilated. This may be a good time to ask how far the broad outlines of such a reinterpretation can already be discerned and where the gaps and muddles still lie.

Cultural history and the problem of causation

Revisionism has provoked considerable debate over whether the Civil War had long-term causes. Did short-term events polarize 'a country in working order, [that] was not on the edge of a revolution', as Russell has insisted, or had significant rifts begun to appear years earlier, as David Underdown has continued to argue?[20] Do we need to explain the gradual formation of two opposing outlooks or the relatively sudden collapse of consensual values under the impact of an immediate crisis? We need not necessarily chose between extreme positions on such questions: the answers may vary depending on which part of the historical landscape we scrutinize. But the problem is obviously a fundamental one, on which historians have sharply disagreed.

The revisionist method of working outwards from focused narratives has injected greater rigour into the discussion. But a certain kind of revisionism that concentrates on high politics has arguably produced an overly constricted view of the issues at stake.[21] Russell has helpfully suggested that to explain the Civil War we need to account for a whole chain of events and 'non-events' leading up to a situation in which fighting became inevitable. To understand that conflict fully, however, the sequence needs to be investigated not only for the leading actors at Westminster and in Scotland and Ireland, but for scores of local communities and thousands of individuals, whose experiences and perspectives inevitably varied.

Revisionists have concentrated on the problem of 'why the middle ground collapsed', so that men who were united in 1640 became antagonists by 1642, as the King overcame his political isolation and gathered a party. This is certainly a crucial issue but it cannot be allowed to obscure altogether the need to understand violent partisans who quickly adopted antagonistic positions. To understand royalism, for example, we have to examine not only relatively moderate men like Edward Hyde but the extremists involved in the first Army Plot and the intrigues of Henrietta Maria. Thanks largely to Caroline Hibbard, historians have learned to take seriously fears of popish court conspiracies in motivating parliamentary opposition.[22] Unlike Hibbard, however, most have continued to view popish plots from the perspective of hostile observers. The mentality of court Catholics and the Protestants who sometimes cooperated with them has received little attention since her pioneering work.[23]

Moreover we cannot always assume that the only attitudes that mattered were those which produced consistent patterns of division. Historical explanation is not a problem in mathematics, in which similar variables on two sides of an equation cancel each other. It is certainly useful to know, as revisionists have shown, that religious attitudes are more reliable predictors of Civil War allegiance than constitutional values.[24] But we still need to understand why belief in the supremacy of the law turned Edward Hyde into a royalist and John Selden into a parliamentarian.[25] Similarly the fact that some courtiers joined the parliamentary side after 1642 does not prove that court culture is irrelevant to explaining the actions of the King and those members of his household who became royalists. Both royalist and parliamentary movements were always coalitions not only of hardliners and moderates but of people with different preoccupations and priorities, and it is only by developing complex and pluralistic interpretations that we will ever adequately understand them.

If older Whig and Marxist explanations of the coming of the Civil War now often seem hopelessly inadequate, this does not mean that we can abandon the search for social and cultural roots of that conflict. The problem may be that we are dealing with historical processes so complex that simple models of causation cannot adequately describe them. What is needed is more nuanced and densely textured analysis.

Religion and society

Perhaps the most important example is the challenge of explaining relationships between religion, social change and politics. Nearly all historians have by now discarded the Marxian view of puritanism as bourgeois ideology and of the Civil War as a class struggle. But many, such as Underdown and Keith Wrightson, continue to see puritanism as connected to a long-term 'crisis in society'.[26] These scholars stress the importance of population growth in sharpening economic polarities and aggravating economic distress throughout the late sixteenth and early seventeenth centuries. As population grew landlords and large tenant farmers prospered from buoyant food prices and abundant supplies of cheap labour, while the land poor suffered from the division of holdings among heirs, stagnant wages and inflation. The former groups enjoyed rising levels of material and intellectual culture, while the latter experienced a declining standard of living and remained overwhelmingly illiterate. Villages across England 'filled up at the bottom' as population pressed against an inelastic supply of land. Migration increased as people left arable villages with inflexible economies, moving towards places with rural industries or more abundant wastes on which they might scratch out a living, or else towards the towns, above all London. Migrants were seen as threats and sometimes prosecuted as vagrants, while even the native poor were treated with suspicion by more prosperous neighbours, fearful of petty crime and increases in the poor rate.

The cumulative result was a growing gap between the upper and middling strata of local society – the gentry, yeomanry, merchants and more successful tradesmen – and the poor. Older ideals of charity and community came under severe strain, as more substantial inhabitants sought to distance themselves from their less fortunate neighbours while emulating the gentry. In doing so they were often strongly attracted to puritanism, with its stress on literacy and discipline.[27] In some places, such as the village of Terling in Essex and the town of Dorchester, a godly group among the local elite consolidated power and attempted to impose its vision of discipline on the entire community.[28] Such reformers invariably encountered resistance, so that arguments over religion became intertwined with other social and cultural differences. 'The division of the English body politic which erupted in civil war in 1642,' Underdown concludes, 'can be traced in part to the emergence of two quite different constellations of social, political and cultural forces, involving diametrically opposed responses to the problems of the time', one involving 'the traditional conception of the harmonious, vertically integrated community', the other more exclusive and divisive concepts of godliness.[29]

Underdown adds the further argument that the relative strengths of puritan and traditional religious cultures correlates with an ecological division between wood-pasture and arable farming communities. 'The arable village was nucleated, tightly packed around church and manor-house (often with a resident squire), the whole firmly bound by neighbourhood and custom, and by powerful mechanisms of social control.'[30] It therefore remained wedded to traditional concepts of order. The woodland village was more dispersed, with an economy permitting greater individualism, and so provided a receptive environment for puritanism.

How convincing are these arguments? There can be no doubt that the social and economic stresses which Underdown and Wrightson emphasize were very real. It is also clear that godly religion did often lead to stringent attitudes towards moral behaviour and campaigns against popular recreations, such as Sunday sports and May festivals, which some villagers still cherished. The issue is how far we can generalize from cases like Terling and Dorchester, where such issues sharply divided local society. Studies by other historians, notably Martin Ingram, have depicted a much less polarized landscape, in which most people shared Protestant values and prejudices against fornication, idleness and drunkenness without necessarily becoming puritans.[31] Underdown's attempt to correlate puritanism with wood-pasture economies has met with particular scepticism from Ingram, John Morrill and Anne Hughes, who argue that it is overly schematic and ignores the important problem of how popular attitudes interacted with those of local gentry.[32]

Underdown's model of two opposing cultures may also need qualification. Puritans shared a commitment to 'traditional' ideals of hierarchical order and community, while some people who rejected puritan theology adopted rigid attitudes towards sin. To a considerable extent, the conflict between godliness and traditional religion involved differing degrees of emphasis placed on commonly held values, rather than a conflict between completely distinct codes. It is also too simple to regard 'traditional' culture simply as a residue of old customs threatened by change. Underdown's treatment of this topic has strong affinities with a model developed by Peter Burke and others in the 1970s, which sees popular culture as something created by the progressive withdrawal of elites from practices in which all ranks of society had once participated.[33] This view has been criticized for failing to recognize the ways in which popular groups were able to borrow elements from elite culture and adapt to changing circumstances.[34] Research by Tessa Watt, Peter Lake and Ronald Hutton, among others, has shown that the relationship between Calvinist attitudes and inherited cultural beliefs was far more complex and dynamic than a bipolar model suggests.[35]

Despite these qualifications, the evidence remains overwhelming that ongoing attempts at cultural and moral reformation, inspired by Calvinist religion but also complicated by social tensions, did frequently generate acrimony within early Stuart communities. Russell has argued that terms like puritan and popery were 'weapons in a struggle for power, and tell us a great deal more about those who used them than they do about those against whom they were used'.[36] It would seem to follow that to understand that struggle we need to examine all the contexts in which those weapons were fashioned, including altercations at the village level.[37] Although no conceptual model has so far succeeded in providing an entirely satisfactory explanation for the sociological or geographic distribution of puritanism, the messiness of the evidence does not diminish the importance of the problem.[38]

Print and the Dissemination of Controversy

Cultural history must also consider the constructions contemporaries placed upon events once the personal rule collapsed, including misunderstandings, myths and fabrications. This requires avoiding the opposing kinds of distortion that come from taking contemporary representations at face value or dismissing them altogether. Achieving a balanced perspective can be difficult because the polemics of the 1640s so often continued to reverberate in later disputes, until images of the Civil War became embedded in a political folklore that we have still not entirely outgrown. Some scholars continue to treat movements of the 1640s and 1650s as precursors of modern causes they favour, while others have reacted against such present-mindedness by minimizing the role of printed controversy in their accounts of the period.[39]

We cannot filter out all the myths and polemical distortions from the story of the Civil War, however, since many of these are integral to it. Knowing what actually happened can sometimes be less important than appreciating what contemporaries believed. In evaluating the impact upon England of Charles's journey to Scotland in the summer of 1641, or the Irish Rebellion in the autumn, the mass of often misleading reports in the press is as crucial as what actually took place in the other kingdoms. Printed sources often provide evidence of both sharper divisions and greater continuity with pre-war attitudes than narratives focused on an exact reconstruction of events will reveal.[40]

The convening of the Long Parliament brought a sharp and immediate increase in the intensity of political newsmongering and debate, centred in London but percolating into the provinces through gentry correspondence and other means.[41] Within weeks the hunger for information was being fed by the press. It is not clear that the number of *pages* printed in London increased significantly, but the number of *items* certainly did – from an average of just over 300 a year before the war, to 700 in 1641 and 2000 in 1642.[42] Printers turned out a flood of short topical pieces, selling for as little as a farthing for one-page broadsides to a penny or two for a quarto pamphlet of eight to sixteen pages. Print runs seem to have averaged about 1000, the number of sheets that two men could print in a working day.[43]

The ending of Star Chamber censorship early in 1641 contributed to this explosion of print, as did the collapse of the monopoly of a small number of master printers licensed by the Stationer's Company. Entrepreneurial journeymen set up their own presses to tap a lively market.[44] Printed matter was sold in shops, hawked by women in London streets and carried into the provinces by porters or in consignments sent through the recently established Tuesday post. Certain inns and taverns became focal points of reading and political conversation, anticipating the later role of coffee houses.

Several older political treatises previously circulated in manuscript now reached print, including a translation of the medieval *Modus Tenendi Parliamentum* and Sir Robert Cotton's *Briefe Discourse concerning the Power of the Parliament in point of Judicature*. Such pieces were greatly outnumbered, though, by more current ones. Twenty-two real or fabricated parliamentary speeches appeared in 1640 and sixty-six in 1641, along with copies of petitions, sermons preached before Parliament or in London, and other political documents.[45] This kind of material had circulated as manuscript 'separates' in earlier decades but it was now being produced in larger quantities and sold for much lower prices. The first newsbooks appeared in the autumn of 1641, taking over a function previously served by manuscript newsletters.[46]

The great variety of pamphlets included numerous satires and fictional works, like *The Description of the Passage of Thomas Late Earle of Strafford over the River Styx*, published shortly after his execution, or the supposititious *Conference between the two great monarchs of France and Spaine, concerning these our present proceedings in England* of 1641.[47] Certain secular issues, notably monopolies, attracted considerable attention. By far the largest volume of print, however, dealt with religion. Over 150 tracts containing attacks on puritans or papists, or commentary on the debate over episcopacy, appeared in 1641 alone, not counting parliamentary speeches and sermons devoted to these topics. In January of 1642 pamphlets on the impeachment of the bishops outnumbered those on Charles's attempt to arrest the Five Members by about four-to-one.[48]

The impact of this material on the country is not easily assessed. Print was most available in London, where nearly all of it was produced until the royalists established their presses at Oxford in 1643. Even in the capital, few people can have kept abreast of more than a fraction of the tracts pouring from the presses. We can undoubtedly assume, on the other hand, that items reaching the provinces were often passed from hand to hand, discussed in social gatherings and read aloud. Print culture had not yet become detached from oral forms of communication. Many tracts recorded speeches, sermons or news initially spread by word-of-mouth, while the ideas and information they contained rapidly passed back into oral circulation, stimulating local discussions of affairs at Westminster.

Anti-popery and the attack on episcopacy

Print disseminated not only information and sober commentary but rumours and polemical stereotypes that proliferated as political deadlock developed. While some tracts appealed through reasoned arguments to uncommitted moderates, many were calculated to reinforce divisive prejudices.[49] One reason may be that partisan and sensationalist material sold briskly. Attacks on papists, Arminian bishops and sectaries; personal satires of the leaders of both the court and the House of Commons; and reports of conspiracies and atrocities all figured prominently in printed tracts.

This partisan imagery generally reflected cultural beliefs of long standing. Consensus did not collapse because entirely new attitudes developed, so much as because old prejudices and animosities were greatly sharpened and intensified by the crisis. The dominant sentiment on the parliamentary side was fear of popery, especially within the court.[50] Fear of subversion by a conspiratorial Catholic court faction had existed at least since the appearance of Stubbe's *Gaping Gulf* in 1575. The role of Henrietta Maria, who actually was engaged in intrigues involving her co-religionists, greatly reinforced this ancient worry. A letter from the Queen's confessor, Father Philip, to the Catholic courtier Walter Montagu, who was residing in Paris, was intercepted by Pym's agents in the summer of 1641 and printed.[51] It had always been assumed that a popish faction would enlist corrupt courtiers and religious neuters as allies. The existence of such a sinister coalition was the main theme of the Grand Remonstrance and a frequent obsession of Pym and his allies.[52]

These anxieties were reinforced from another angle by several rumours during the spring and summer of 1641, widely reported in the press, of popish plots to murder Protestants.[53] These fed on other ancient prejudices concerning the cruelty of papists and their settled hatred of 'heretics'. The outbreak of the Irish rebellion (October 1641) enhanced the terror by giving rise to greatly exaggerated reports of atrocities. Some forty-one tracts dealing with the rebellion or Irish conspiracies had already appeared by the year's end.[54] As a recent study has shown, most followed stereotyped formulas deriving from Foxe and other early Protestant propaganda, which emphasized popish fanaticism and sadism. Another category of tracts, however, minimized reports of cruelty, glossed over religious divisions and stressed instead the rebels' violation of royal authority. These invoked traditional images of peasant rebellion going back to Jack Cade and 1381. Purported eye-witness accounts therefore actually confirmed preconceived biases.[55]

Laudians and Arminians, who had been accused of popery as early as the 1620s, inevitably came under attack in the Long Parliament, the press and London's streets.[56] Laud's party found few friends but a wider 'roots and branches' campaign to extirpate episcopacy did more than anything else to precipitate the formation of antagonistic parties.[57] The assault on episcopacy derived its wide appeal from reactions against Laudian innovations, although separatist minorities sometimes helped spearhead the movement.[58] The famous London Petition for the extirpation of episcopacy with all its roots and branches, bearing 15,000 signatures and presented to Parliament by a procession of 1500 men in December of 1640, resulted from a well-organized campaign.[59] It was soon seconded by provincial petitions complaining of misdeeds of bishops and Arminian clergy. The earliest arrived in January, and over the next two years a total estimated at about 800 came in.[60] The petitioners turned traditional anti-popish arguments against the English bishops. The existing Church perpetuated popish superstitions and restrained 'godly and able men' from preaching, while subordinating religion to 'the pride and ambition of the prelates... unwilling to be subject either to man or laws'.[61] Milton's anti-episcopal pamphlets echoed these charges, refusing to distinguish between medieval and post-Reformation bishops.[62] Milton modified Foxe's chronology by dating the corruption of Christianity from Constantine's conversion rather than the Middle Ages.[63] The resulting alliance between the clergy and the Empire resulted, he argued, in a loss of political rights and the debauching of true devotion by carnal ceremonies.[64] This effectively undercut Elizabethan arguments for an episcopal Church under the monarch. Conventional lines of Protestant argument were being pushed beyond the boundaries within which they had normally operated and turned into weapons against royal, no less than episcopal, authority.

A related development was an intensification of eschatological preaching and writing. Millenarian tracts written in earlier decades by writers like Joseph Meade and Thomas Brightman saw print for the first time, and a number of new eschatological sermons were published.[65] Belief that the final days of the world might be drawing near intensified demands for godly reformation, and sometimes blended with a proud sense of England's godly mission. As Milton wrote in *Areopagitica*:

> God is decreeing to begin some new and great period in his Church, even to the reforming of Reformation itself. What does he then but reveal Himself to his servants, and as his manner is, first to his Englishmen.[66]

This sense of being engaged in a providentially inspired work of overthrowing centuries of oppression and corruption provided the ideological core of parliamentary activism.

Such attitudes unleashed considerable experimentation and speculation, much of it pushing well beyond the boundaries of conventional puritanism. Some people, of whom the Milton of *Areopagitica* is an especially articulate example, welcomed this development as a sign that God's spirit was at work in the nation. They identified religion with a life spent seeking God rather than with outward forms of worship and discipline: 'to be still searching what we know not by what we know, still closing up truth to truth as we find it... makes up the best harmony in the Church; not the forced and outward union of cold and neutral and inwardly divided minds'.[67] Error itself must be granted free expression, Milton argued, so that men may learn to engage and overcome it.[68]

Defences of order and anti-puritan polemic

Even among Parliament's adherents, however, such attitudes were minority beliefs. For most people the collapse of religious uniformity presaged spiritual and social anarchy (see plate 5). The freeing of the pulpit and the press, together with the appearance of the newsbooks, meant that wilder sectarian excesses became widely known. Indeed, the simple act of reporting unusual opinions and behaviour was one of the most effective tools of anti-sectarian propaganda. 'I have been a faithful gatherer and storer up, remembrancer and treasurer of these errors and practices', Thomas Edwards wrote in *Gangraena*, 'that I might in a good season bring out of my treasure these things, and discover these monsters and rocks, so that they might be of some use to godly people, to make them afraid of forsaking the public assemblies and forming separated churches'.[69] Belief in order, discipline and subordination ran deep in this society, so that large doses of intellectual freedom – especially among the middling and lower orders, the young and women – triggered reflexive hostility.[70]

Although many of the godly shared the horror of sectarianism, royalist publicists first exploited it systematically. In the opening months of the Long Parliament, attacks on popish bishops were quickly answered by satires and invectives against puritans and sectaries. Here again, the groundwork had been prepared by earlier controversialists. The equation of puritan religion with demagoguery, developed by Bancroft in the 1590s, now became a central motif in defences of the Episcopal Church.[71] Several developments breathed new life into old stereotypes. Reports of public demonstrations and iconoclasm by crowds in London and elsewhere fed perceptions of the dangerous volatility of the lower orders.[72] Meanwhile ruthless tactics adopted by Pym and his allies provoked mounting disquiet. 'The myth of a small clique engaged in a conspiracy to overthrow monarchical authority was born during the spring and summer of 1641.'[73] Finally a well-publicized rash of public preaching by London sectaries, many of them self-educated tradesmen of modest income, alarmed the public. John Taylor's influential *A Swarm of Sectaries and Schismatics*, followed by his *Tale in a Tub, or, a Tub Lecture*, disseminated images of lay preachers spreading bizarre and dangerous doctrines to gullible popular audiences.[74] Invocations of Jack Straw and Jack Cade, by the King's *Answer to the Nineteen Propositions* and several royalist tracts of the autumn and winter of 1641–2, played upon such fears.

5. *Heraclitus Dream* (1642), a satire of sectarian and anti-clerical agitation. Copyright the British Library.

Satire and the fabrication of stereotypes

Although the events of 1641 were unprecedented, at least in England, the constructions placed upon them were usually rooted in older cultural typologies, associated with familiar figures like the evil favourite, the popish conspirator and the demagogue. Some polemical techniques were also indebted to past models. The war years saw a revival of a style of satire that had first emerged during the Marprelate controversy, which drew upon popular forms of slander and insult prevalent in village culture.[75] The techniques included a penchant for sexual slander and scandalmongering, as in Taylor's repetition of stories of illicit liaisons involving lay preachers and their female auditors. The most accomplished royalist satirist was John Cleveland, who mercilessly ridiculed puritans, parliamentary leaders and Scots:

> Nature herself doth Scotch-men beasts confess
> Making their country such a wilderness:
> A land that brings in question and suspense
> God's omnipotence, but that Charles came thence.
> ...
> Had Cain been Scot, God would have chang'd his doom
> Not forc'd him wander, but confin'd him home.[76]

Cleveland often employed heavy burlesque description of appearances and linguistic forms, such as the scripture-quoting idiom of puritan saints. Sneers based on social stereotypes are ubiquitous.

The most common and enduring caricatures created in this period are the Roundhead and the Cavalier. Roundhead was a derisive nickname for a London apprentice, applied indiscriminantly to parliamentarians as a social smear.[77] Although a gross distortion of reality, the image reflected a bias of many royalists against urban populations, as prone to vice, hypocrisy and sedition. This prejudice had already developed in pre-war culture and now acquired partisan overtones. Cowley's uncompleted epic, *The Civil War*, sharply satirizes parliamentary towns like Exeter and Birmingham, mocking the latter as a place renowned for making but not using swords, whose cowardly citizens easily succumb to Welsh royalist soldiers.[78] Like most royalists, he was especially antagonistic towards London.

In origin the image of the Cavalier was equally a symbol of social and moral disorder, though rooted in a different set of preconceptions.

Much meate doth gluttony produce.　　Hee needes no napkin for his handes
And makes a man a swine　　　　　　His fingers for to wipe.
But hee's a temperate man indeed　　Hee hath his kitchin in a box
That with a leafe can dine　　　　　His Roast meate in a pipe

6. *The Sucklington Faction or Suckling's Roaring Boys* (1642), an early satire of the Cavalier. Copyright the British Library.

7. Engraving of Sir John Hotham, commander of the garrison at Hull. A parliamentarian image of the virtuous gentleman soldier. Copyright the British Library.

It resulted from a fusion of negative stereotypes of soldiers, Roman Catholics, dissolute young gentlemen and corrupt courtiers, projected onto the royalist swordsmen involved in the Army Plot and the street confrontations of 1641. *The Sucklington Faction, or Suckling's Roaring Boys* captures this image, using as its model a court poet known for jocular amatory verse and alcoholic excess (*see* plate 6). In parliamentary literature the Cavalier is an arrogant womanizing swordsman, fond of drink and blasphemy, who relishes war because it provides him with opportunities for robbery, debauchery and rape. He is a figure from whom all propertied and sober householders need protection, the incarnation of the chaos that a victory by the malignant party will unleash.[79] This stereotype was contrasted with positive images of patriotic lords and disciplined soldiers on the parliamentary side, who embodied the virtuous features of an aristocratic and military culture (*see* plate 7).

Forms of royalist culture

Despite its origins as a hostile caricature, many royalists soon adopted the Cavalier stereotype, playing up its aristocratic associations and the ways in which it represented an inversion of godly values. Some supporters of the King complained of the damage done to the cause by the hard drinking, womanizing and blasphemy of 'damme cavaliers'.[80] But other publicists cultivated an air of aristocratic libertinism:

> Down Dagon Synod with thy motley ware,
> Whilst we do swagger for the common prayer.[81]

Instead of sour piety, Cavaliers exalted honour and personal loyalty – to friends, the royalist cause and above all to the King himself. As a sermon preached before the royal army put it, 'a complete Cavalier is a child of honour, a gentleman well born and bred that loves his King for conscience sake, of a clearer countenance and bolder look than other men, because more loyal at heart'.[82] The ritual of drinking to the King's health – and sometimes forcing others to join in – provided another way of asserting these values, particularly after Naseby.[83]

Allegiance to the King's person, attachment to the established Church and mistrust of the Scots and the parliamentary 'junto' were fundamental values shared by nearly all Charles's adherents. Beyond this it is risky to generalize. Royalism, even more than parliamentarianism, has too often been characterized in monolithic terms, even though scholars have disagreed on the movement's chief characteristics and the best sources for reconstructing it.[84] Some have turned to royalist literature, especially by writers like Thomas Carew, Robert Herrick, Richard Lovelace and Isaac Walton,[85] while others have concentrated on the moderate constitutionalism of men like Edward Hyde and Sir John Culpepper.[86] But since little systematic work has been done on the rank and file of the movement, it is difficult to be certain exactly what a typical royalist mentality was like.[87] In the present state of our knowledge it is safer to avoid sweeping characterizations and concentrate instead on delineating a variety of positions articulated by the King's advocates.

During the War an active royalist press emerged at Oxford.[88] Courtiers, university wits, professional writers, clergymen and lawyers were all pressed into service producing propaganda for the cause. The King's official responses to parliamentary acts were generally crafted by moderates like Hyde and Culpepper, who depicted Charles as the defender of the ancient constitution against Parliament's illegal actions.[89] This position was developed in a number of pamphlets, many written against Henry Parker's anonymous *Observations upon some of His Majesties late answers and expresses* (1642), which asserted Parliament's right, as representative of the people, to act in any way necessary to protect the public interest even when it meant violating the law.[90] The emergence of a parliamentary absolutism facilitated the elaboration of royalist constitutionalism. So, even more, did arbitrary actions by Parliament, its county committees and its army.[91] Legalistic arguments were obviously calculated to appeal to the middle ground. After 1646 the old courts and local juries were also far more likely to give royalists sympathetic treatment than parliamentary committees and tribunals.[92] On some issues, including liturgical practices, it was possible to appeal to an unrepealed statute against a policy prescribed by parliamentary ordinance. Royalists therefore had good tactical reasons for stressing legality.

One particularly effective means used to drive home the argument that Parliament, rather than the Crown, now represented the chief threat to constitutional liberties was the theatrical publicity given to the trials and executions of victims of irregular parliamentary justice. Charles himself eventually became the most conspicuous of these martyrs but he was neither the first nor the last. Others included both conspicuous figures like the Earl of Holland, executed for his role in the Second Civil War and lesser men like the former soldier James Hind, who turned highwayman and was executed in 1652 after inspiring at least seventeen pamphlets celebrating him as a Robin Hood character who victimized lawyers, parsons and committeemen while befriending the poor.[93] The radical John Lillburne also turned himself into a symbol of the Englishman's violated liberties in theatrical pamphlets recording his trials by the House of Lords in 1646 and the Commonwealth in 1649.[94] But even Leveller pamphlets were now directed against Parliament rather than the King's justice.

Even so, serious royalist tracts on constitutional issues were always outnumbered by satires and journalistic works, notably the official court newsbook, *Mercurius Aulicus*. Initially directed by the Laudian cleric Peter Heylin, this soon passed under the able control of Sir John Berkenhead.[95] *Aulicus* specialized in commenting on reports from other publications, exposing false statements, ridiculing opponents' claims and caricaturing parliamentary leaders.[96] Berkenhead quickly recognized the propaganda value of racy verse in a doggerel style that was already developing among university wits in the 1630s.[97]

There was also an appreciable quantity of more serious poetry associated with the King's cause.[98] Paradoxically 'Cavalier' verse is a product of both the pre-war and immediately post-war periods, more than of the years 1642–6. It is a pre-war phenomenon insofar as most of it was written before 1642, including all the poems of Carew, most of those by Herrick and Suckling and many poems by Lovelace, Richard Fanshawe and Edmund Waller. This was also a poetry that looked back to Jonson, Donne and classical models like Horace, Virgil, Catullus and Ovid. But it is a post-war phenomenon in the sense that most of it was first published between 1647 and the early 1650s, in volumes deliberately constructed to commemorate the royalist cause and Cavalier values. In addition, new poetry that consciously sought to carry on the traditions of Caroline court writers continued to appear. One publisher, Henry Moseley, accounted for the lion's share of printed anthologies, producing collections by Edmund Waller (1645), Richard Crashaw (1646 and 1648), Sir John Suckling (1646, 1648 and 1658), Abraham Cowley (1647 and 1655), Thomas Carew (1651), Thomas Stanley (1651) and Henry Vaughan (1651 and 1654), in addition to a folio edition of Beaumont and Fletcher plays (1647). Robert Herrick's *Noble Numbers* (1647) and *Hesperides* (1648) appeared from a different publisher in the same period.[99]

Several of these collections began with prefatory poems commemorating a community of writers and literary patrons that had first come together at the Stuart court and was now perpetuating itself in adversity.[100] Even without this framework, many pre-war poems assumed fresh partisan meanings during the years spanning the King's defeat and execution and the establishment of a puritan Commonwealth.[101] This was the case with panegyrics to Charles, Henrietta Maria and other prominent royalists, as well as poems celebrating rural customs puritans disliked and religious verse exhibiting a taste for ceremony. Even verse lacking overt political or religious content, on topics like love and friendship, was read as expressing the cultural ethos of the King's party.[102]

In short, certain royalist poets and publishers reacted to the trauma of the King's defeat by constructing a partisan myth of royalist civilization shattered by rebellion and puritan philistinism.[103] They celebrated characteristics that allegedly distinguished the loyal gentry from the rebel party. In addition to the ideals of honour and loyalty, these traits included frank sensuality, which shows up most obviously in love poems, a staple of nearly all royalist anthologies. Although godly poets also wrote erotic verse, as can be seen in several passages of *Paradise Lost*, the royalist poets' ongoing fascination with feminine beauty and the rituals of courtship has no parallel in puritan literature.[104] It sometimes passed into prurience tinged with misogyny, especially in work by Carew and Suckling, and even more in obscene verses circulated anonymously in manuscript before the war and printed in the late 1650s. As Marotti has written, these convey a 'sexist and classist condescension' that Restoration rakes like Rochester would inherit.[105]

In addition Cavalier verse sought to exhibit social and linguistic codes associated with superior rank. The desire to distinguish polite from vulgar language and manners was a marked feature of European culture in the seventeenth century, connected to the evolution of the French concept of *honnêteté*, the development of academies for training young nobles and the publication of manuals of gentlemanly deportment.[106] The Cavalier ethos was rooted in this cosmopolitan tradition, although it also represented a reaction against the destruction of the royal court and House of Lords, the displacement of leading families from their traditional role of leadership in provincial society, and the promotion of men of humble origins through the Army and the County Committees. These challenges to principles of hierarchy made it all the more crucial to uphold the unwritten social codes that differentiated gentlemen from commoners. As Dudley, Lord North put it:

> a gentleman...stands ever bound to his good behaviour...for if outwardly he be incomposed in his carriage and civil respect, he will appear to men that understand good fashion as full of solecism and more absurd than the arrantest clown...and therefore he will make it a business, so much to frequent companies of the best respect and season himself with their fashions, as that thereby he may avoid in the least sort to become ridiculous.[107]

North echoes the old courtly manuals on the importance of pleasing others but replaces the prince with a collectivity of 'men that understand good fashions' as the arbiter of manners.

It would be grossly misleading to suggest that only royalists cared about fashion and civility. But royalist writing sometimes tried to foster this misconception by emphasizing concepts of gentility that contrasted with republican and puritan values of personal rectitude and public duty. 'Thou'rt careful, frugal, painful,' Cowley once remarked: 'we commend a servant so, not a friend.'[108] The qualities prized by Cavaliers remained strongly tinged with self-assertiveness and hedonism, which good manners tempered but did not displace. 'Civility is an important piece of society, especially among the better sort', North wrote, because 'high and braving spirits unseasoned therewith would like cocks and mastiffs, impatient of the fierceness of one another's eyes, uncollected and unrecalled assault each other with blows instead of salutes.'[109] Behaviour reflecting this outlook, such as duelling, drinking and condescending mockery, served as symbolic protests against the victorious puritans.

A related attitude was pronounced mistrust of religious enthusiasm, which Cavalier publicists usually depicted either as canting hypocrisy or a kind of madness. A view of the Great Rebellion as the product of a collective madness characterized many royalist accounts, including the opening books of Clarendon's *History of the Great Rebellion* and the first chapter of *Eikon Basilike*. It is strikingly foreshadowed in the last Caroline masque, *Salmacida Spolia*, in which Furies try to foment war in England.[110] Some writers attempted to undercut appeals to inspiration by advancing values of rationality, balance and clarity. The most systematic and radical was the philosopher Thomas Hobbes (1588– 1679), who developed an extended linguistic and philosophical critique of claims to religious inspiration and their use in the political sphere. Hobbesian politics is motivated by natural passions, especially the greatest passion, fear. Religion itself derives psychologically from the 'fear of things invisible', which instils dependence on those who seem to possess an ability to interfere with the supernatural or predict its course.[111] Pretences to supernatural knowledge, given credence by popular ignorance, have been a potent source of political mischief throughout history. The removal of this evil was one of the chief goals of the rational science of politics that Hobbes claimed to have founded.[112]

Hobbes was far from being a typical royalist, especially in dismissing all forms of clerical influence, including that of the episcopal Church. But others shared his dislike of enthusiasm and his quest for a rational concept of politics as rooted in the operation of passion.[113] William Davenant mistrusted inspiration in both religion and poetry, and indeed drew a connection between the two:

> inspiration [is] a dangerous word, which many have of late successfully us'd... a spiritual fit, derived from the ancient ethnic poets who then, as they were priests, were statesmen too, and probably lov'd dominion; and as their well dissembling of inspiration begot them reverence then, equal to that which was paid to laws; so these who now profess the same fury, may perhaps by such authentic example pretend authority over the people.[114]

In place of inspiration he elevated wit, defined as 'the dexterity of thought, rounding the world like the sun... and bringing swiftly home to the memory universal surveys', a faculty that 'removes, uncovers, makes way for light, where darkness was enclosed'.[115] He rejected obscure mystical flights of imagination, as well as the traditional apparatus in epic poetry of mythic creatures and gods. In their place Davenant advocated a new kind of 'heroic poem', devoid of implausible fantasies, written in a lucid style perfected through 'time and labour', in which the depiction of character and action derived from the poet's careful observations of life.

The epic was a less characteristic royalist genre, however, than the short lyric, the tragi-comedy and the romance. Romances appealed to Cavalier writers partly because they revolved around stories of patient endurance and emotional constancy under adversity, which suited the polemical and emotional needs of a defeated party. *Eikon Basilike*, for example, continuously evokes themes and images from the romance tradition in describing Charles's sufferings during and after the Civil War. But this is not the only explanation: romances and romance plots had already become popular at court in the 1630s, and the 'noble' passions of love and ambition, which Davenant placed at the centre of *Gondibert*, were equally pivotal in the French classical drama developing in this period. Royalist literature, while in part a response to traumatic events at home, also reflected larger European fashions.

Another international influence was a Christianized version of Epicureanism, associated especially with the French Catholic theorist Pierre Gassendi.[116] It is especially evident in the work of royalists resident in Paris, who were in touch with Gassendi himself. Margaret, Duchess of Newcastle, who presided over the largest English royalist household in Paris after the Queen's court at St Germain, later published the most thoroughly Epicurean collection of English verse of the century. Epicurean physics, ethics, religious scepticism and politics are also very evident in the work of other writers, including Cowley and Davenant. Epicureanism's materialist physics and psychology was developed in antiquity as an antidote to religious fanaticism. Gassendi had adjusted Epicurean doctrine just enough to make it compatible with an optimistic Catholic theology, but not with predestination, millenarianism or belief in mankind's natural depravity. It took little imagination for anti-puritan writers to grasp the utility of this philosophy.

Ancient Epicureanism was also associated with ideals of retirement and private friendship, which had strongly influenced Virgil, Horace and other Roman poets. These values, which had already been absorbed into English culture in the pre-war period, seemed particularly suited to the circumstances in which royalists found themselves after 1648 and were readily adapted as Cavalier tropes.[117] Isaac Walton even managed to infuse the sport of angling with a royalist colouration.[118] We do need to make allowances for a few parliamentarians who retreated to their country estates to cultivate pleasures like philosophy, painting and gardening after becoming alienated from the government of the moment. The ideal of country retirement was too deeply rooted to be entirely monopolized by one party. But rural beatitude was recognized as an essentially royalist – or at least an anti-republican – theme even by some writers on the other side. In 'Upon Appleton House' and 'An Horatian Ode upon Cromwell's Return from Ireland', Andrew Marvell deliberately juxtaposed the private pleasures of gardening (an Epicurean preoccupation) and housekeeping to images of military and political activity.[119]

Millenarianism, Republicanism and Cromwellianism

Whereas the defeated royalists managed to portray themselves as defenders of the law and ancient concepts of gentility, defenders of the new Commonwealth faced an altogether more difficult predicament, since Pride's Purge and the regicide had effectively destroyed most of the principles for which the Long Parliament had claimed to be fighting.[120] Even the Levellers had been alienated by the Army grandees. Yet the ultimate military outcome remained in doubt until the defeat of the Scots and English royalists under Charles II by Cromwell, at Worcester in August of 1652.

These conditions offered numerous opportunities to royalists and other hostile writers, which they quickly exploited. The regicide inspired numerous tracts, including the century's single most successful work of propaganda, *Eikon Basilike*. Purportedly a memoir of the King during his 'solitudes and sufferings', it was probably written by the clergyman John Gauden from notes left by Charles.[121] Milton's *Eikonoklastes* and other pamphlets quickly answered it, and modern accounts sometimes give the impression of a fairly even exchange. But in terms of impact there was no contest. Milton's pamphlet had two English and one Latin edition before 1660, while the 'King's book' went through thirty-five English impressions and twenty-five abroad during 1649 alone.[122] Other tracts reinforced its message by portraying Charles as a man of great humanity, saddened by the plight of his people more than by his own misfortunes. One described miracles performed by his blood.[123] This publicity compounded the shock and horror caused by the King's execution.

One common reaction to political upheaval was a heightened sense of eschatological expectation. This took many forms and often remained sufficiently open-ended to accommodate considerable ambivalence. Royalists saw the Army's triumph as a chastisement visited upon the nation for its sins that would eventually end in the King's providential return, once guilt had been sufficiently expiated. Some of the Army's more enthusiastic supporters looked forward to the imminent dawn of the millennium. The Fifth Monarchists, who emerged after the battle of Worcester as a movement among army officers and gathered congregations in London, Wales and elsewhere, were the most outspoken advocates of such views.[124] Millenarian speculation coloured a variety of sermons and tracts of the period, however, including the works by orthodox figures like Richard Baxter, who opposed the regicide and the sects but devoted much of the 1650s to scriptural research concerning the end of the world.[125]

Alongside apocalyptic visions grounded in scripture, there proliferated a large number of astrological predictions and prophecies attributed to Merlin, Nostradamus and Mother Shipton, whose riddling account of a general alteration of Christendom, ostensibly written in the reign of Henry VIII and newly rediscovered, was applied to current events. The parliamentary astrologer William Lilly produced a popular annual almanac larded with predictions favourable to the government, which earned him a pension of £100.[126] But royalists also used astrology and prophecy, as did writers whose allegiances remained indeterminate or muddled. One predicted that Cromwell would eventually restore Charles II; another published prophecies by Merlin, Mother Shipton, the puritan millenarian Joseph Meade and Ignatius Loyola, with no apparent sense of inconsistency.[127] Political instability encouraged a desire to peer into the future and anticipate events that cut across party lines.

Another response was to wait upon events until God's intentions became clearer. Oliver Cromwell was famously given to bouts of uncertainty and inaction as he searched out God's providences, punctuated by periods of intense energy once he felt confident of the Almighty's intentions.[128] But a similar attitude of worried anticipation also characterized the responses of many others to events following the regicide, as the new Commonwealth struggled to rally support and defend itself from renewed military threats in Scotland.

Two of Marvell's poems written during these years – 'An Horatian Ode upon Cromwell's Return from Ireland' and 'Upon Appleton House' – provide finely calibrated expressions of the mingled hopes, fears and uncertainties of this period.[129] Worden has dated 'An Horatian Ode' to the weeks immediately after 28 May 1650, when Cromwell entered London to take command of the forces being prepared for the invasion of Scotland that would culminate in the victory at Dunbar in September. He owed his elevation to the fact that Fairfax, who became Marvell's patron at about the time of the poem's composition, refused to lead the Army against the Scots. Cromwell had thus become the man of the hour, attracting both praise and vilification. To many supporters of the Commonwealth he was a hero providentially chosen to overturn monarchy in England and perhaps ultimately in all Europe. Marchamont Nedham, whose work we will examine shortly, predicted that Cromwell might soon lead the New Model Army on a campaign against the continental strongholds of popery and tyranny. In a more secular vein, Nedham also depicted Cromwell as a Machiavellian hero, destined to found a new republican state through his active *virtu*. Royalists were meanwhile portraying him as a Machiavel in the conventional sense, who had murdered the King and destroyed the constitution from a ruthless lust for power.

Marvell echoes both views, describing a 'restless Cromwell' purging parliamentary rivals before ruining 'the great work of time' that was the ancient constitution. The violence is accompanied by guile: Cromwell ensnares the King with 'subtle hopes and fears' before destroying him. In contrast to Charles, who is portrayed accepting his fate with a dignity reminiscent of *Eikon Basilike*, Marvell alternately associates Cromwell with images of natural violence (three-forked lightning), conquest (a Caesar and a Hannibal), or the hunt (chasing the King to Carisbrooke; perching like a falcon over its prey; pursuing Scots like 'Caledonian deer'). The imagery is given a deeper resonance by an allusion in the poem's opening to the account in Lucan's *Pharasalia* of Caesar's crossing the Rubicon.[130]

If there is no doubt that Cromwell stands for a power forged by violent action, Marvell repeatedly suggests both that this may be what Providence intended and that in times like the present such ruthless energy is required. Ancient rights

> ...do hold or break
> As men are strong or weak.
> Nature, that hateth emptiness,
> Allows of penetration less:
>   And therefore must make room
>   Where greater spirits come.

Here the poem gestures toward a more positive Machiavellian imagery, along the lines explored by Nedham. As Worden and others have argued, Marvell appears to suggest that the 'ancient rights' and decorum associated with Charles are now irrevocably doomed, so that hesitation can only make matters worse.[131] Yet there is at least a hint of equivocation in the celebration of Cromwellian activism:

> A Caesar, he, ere long to Gaul,
> To Italy an Hannibal,
>   And to all states not free
>   Shall climacteric be.[132]

This sounds like a prediction of European conquest – until we remember how Caesar and Hannibal ended up.[133] If Cromwell is 'the force of angry heaven's flame', it is not absolutely clear whether this means he is a godly leader destined to hasten the millennium, or a Nimrod scourging God's people for a season before meeting destruction himself. No one could know in June of 1650 what the next few months would bring. Marvell's equivocation is perhaps intended to convey the uncertainty of a man facing a portentous but unknowable future, in which the meaning of the present still lay hidden.[134]

Derek Hirst and Steven Zwicker have recently placed 'Upon Appleton House' in the equally precise context of the following summer of 1651, when the defeated Scots regrouped and prepared the campaign that ended at Worcester.[135] Fairfax was being pressed by the regime in London and others to resume a more active role. 'At the epicentre of the poem', Hirst and Zwicker comment, 'is a man facing a very specific decision, whether or not to take up arms for an uncertain cause.' Around that centre cluster incidents involving other members of the Fairfax household, references to current events such as a small Leveller outbreak a few miles from the estate, and allusions to larger themes of rustic retirement and military action. These are interwoven with allusions to Fairfax family history, classical and biblical literature and Hermetic philosophy, which Fairfax was studying at the time.[136] The result is a densely textured poem whose meaning again remains highly elusive, though Marvell does appear to tactfully advocate action more than withdrawal.[137] As with 'The Horatian Ode', although in even more complex ways, the poem is a meditation on whether and how to act in the face of political uncertainty and moral ambiguity, which make God's purposes extraordinarily difficult to read.

The most widely persuasive secular arguments for the commonwealth were based on the right of conquest and the duty of submission to *de facto* authority. Even some royalists acknowledged the force of this position, especially after Dunbar and Worcester. Hobbes's *Leviathan*, published in 1651 on the eve of these Cavalier disasters, was widely regarded as justifying submission to the new government.[138] At the other end of the spectrum some people, including but not confined to the Levellers, argued that the New Model Army's victory had finally shattered the 'Norman Yoke' imposed on England in 1066, freeing her people to restore a mythic Saxon constitution or else create an entirely new government.[139]

Meanwhile a handful of writers – Marchamont Nedham, John Milton, James Harrington and Henry Vane – developed explicit republican theories. They did not always agree with each other and their views were in some ways untypical even among supporters of the regicide. Their writings did, however, represent a bold new strain in English political discourse, which broke free from the dominant frameworks of the early Stuart period and the Civil War itself. Republican ideas appear so anomalous, in fact, that historians have shown some perplexity over their origins.

Thomas Hobbes supplied one answer in an often quoted dictum, blaming the Civil War on ideas inculcated by the humanist education the gentry received in the universities.

> There were an exceeding great number of men of the better sort that in their youth having read the books written by famous men of the ancient Grecian and Roman commonwealths concerning their polity and great actions, in which books the popular government was extolled by the glorious name of liberty and monarchy disgraced by the name of tyranny, they became thereby in love with their forms of government. And out of these men were chosen the greatest part of the House of Commons, or if they were not the greatest part, yet by advantage of their eloquence, were always able to sway the rest.[140]

Most historians have discounted this assessment, arguing that republican principles had little impact before 1649. Blair Worden and Markku Peltonen have recently sought to qualify this view, however.[141] Peltonen has shown that certain generically republican ideas were central to English humanist thought from the earlier Tudor period onwards. These included a Ciceronian ideal of service to the state and commonwealth; Aristotelian and Polybian concepts of mixed government, which many thinkers applied to the English constitution; admiration for foreign republican states, especially Venice; arguments that virtue and merit, rather than birth and royal favour, provided the only true claim to nobility; concern over political and moral corruption at court; and a belief that liberty and security of property were essential to the preservation of valour and civic virtue. These attitudes were never integrated into an overtly republican ideology but they did remain widely available. Foreign republican and resistance theorists – including George Buchanan and Machiavelli – were known in England.[142] Republican values were, in addition, portrayed in imaginative literature, for example Shakespeare's *Julius Caesar*.

In the 1620s we find a few instances of republican writings being deliberately reinterpreted to provide *anti*-republican arguments. Hobbes's preface to his 1627 edition of Thucydides argued that Periclean Athens was a *de facto* monarchy, since Pericles had achieved a position of supremacy over the democracy. In 1628 Peter Heylin employed a Polybian analysis to explain (approvingly) how Augustus had subverted the Roman constitution by manipulating its republican forms to cloak his monarchical power.[143] The court poet, Thomas May, placed a royalist gloss on Lucan's republican epic, *Pharsalia*, which he translated into English. May ended up abandoning his master in 1642, however, claiming that he had been persuaded by Lucan's position.[144] Republican ideas did arouse speculative interest in early Stuart England, apparently with mixed results.

Yet there is little evidence to support Hobbes's contention that reading classical sources converted many gentlemen into overt republicans, even after 1641.[145] Although Henry Parker and other parliamentary publicists advanced concepts of popular sovereignty, few explored the possibility of dissolving the ancient constitution and replacing it with new structures of free government.[146] Secular political theory may actually have done less to prepare the ground for republicanism than certain strains of religious argument. The defence of political freedom was closely bound up with pleas for freedom of conscience, just as the claim that freeborn Englishmen had the right to elect their governors was anticipated by assertions that Christians should be free to gather their own churches. The links seem particularly clear for the Levellers, whose leaders all had earlier connections to radical religious sects, and who drew most of their support from separated congregations and army regiments infected with sectarianism. David Wootton has noticed that Edwards, the great chronicler of sectarian heresies, correctly predicted the rise of the Levellers in the third part of *Gangraena* (1647). He named several future Leveller leaders and asserted that they had recently moved beyond their subversion of the Church to advocate 'democracy' in the state.[147] Other advocates of popular sovereignty – notably Parker, Marchamont Nedham and James Harrington – were anti-clerical erastians rather than sectarian enthusiasts. But they shared an antipathy towards both episcopal and presbyterian authority that seems characteristic of thinkers attracted to Leveller or republican positions.

The political eclipse of the parliamentary peerage, culminating in the abolition of the House of Lords in 1649, also crucially shaped the context in which republican thought developed. In pre-war culture it was often possible to absorb republican ideals of liberty and patriotism within a discourse structured around aristocratic concepts of honour, traditional notions concerning the importance of good counsel and medieval constitutional precedents.[148] After the Restoration Algernon Sidney would similarly combine republican values with belief in the role of the feudal nobility in preserving liberty in medieval England.[149] The elimination of the peerage along with the monarchy effectively precluded this kind of synthesis, clearing the way to a much bolder and purer variety of classical republican thought.

The pioneer theorist in this respect was Marchamont Nedham, previously editor of the leading parliamentary newsbook, *Mercurius Britanicus*. Nedham had gone over to the royalists in 1646 but then changed sides again in 1649 and was given control of a new government journal, *Mercurius Politicus*.[150] Between September 1651 (the month of Worcester) and August 1652 he published a series of editorials which expounded republican ideas through commentaries on history, in the manner of Machiavelli's *Discourses on Livy*.[151] Nedham drew upon a much wider range of sources, however, including the Bible, medieval chronicles and classical historians. Like Machiavelli, he admired military expansion and advocated arming the citizenry, from whom a free state had nothing to fear. He wanted political offices thrown open to talent, which would encourage virtue and public service. Republican government, he urged, would allow the genius of the English people to flourish as never before.

The assumption that free states encourage talent and virtue more effectively than monarchies, 'where the prince's pleasure usually weighs down all considerations of the common good',[152] is one that Nedham shared with the Commonwealth's Latin Secretary and official censor, John Milton, with whom he formed a close friendship.[153] Royal government, both men believed, is characterized not only by despotism but pomp, luxury and corruption. These vices flourish in courts and spread to deprave and enervate the people, who, as they become 'slaves to their own lusts, they become the more easily enslaved unto the lusts of another'.[154] Monarchies foster sloth and languor, whereas republics promote action and vitality. These arguments drew upon Machiavelli and a number of classical sources, including Aristotle, Cicero and Sallust, whose depiction of imperial corruption provided a rich source for Milton's anti-royalist tracts.[155] But they also paralleled puritan attacks on popery. Just as papists keep the Word of God from the people and turn religion into priestcraft, so Kings use ceremony and the doctrine of the *arcana imperii* to discourage citizens from political engagement. If God wishes people to abandon superstition and join in building his Church, He also wants them to cast off their servility and employ their reason and energy in public life.

There were consequently numerous points of contact between republican and eschatological languages, making the passage from one to the other relatively easy.[156] After Dunbar, Steven Pincus has written, 'it had become quite fashionable to preach an aggressive apocalyptic republicanism – a republicanism derived not only from an analysis of classical texts but from a conviction that God would replace the rule of earthly kings with that of Christ in the last days'.[157] This fusion of religious and secular arguments is especially evident in polemics against the Dutch, who had allegedly betrayed both Protestantism and republicanism by embracing the monarchical House of Orange, supporting the exiled Stuarts and placing trading interests above religion. Like the Scots, who had similar vices, they needed to be chastised and compelled to join England in a free and godly state, which could then proceed to the great work of destroying the anti-christian kingdoms of Europe.[158]

All British governments of the 1650s sought to justify themselves through a blend of religious and republican rhetoric, invoking godliness, liberty and military success. This stance was defined not only through written argument but gestures and symbolic rituals. In 1655 the Venetian ambassador described Cromwell making a great public show of religious zeal, going 'every Sunday to preach to the soldiers and exhort them to live after the Divine Law. He does this with fervour, even to tears, which he has ready at a moment's notice.'[159] Earlier in the year a day of public prayer had been declared 'for the ill used Protestants in the valleys of Savoy...the preachers make much of the outrage and martyrdom of so many'. Cromwell initiated a public contribution for their aid, promising to give £2000.[160] The next March a day of public fasting was declared 'to implore the favour of the Almighty' for the fleet that had just departed to attack Spanish America; for good measure the sufferings of Savoyard Protestants were again remembered.[161] Through events like this the Protectorate sought to enliven Protestant and patriotic sentiments and direct them at external enemies, rather than at domestic politics.

The republicans never entirely overcame certain latent weaknesses in their position, however. If, as Nedham and Milton argued, free government depended on the virtue of its people, then it could not work among a debased population. It was always difficult to decide how far political rights might safely be extended beyond a godly and virtuous minority of committed supporters, to presbyterians, neutralists and crypto-royalists. This was at once a practical problem – since most of the political nation continued to desire some sort of restoration of the old constitution – and a theoretical one, requiring attempts to decide just how rights to political participation should be defined. We can think of the available positions as being arrayed within a triangular space whose corners were represented by the old constitution, Leveller democracy and the Fifth Monarchist ideal of a republic of saints. By late 1653 each of these extreme positions had been repudiated but attempts to work out some sort of compromise between them continued until the Restoration. The quest for 'settlement' and reconciliation of former opponents conflicted with the convictions of many ardent supporters of the regicide, whose dislike of aristocratic government and desire for further reforms threatened to further alienate the conservative majority.

Every government of the 1650s had to wrestle with these tensions and contend with the bitter disillusionment of erstwhile supporters who felt their ideals had been betrayed. Those who remained loyal to Cromwell, including Milton and Marvell, continued to employ a republican rhetoric of liberty and public service, often tinged with eschatological language. But many commonwealthsmen turned against the Protector, converting republicanism into a vehicle of opposition. In 1656 a military defeat on the Caribbean island of Hispaniola tarnished the Protectorate's image, causing even sympathizers to wonder if it had not angered providence.[162] The parliamentary elections of that year witnessed numerous partisan contests and gave rise to three major republican tracts: Nedham's *The Excellency of a Free State*, Henry Vane's *A Healing Question* and James Harrington's *Oceana*.[163] The last of these was by far the most original republican work of the period and the only significant one to break with the assumption that a free state depends upon the moral virtue of its citizenry. Harrington analysed politics though a language of public and private interest shared by other republican theorists. But he argued that in a properly constituted commonwealth, the public good could be made to coincide with the private interest of the majority.[164] Devotion to the state would not, therefore, require any extraordinary capacity for self-sacrifice.

Harrington associated states dedicated to achieving this result with an 'ancient prudence' revealed directly to the Jews 'and afterward picked out of his [God's] footsteps in nature and unanimously followed by the Greeks and Romans'.[165] It consisted of 'an art whereby a civil society of men is instituted and preserved upon the foundation of common right or interest...the empire of laws and not of men'. He contrasted this with the 'modern prudence' which had developed after the fall of the Republic and triumphed decisively with the barbarian invasions of the fifth century. Modern prudence is 'an art whereby some man, or some few men, subject a city or a nation, and rule it according unto his or their private interest...an empire of men and not laws'. It is inherently unstable because it creates conflicts of interest not only between rulers and subjects but within the governing elite itself.[166] Modern constitutions, including that of England, are in reality 'no other than a wrestling match, wherein the nobility, as they have been stronger, have thrown the king, or the king, if he have been stronger, hath thrown the nobility; or the king, where he hath had a nobility and could bring them to his party, have thrown the people, as in France and Spain; or the people, where they have had no nobility, or could get them to be of their party, have thrown the king, as in Holland or latter times in Oceana [England]'.[167]

Harrington explained the collapse of this constitution in the English Civil War through a now famous analysis of economic history.[168] Stable government, he argued, depends upon a proper alignment between political power and landed property. In the short term a ruler may depend on the sword to preserve his power, 'but an army is a beast that hath a great belly and must be fed' and 'he that can graze this beast' will ultimately prevail.[169] An absolute despotism can only endure in a state like Ottoman Turkey, where all land is held at the Sultan's pleasure. The old English constitution rested on feudal tenures through which the King parcelled out the land to nobles in return for military service. Although individual kings were often at the mercy of their own armed followers, the throne itself had survived because it was essential to the system of property on which the nobility depended. Drawing heavily upon Francis Bacon's *History of King Henry VII*, Harrington argued that the early Tudors had altered this balance by establishing a class of middling freeholders possessing sufficient land to remain independent of the great lords.[170] In doing so they had unwittingly undermined monarchy itself, for 'whereas nobility striketh not at the throne, without which they cannot subsist, but at some king that they do not like, popular power striketh through the king at the throne, as that which is incompatible with it'.[171] Elizabeth postponed the reckoning with her 'love tricks' but under Charles I, a king 'as stiff in disputes as the nerve of monarchy was grown slack' the old government had dissolved.[172]

It remained to settle the state on new foundations. To this end Harrington proposed an 'agrarian law' prohibiting estates worth more than £2000 *per annum* to preserve a republic of relatively equal independent proprietors, and an elaborate institutional apparatus designed to hold in check the elite that he thought would inevitably emerge, since about one third of any population will always be found more intelligent and resourceful than the rest. These reforms, he argued, would produce an egalitarian republic of self-sufficient agriculturalists, which Aristotle had described as the best commonwealth. With the elimination of both political and economic servitude, the people would be free to pursue a government based on reason, rather than private interest.[173] At this point Harrington's thought acquired Platonic and vaguely millenarian dimensions. Since reason derives from God, the commonwealth will be doing His work. For Harrington, no less than Milton or Vane, republicanism was ultimately a kind of political theology with eschatological overtones.[174]

A final great flurry of republican speculation occurred in 1659, after the fall of Richard Cromwell. Much of it was heavily influenced by Harrington, who formed the Rota Club at a London coffee house to discuss schemes for a new commonwealth. Events soon truncated these discussions, but a republican intellectual legacy survived into the eighteenth century.[175]

An Ambiguous Restoration

The Restoration has been less intensively studied than the collapse of royal government in 1641 and has therefore often seemed more straightforward. Viewed from a distance, it can look like a return to the *status quo ante bellum*, soon followed by a resumption of earlier conflicts in slightly modified form. But events were actually more complex than this characterization suggests. Like the Civil War itself, the King's return resulted from both long-term and short-term causes. The former included several fundamental political weaknesses that none of the post-regicide regimes ever solved. After 1649 no government enjoyed majority support and the minority that had accepted the regicide showed an incurable tendency to splinter into antagonistic factions. The fiscal burden of an unpopular army, whose wages were often in arrears, generated further antagonisms between soldiers and civilians that surfaced in every parliament of the protectoral period. But although these problems caused a series of political headaches, every Cavalier plot to restore the monarchy had quickly collapsed. By 1659 most royalists were demoralized, quiescent and seemingly incapable of reversing the outcome of the Civil War, no matter how unpopular republican government became.

Richard Cromwell's deposition by the Army in April 1659 unleashed a period of acute instability. The infighting mostly involved politicians associated with the Protectorate, the Army or the Republic, however, who nearly all opposed the King's return. Although royalists tried to exploit feuds among their enemies, they seemed unlikely to succeed even as late as January of 1660, when General Monck remained allied with a republican faction headed by Arthur Haselrig. Only in February, when Monck stopped enforcing the Rump Parliament's suppression of protests in the City, did events begin to move decisively in favor of monarchy.[176]

The political turbulence of 1659 was accompanied by an upsurge of controversy in the pulpit, London streets and the press, whose output again reached levels unseen since the early 1640s. As Ronald Hutton has written, this printed literature is among the most understudied features of the period.[177] It ran the gamut from royalism to extreme sectarian and republican tracts, and included a large volume of abusive polemic. Until 1660 the main controversies centred not on the King but the army's role in politics, the kind of republican state that would succeed the Protectorate, the status of religious sectaries (particularly Quakers) and radical reforms like the abolition of tithes. The northern Quakers gathered 15,000 signatures on petitions supporting this last proposal in Westmoreland, Cumberland, Lancashire and Cheshire in June of 1659.[178] There were also demands for sweeping legal reforms.

These proposals, which threatened the interests of the two largest professional groups in England, fuelled a backlash against Quakers and other radicals that had already been gathering momentum in Cromwell's last years. As Barry Reay has argued, the swing of opinion away from the republican regime that climaxed early in 1660 was inspired as much by hatred of extremist minorities as by royalist sentiment.[179] Even many Independents and some Baptists now sought to close ranks against a common enemy who threatened to subvert any settled religion.[180] Animus against Quakers was reinforced by dislike of the Army and republican politicians in Parliament, by economic grievances aggravated by a trade depression and by sensationalist rumours spread through the press and the pulpit. A London broadside warned that Henry Vane and the Fifth Monarchists were plotting a massacre of the citizenry, and panic caused by rumours of sectarian risings broke out in several provincial settings. Increased co-operation between the regime and the sects following the suppression of George Booth's Presbyterian rebellion in the summer added to the climate of anxiety.[181]

Resentment also inspired a flood of satires, described by Hutton as perhaps 'the most vulgar collection of writing in English poetical literature'.[182] The purged Parliament acquired the title of 'the Rump', associated with all manner of scatological imagery. When Monck refused to suppress agitation for a free Parliament in the City in February 1660, the populace celebrated by roasting the rumps of chickens, cows and sheep over bonfires in the streets. Individual politicians and the soldiery were subjected to abusive and vulgar mockery, which emphasized well-worn themes concerning the selfishness, hypocrisy, sexual licence and low social status of the Commonwealth's rulers. The stream of invective continued into the early months of the Restoration, spreading to the newly reopened theatres, which staged a number of anti-puritan and anti-Commonwealth satires, including both old works, like Jonson's *Bartholomew Fair*, and new plays set in the 1650s.[183]

Among the latter was John Tatham's *The Rump; or the Mirrour of the Late Times*, a satiric account of high politics in 1659. The plot centres on the machinations of civilian and Army grandees, especially Bertlam (Lambert) Lockwhit (Whitelock), and Stoneware (Lord Wareston), who form a cabal that easily outmanoeuvres Woodfleet (Fleetwood), whom everyone regards as an ineffectual fool. The true force behind the cabal is Lady Bertlam, who goads her husband on to satisfy her insatiable ambition to be called her highness. Her upwardly mobile ambitions infect other women, such as the maid Prue, who dreams of being 'ladified'.[184] Inevitably, feminine pride is linked to promiscuity. Lady Bertlam hints that she was formerly Cromwell's mistress – a widely disseminated slander – and presides over a council of grandee's wives whose chief demand is the repeal of a law against fornication, since 'society is the life of republics'.[185] At the end of the play, after all their plots have failed, the main characters return as London street peddlers.[186]

Hatred of the republic and its leaders found additional outlet through public demonstrations, from the hanging in effigy of Cromwell and other Army leaders by London crowds to the anti-Quaker riots that accompanied rejoicing over the King's return in at least fifteen counties during May and June of 1660.[187] The trials and public execution of regicides and the grisly hanging of Cromwell's exhumed body provided a further grim counterpoint to public joy at the Restoration. London celebrated for three days following the King's arrival in the City on 29 May, while Norwich did so for a full week. Everywhere church bells rang out in commemoration.[188] Maypoles were a common prop in these festivities, symbolizing the popular association of the return of monarchy with the end of puritan morality.[189] People drank and feasted at public expense: in several cities the fountains ran with wine, while cakes and ale were ubiquitous.[190] Celebratory prints ranged from formal panegyrics to romantic accounts of the King's escape in disguise after the Battle of Worcester and engraved portraits adorned with royalist symbols.[191]

Widespread rejoicing might seem to betoken a national repudiation of puritan and parliamentary principles. Yet what had actually been rejected was less the 'good old cause' of the 1640s than the power of soldiers, republican politicians, Quakers and Fifth Monarchists: groups many of Parliament's original supporters had long detested. The line dividing royalists from parliamentarians had often blurred considerably in the 1650s, as Cavaliers reconciled themselves to the *de facto* power, while erstwhile Roundheads found themselves opposing protectoral policies. The Restoration was itself brought about almost entirely by former supporters of Parliament. Some embittered Cavaliers certainly hoped for vengeance but many people looked forward instead to rebuilding the shattered centre that had collapsed so disastrously in 1642.

Charles II and his entourage encouraged this hope with moderate words and gestures, especially the promise to respect tender consciences made in the Declaration of Breda, before the King's embarkation for England. The new court encouraged negotiations between episcopal and presbyterian divines over a new Church settlement, while panegyrics praised Charles's forgiveness of the sins of rebellion and his efforts to subdue the spirit of discord. The London mayoral entries of the early 1660s generally followed this formula, as did the pageants staged in London to celebrate the King's coronation in 1661, a spectacular show of royal splendour, for which the Crown was granted £70,000 – roughly double the expenditure of the last great coronation entry of James I in 1604. Speeches and iconography stressed the healing of wounds and prospects for renewed economic prosperity under royal government. The vanquished forces of rebellion were represented in sufficiently general terms to avoid needless provocation.

Even the widespread reaction against puritan 'fanaticism' did not invariably engender harsh partisanship. Several leading figures at the new court had developed a strong dislike for *any* sort of religious dogmatism and intolerance and so favoured toleration for all peaceable consciences.[192] The Duke of Buckingham was the most consistent champion of this attitude but the King's own views were not fundamentally different. Although he did not always support toleration, Charles invariably based his ecclesiastical policies on pragmatic political calculations.[193] In contrast to his father, he had no instinctive inclination towards religious partisanship.

The Renewal of Partisanship

The ultimate failure of reconciliation and persistence of partisan divisions rooted in the Civil War was caused partly by conflicts over the detailed shape of the Restoration settlement, especially in the ecclesiastical sphere. But it was due even more to a resurgence of hardline Cavalier and Anglican sentiment, not only among the gentry and clergy but a substantial portion of the general population. Especially at the popular level violent royalist sentiment was associated with loyalty to the old Church. Once the King's return began to appear inevitable, a spontaneous religious reaction developed in many communities, including London. Here, as Tim Harris has shown, hatred of the sects sometimes passed into a broader revulsion against all forms of puritanism, while 'ballads and prints often portrayed an uncompromisingly anglican vision of the Restoration'.[194]

Once the initial euphoria of 1660 had subsided, the new regime found it needed to placate not only former enemies but a vocal segment of the nation that was, in certain respects, more royalist than the King. This was, however, a royalism defined by memories of the 1640s rather than blind support for Charles II. Positively, it was characterized by a commitment to monarchy as the lynchpin of a hierarchical social and ecclesiastical order. Negatively, it rested upon visceral loathing for puritanism, rebellion and disobedience. People holding these attitudes refused to distinguish between sober presbyterians and the wildest sectaries, treating both as seditious 'fanatics'. But they were usually not absolutists, since they regarded kingship as entirely compatible with the rule of law, and they soon showed a willingness to obstruct royal policies that conflicted with their perceptions of the monarchy's true interests. Any signs of activism on the part of groups associated with the old parliamentary cause naturally reinforced Cavalier prejudices. In 1661 the election of a presbyterian slate of representatives to Parliament in London, by crowds chanting 'No Bishops, No Lordly Bishops' provoked an angry reaction elsewhere, while Venner's Fifth Monarchist uprising in January 1661, the Northern Rising of 1663 and a serious rebellion in southwestern Scotland in 1667 all helped sustain fears of a revival of the old parliamentary cause.

Intransigent Cavalier partisanship was never entirely dominant among the political nation, however, or even within the so-called 'Cavalier Parliament' elected in 1661.[195] Many people who detested puritan government still shrank from rigorous prosecution of peaceful dissent, which could severely disrupt local communities. By the late 1660s sentiment was growing for some relaxation of the penal laws passed earlier in the decade.[196] But this softening inspired redoubled efforts by an energetic minority of committed partisans, determined to prevent any relaxation of vigilance against the old enemies of the 1640s. The celebration of significant anniversaries – especially of the regicide (30 January), and the King's birthday (29 May) – provided one means of perpetuating partisan memories. Another was anti-puritan satire and polemic. Samuel Butler's *Hudibras* and tracts by clerical writers associated with Bishop Gilbert Sheldon, such as George Stradling, Thomas Tomkins and Samuel Parker perpetuated stereotypes of 'the disloyal, hypocritical, untrustworthy and covertly anti-monarchical character of Nonconformity... *ad nauseam*'.[197]

If Restoration England was a nation unable to forget the Great Rebellion, this was at least partly because of publicists who refused to let it do so.[198] The obsession of these partisans with the past sustained a climate in which, as Steven Zwicker has written, polemic 'engulfed the literary and tempered all idioms of culture'.[199] For Thomas Hobbes, even scientific experiments with air pumps had potentially dangerous political implications.[200] But if the Restoration was for some people an age of intense partisanship, it was not yet one of formed parties, since the actual conduct of politics did not consistently conform to any single pattern of alignments. The ideological diversity and policy fluctuations of the royal court, especially the Declaration of Indulgence of 1672, confused the political situation. In addition the line between the restored Church and Dissent, which the Uniformity Act of 1662 had attempted to define sharply, was blurred in practice by the outward conformity of gentlemen who remained sympathetic to puritan religion and the attitude of divines like Richard Baxter, who refused to accept the permanence of their expulsion from the Anglican fold.[201] It was by no means inevitable that English society would remain indefinitely divided by the antagonisms of the 1640s. Intransigent Cavaliers like the King's censor, Roger L'Estrange had to worry, not only about the old republican enemy, but Anglican royalists who were prepared to put the Great Rebellion behind them.

Yet by Charles II's death in 1685 men like L'Estrange had triumphed: fierce partisanship, defined through memories of the Great Rebellion, had been reinscribed in English political culture. The persistence of divisions rooted in the Civil War certainly helps to explain this result, as recent work has repeatedly emphasized.[202] But Restoration history was not a high road from civil war to the age of party. Memories of the recent past deeply shaped the political culture of this period but they did not rigidly dictate its evolution.

Society, Culture and Politics

Court, town and fashion

We have already noticed that many royalists regarded the Civil War as an unmitigated cultural catastrophe. Military conflict and political upheaval certainly had been destructive. The Commonwealth auctioned off Charles I's great art collection, selling most of the choice pieces to foreign buyers.[203] The London season was disrupted; building activity was for a time depressed; cathedral choirs were dispersed, church organs destroyed, and a rich tradition of liturgical music interrupted. Yet the break with the past was less complete than this litany of disasters suggests and the 1650s witnessed a significant revival of metropolitan culture, albeit with some different emphases. The coffee house developed as a venue for a lively intellectual debate and the Cromwellian court, while less opulent than its royal predecessor, still provided a centre for social life. Royalist poets – Abraham Cowley, Edmund Waller and William Davenant – made their peace with the new regime. Even theatrical performances reappeared, despite their illegality. Davenant attempted to get around the prohibition on plays by having a tragedy set to music and calling it an opera, anticipating the later Restoration fashion for musical plays. On a less refined plane, 1658 also saw the appearance of the first published guide to London houses of prostitution.[204] The social and cultural life of the British capital in this period still awaits its historian, but it is clear that a metropolitan high society, with its fashions and its vices, had already begun to rise from the ashes before May 1660.

The return of the royal court accelerated this revival. A West End that had already begun to develop before the war, in places like Covent Garden and Lincoln's Inn Fields, expanded much further after 1660, as Bloomsbury, Leicester Fields, Soho and St James's Square were developed in the 1660s and 1670s. The main innovations of the new urban landscape were the classical brick town house, the rectilinear street plan and the uniformly built square. These features were associated with an equally important movement towards greater social segregation, achieved by preventing the erection of cheap tenements in back alleys.[205] The new neighbourhoods were therefore less crowded and preserved open spaces filled with greenery, fresh air and light, where people of quality might congregate. Even more important, in this respect, were St James's and Hyde Park, which lay immediately adjacent to the new neighbourhoods. One of Charles II's first acts after returning to England was to construct a canal in St James's Park for water fowl given him by Louis XIV and the Russian ambassador, which remains a popular attraction to this day.

The West End supported a variety of social, economic and cultural amenities, from theatres and upmarket shops to brothels and coffee houses, which were especially numerous around Covent Garden. It provided the setting for an urban milieu adjacent to the court and closely associated with it, but essentially independent. Even before 1642, 'court' culture had been supported not only by the King's patronage but by the expenditures of peers and gentry in London.[206] The relative importance of direct royal patronage diminished further after 1660, since the royal budget remained straitened as the prosperity of the 'Town' grew. The King had become simply the wealthiest and most conspicuous member of a community of patrons and virtuosi concentrated near his palaces; he could wield considerable influence but never completely dominate.

There was, however, a tendency, especially in the early Restoration, to disguise this fact by advertising royal patronage and leadership. The foundation of the Royal Society, to facilitate communication and experimentation in natural philosophy, provides one example. Charles II did not participate actively and failed to provide generous financial support, while the Society itself never fully displaced other centres of scientific discussion.[207] Yet the King did provide an official imprimatur for an organization whose meetings and publications helped focus and stimulate wider interest in scientific topics, chiefly among the gentry, the medical profession and a handful of university academics. He was a symbolic rather than an actual leader of the new philosophy.

The stage presents a more complex case. Shortly after the Restoration the Crown licensed two new companies, under the patronage of the King and his brother, the Duke of York. Charles thereafter took an active interest, reading some plays before production, attending the theatres and conducting public affairs with actresses like Nell Gwynne. As Nancy Maguire has shown, the ties between the court and the stage go well beyond this personal royal involvement. The directors of both companies – Davenant and Thomas Killigrew – were old courtiers with solid records of wartime royalism. Many playwrights also came from families with close connections to the pre-war court or the royalist cause. They included the sons of a Secretary of State, a Gentleman of the Bedchamber and the Vice-Chamberlain of Henrietta Maria, and aristocrats with court connections like the second Duke of Buckingham, the Earl of Orrery and several members of the Howard family. Out of a sample of thirty playwrights, Maguire found that at least nineteen were either early Stuart courtiers, active royalists or both. Several also held court posts after 1660.[208]

In terms of its leading personnel the theatre was, therefore, significantly more courtly and aristocratic than in the pre-war period. Court influence was also evident in the use of stage scenery and musical accompaniments descended from the masque, the imitation of Spanish and French dramatic models and the introduction of actresses. Davenant, author of three masques in the 1630s, was the most audacious innovator.[209] In addition the price of theatre admissions had risen substantially, restricting the audiences.[210] This marked the culmination of a trend already under way before 1642, as more expensive indoor 'private' playhouses slowly supplanted the older 'public' theatres.[211]

Had the theatres therefore become partisan royalist institutions, as Maguire and others have claimed? The answer depends on the context in which the question is asked. We have already noted the anti-puritan dramatic satires that marked the Restoration, and Maguire has plausibly argued that the tragicomedies popular throughout the 1660s provided a response to the experience of political catastrophe followed by an unexpected and seemingly providential recovery that Cavaliers had experienced.

But the theatres did not support a consistent political line thereafter. They could not have done so, since the fashionable society in which they were embedded was soon riven by political infighting. Plays thus became weapons through which court politicians defamed each other. In 1667 Robert Howard's *The Great Favourite or The Duke of Lerma* struck at Clarendon, shortly after the former Chancellor had fled England to avoid impeachment.[212] Two years later Buckingham attacked his rival on the privy council, Sir William Coventry, and Coventry's ally Sir John Duncombe, by inserting a scene into Howard's *The Country Gentleman* that mercilessly ridiculed them as Sir Cautious Trouble-all and Sir Gravity Empty.[213] Coventry threatened to slit the nose of the actor who had impersonated him and challenged Buckingham to a duel, an action which caused his dismissal from office.

Court playwrights and poets had divided into rival factions. Some, including John Dryden, Poet Laureate after Davenant's death in 1667, were allied to the Duke of York, while an anti-Yorkist group around the Duke of Buckingham included Robert Howard and Rochester. Although Buckingham had connections with the former Leveller John Wildman, his father-in-law General Fairfax and other former parliamentarians, too much should not be made of this. He had fought for the King in both the first and second Civil Wars and his own lifestyle was the reverse of godliness.[214] Rochester – the major literary talent of Buckingham's group – specialized in obscene verse libels of other courtiers, including the King himself. Literary attacks on immoral courtiers did not always reflect principled moral or political opposition. They were often a product of the same cynical and licentious environment they described.

Publicity and censorship

Such hypocrisy did not prevent satires from damaging the court's moral reputation, however, among pious Anglicans no less than Nonconformists. Political discussion remained significantly more open and fractious in the Restoration than before 1640 and the habitual irreverence towards political opponents that had flourished during the Civil War never fully subsided, despite the Crown's efforts to regulate expression. From 1660 until 1679 the only newsbooks were official government publications.[215] The Licensing Act of 1662 revived and extended the old censorship regulations of the early Stuart period, with much stiffer penalties for violations, including those of treason for the publication of seditious material. The task of enforcing this legislation fell to L'Estrange, who launched a series of prosecutions that resulted in the execution or death in prison of several offending printers by 1664[216]. He would later claim to have suppressed over 600 seditious works in the period 1663–70.[217] But even he could not prevent large numbers of works hostile to the government, the bishops and specific Crown policies from being printed, mostly by clandestine presses or houses in the Netherlands. Dissenters were responsible for the writing and distribution of many of these, through organized networks linking the capital to other parts of the British Isles, Dutch printers and English exiles abroad.[218] Although they numbered only somewhat above 100,000 in a nation of nearly five million, and probably represented more than 10 per cent of the population only in a handful of counties and Bristol, dissenters were more literate and bookish than the general population. They could normally count on the sympathy of many nominal conformists, including pious gentry of both sexes, and on some issues, such as opposition to lax morals and Catholic influence at court, they might elicit support from a majority of politically informed opinion. Their potential influence was, therefore, disproportionate to their numbers, especially when the court's prestige had suffered a reversal for other reasons, like defeat in war.[219]

In addition to printed material there was a considerably expanded market after the Restoration for scribally published tracts.[220] L'Estrange thought manuscript libels almost as dangerous as printed works and strove energetically to suppress them, without much success. Scribal texts remained free not only from censorship but, when produced anonymously, the constraints of decorum limiting what gentlemen felt able to say openly in public. Indeed, consumers expected and writers often deliberately cultivated a tone of familiar vulgarity while spreading sexual gossip and personal lampoons through manuscript libels.[221] Newsletters and serious records like parliamentary speeches were also scribally published. By the late 1670s, and possibly for some time before, two London booksellers, Thomas Collins and John Starkey, specialized in this last kind of tract.[222]

Alongside the private networks of friends and associates through which manuscript materials had always circulated, more public venues now emerged, especially the coffee house. People gathered in coffee houses to discuss everything from literature to natural philosophy but news and politics were normally the favourite subjects. Although associated with the beau monde of the court and town, these establishments remained open to a fairly heterogeneous clientele, including women.[223] Their proprietors often purchased printed tracts and sometimes manuscripts for the use of patrons. Other centres of dissemination included taverns, bookshops and the court itself, where people liked to amuse themselves during boring intervals by reading libels of their colleagues.[224] This lively and scurrilous political culture easily penetrated into the provinces as well, through provincial booksellers and gentry social networks.

Despite a seventeen-year interval between 1661 and the next general parliamentary election, Restoration politics continued to inspire polemical commentary. Three broad issues emerged as particularly important: the position of Protestant dissent and question of toleration; the moral and political shortcomings of the restored court; and perceptions of a renewed threat of popery and arbitrary government.

The problem of dissent

An activist religious minority had always regarded the Restoration as a humiliating disaster, while many moderate puritans who initially welcomed the King's return were soon bitterly disillusioned.[225] Those on the losing side faced decisions of whether to submit to the King or engage in political resistance. This was as much a moral and religious as a political choice, involving questions about whether men should take it upon themselves to achieve God's purposes through secular action, and often painful assessments of why God had allowed the cause to fail. For a few conspicuous figures immediately after the Restoration, it also meant deciding whether to forestall personal retribution by obsequious submission to former enemies. The executions of the regicides and the New Model Army's chaplain, Hugh Peter, were followed, in 1662, by that of Henry Vane, who was killed because he seemed too dangerous to be left alive and refused to beg the King for his life. His courageous defiance made him a martyr, extolled in several pamphlets. Other commonwealthsmen, however, saved themselves through a show of repentance, a judicious distribution of bribes and the intercession of friends with influence in the new court.

Worden has recently argued convincingly that the moral dilemmas of this period lie behind Milton's *Samson Agonistes*. Although the date of this closet drama remains controversial, he identifies several features that seem to point to the early 1660s, especially Samson's protests, which have no counterpart in Milton's sources, against his father's attempts to procure his release by interceding with the Philistines. Several of Milton's friends had worked on his behalf in much the same way to prevent him being executed for his regicide tracts. Samson's agony over his personal humiliation and Israel's defeat, and his struggle to discern God's providence in the catastrophe that had befallen him, closely parallel the recent experiences of Milton and his republican colleagues. The poem's close, with Samson following what he clearly regards as God's design in pulling the temple down on himself and his captors, signals Milton's hope that the verdict of the 1660s would soon be reversed, perhaps through some act of self-sacrifice.[226] It also suggests, however, that outward submission to hated authority had now become the saint's only option.

The choice of how to respond to an ungodly persecuting regime ultimately faced all Nonconformists, although the actual extent of persecution varied substantially from region to region and over time. Quakers suffered far more heavily than other denominations, both because they were more feared and detested and because they refused to run away when arresting officers showed up.[227] Yet even some moderate clergy, like Richard Baxter, suffered long spells of imprisonment in unhealthy jails. Responses varied enormously. A few dissenters went into exile, where some continued to write and plot, foremost among them Algernon Sidney, whose career has recently been reconstructed by Jonathan Scott.[228] But the great majority resisted Anglican hegemony solely through non-violent means.[229] They kept alive older forms of puritan piety and probity through corporate worship in individual households – involving regular reading of the Bible, collective prayers and the catechizing of children and servants[230] – and illegal conventicles. Dissenters responded to their exclusion from the universities by organizing their own schools.[231] A remarkable number also resorted to print. The Quakers alone, by one estimate, produced nearly 650 authors, including 82 women, by the year 1700.[232] Just as Parliament's victory in the Civil War led to an outpouring of published 'Cavalier' verse, so the defeat of 1660 initiated the most fertile period of puritan literature.[233]

The experience of defeat and persecution provided a major theme for this culture. Nonconformists wrote many trial narratives, just as royalists had done after 1646, recording prosecutions under the Clarendon Code and the sufferings of the victims in prison. The Quakers formed a national network for the collection and dissemination of information about persecutions.[234] John Foxe's Elizabethan martyrology provided a favourite model for narratives recounting the spiritual triumph of humble believers over vindictive authorities.[235] This imagery reinforced the equation increasingly drawn in Nonconformist writing between the persecuting episcopal Church and popery. However, trial narratives also frequently stressed legal procedures and the rights of Englishmen, appealing to values transcending denominational boundaries.[236]

Above all, Nonconformist writing stressed the need for perseverance in the face of adversity and introspective critical reflection. Persecution and temptation were tests that challenged believers to deepen their faith.[237] This emphasis owed something to the tradition of practical divinity developed by Perkins and his followers from the late sixteenth century. But it was also shaped by the need to reinvigorate religious values in a time of disillusionment and defeat, when even many Nonconformists regarded spiritual enthusiasm with suspicion.[238]

The challenge of distinguishing true from false values is central to the three great puritan masterpieces of the 1660s: Bunyan's *Pilgrim's Progress* and Milton's *Paradise Lost* and *Paradise Regained*. Milton, especially, challenged his readers by moral ambiguity.[239] In *Paradise Lost*, as critics have long recognized, the party of Satan articulates the republican principles Milton himself had defended in the 1650s. The fallen angels not only defy God's monarchy but expound the ideals of liberty, reason and self-reliance with stirring rhetoric:

> Let us not then pursue
> By force impossible, by leave obtain'd
> Unacceptable, though in heav'n, our state
> Of splendid vassalage, but rather seek
> Our own good from ourselves, and from our own
> Live to ourselves, though in this vast recess,
> Free, and to none accountable, preferring
> Hard liberty before the easy yoke
> Of servile pomp. Our greatness will appear
> Then most conspicuous, when great things of small,
> Useful of hurtful, prosperous of adverse

We can create, and in what place so'er
Thrive under evil, and work ease out of pain
Through labor and endurance...[240]

The fact that this argument is articulated by Mammon, the incarnation of greed, warns the reader not to take it at face value. But the arguments themselves are not easily dismissed. They underline the point Milton had made in *Areopagitica*, that in a postlapsarian universe truth always appears thoroughly interwoven with falsehood, requiring keen powers of discrimination.

If dissenters emphasized the need for individual judgement and the rational examination of religious belief, conformists sometimes countered by denigrating the ordinary human capacity for reason and arguing that conscience is often a name given to self-interest and self-delusion.[241] This view was accompanied by images of the common people as a rabble, with the 'trading part of the nation' particularly stigmatized for hypocrisy and devotion to gain.[242] The debate over toleration therefore broadened out into disagreements over whether individuals possessed a significant capacity for autonomous moral judgement. Perhaps ironically, dissenters appealed to Richard Hooker and advanced arguments savouring of Arminian confidence in the freedom of the will, against conformists who insisted on human depravity.

There is, however, a danger in stereotyping the debate over toleration, since neither conformists nor the Nonconformists ever adopted a single coherent position.[243] The Clarendon Code, more than any fundamental polarization of opinion, had reduced the religious diversity of the 1650s to an artificially tidy division between Church and dissent. But if that division was a fundamental one in Restoration society, it did not always appear destined to remain permanent. In 1672 the Crown's Declaration of Indulgence suspended the penal legislation against religious nonconformity. Although it was soon revoked, in most localities persecution declined in the 1670s. The old pattern of animosities and alignments appeared to be gradually weakening. Why then did partisanship revive in the 1680s?

Revulsion against the court

One reason is that every attempt at promoting toleration or comprehension provoked a fierce response from conformist partisans, which in turn hardened Nonconformist resentment. Thus debates over toleration also reinforced intolerance. Some weight must also be given, though, to Charles II's failure to maintain sufficient credibility to heal the divisions of the past. Within a few years of the Restoration devotion to the King had cooled appreciably. Charles's prestige was harmed not only by the court's extravagance and immorality, but the monarchy's apparent weakness in the international arena, which contrasted with the military strength of the Protectorate. Several panegyrics of 1660 had stressed the vigour and martial proclivities of the new king. Dryden proclaimed:

> Tremble ye nations who secure before
> Laught at those arms that 'gainst our selves we bore;
> Rous'd by the lash of his own stubborn tail
> Our lion now will foreign foes assail.[244]

Instead the greater part of the army was disbanded and Dunkirk, the one significant European conquest of the Cromwellian period, sold to the French. The arguments of writers like Nedham, that republics are virtuous and militarily strong while monarchies are naturally corrupt, extravagant and weak, seemed vindicated by events.

Historians have always seen the Second Dutch War that broke out in 1665 as a conflict over trade, although Pincus has argued persuasively that it also possessed important ideological dimensions.[245] The Dutch republic, dominated by a faction hostile to the Stuart's traditional allies, the House of Orange, had provided a refuge for English exiles. Many Anglicans associated the Netherlands with religious pluralism and commercial values reminiscent of the English regimes of the 1650s. War against them was, therefore, easily associated with royalist and Anglican values.[246] Commercial considerations were integrated within this larger ideological framework, through the argument that the Dutch sought world dominion by monopolizing oceanic trade. In opposing them Charles therefore defended the vital economic interests of his subjects, while punishing a venal, hypocritical and republican people.[247] This complex message was promulgated through printed and oral media, from almanacs and recruiting ballads to plays and the nasty satire of the Dutch character contained in Dryden's *Annus Mirabilis: The Year of Wonders, 1666*.[248]

For neither the first nor last time in British history, chauvinistic patriotism supplied a potent weapon against domestic enemies.[249] The Crown capitalized on early victories in 1665 and 1666 by ordering national celebrations. Unfortunately events then turned against Charles II. The Great Plague of 1665 and disastrous fire of 1666 devastated London, compromising the Crown's ability to raise loans. Both events were widely interpreted as providential chastisements, though whether for the sins of disobedience in the 1640s or the vices of the new age remained a matter of dispute. Louis XIV's entry into the war on the Dutch side aroused strong hostility to the French, which spilled over into renewed suspicions of popery and French influence at the Stuart court. In 1667 the nation suffered a humiliating defeat after the government, erroneously assuming that the war was winding down, failed to put the fleet out to sea, enabling the Dutch to sail up the Medway and destroy a large part of the English navy at anchor.

Although Clarendon became the main scapegoat, the King's own prestige had suffered a severe blow. Reports spread that as the Dutch struck he was busily chasing a moth in the company of his Catholic mistress, Barbara Castlemaine. Satires began associating the personal vices of Charles and his entourage with national weakness – and often with divine disfavour. Although especially prevalent among dissenters, these attitudes affected many conformists.[250] Charles's sexual dalliances were starting to be perceived as signs not only of immorality but political weakness.

The problem was compounded in the early 1670s when Castlemaine was supplanted as the King's favourite mistress by the French Duchess of Portsmouth, who had been sent to England by Louis XIV to provide him with an agent in Charles's bed. Portsmouth has rarely figured prominently in modern political histories. A recent study has presented substantial evidence, however, that she was a skilled court politician who parlayed her relationship with the King into considerable influence.[251] Whatever the ultimate extent of her power, she certainly figured prominently in the political libels of the 1670s, as a French whore who swayed the British sceptre. In 1679 she became the object of an attempted parliamentary impeachment.[252]

Charles's mistresses aroused as much concern as they did only because people had other reasons to believe he was unduly influenced by Louis XIV and all too inclined to experiment with more autocratic methods of government.[253] The court's canvassing of plans to enlarge the small English army after the disaster at the Medway, and more aggressively when renewed war broke out with the Netherlands in 1672, increased these fears.[254] By 1673 it had become clear that the King's policy of toleration had alienated intransigent conformists without winning enough countervailing support to procure supply from Parliament. His alliance with Louis XIV meanwhile aroused widespread misgivings.

During the Third Dutch War loyalist writers attempted to play once again upon the old anti-Dutch sentiments.[255] But although anti-Dutch prejudice remained alive, most informed observers now saw the French as the greater threat, particularly after Louis XIV's armies swept through the Netherlands in 1673.[256] The English public was also aware of violent persecutions of local Protestant populations on the European continent from Portugal to Poland, many at the behest of Louis XIV or his ally, Victor Amadeus of Savoy.[257] Dutch pamphlets skilfully fuelled English fears of French armies, Catholicism and foreign influence at Whitehall. Pierre du Moulin's tract, *England's appeal from the private cabal at Whitehall to the great council of the nation* portrayed Charles's French alliance as the policy of a court faction opposed to the nation's interests. It was devastatingly effective because it expressed what many people already believed. News of the Duke of York's conversion to Catholicism in 1673 simply added one more element to a whole chain of circumstances reviving ancient prejudices against popery, arbitrary government and corrupt courtiers.

The deliberate playing up of Cavalier sentiment by Danby and other court spokesmen following Charles's abandonment of toleration was, in these circumstances, more symptomatic of the court's vulnerability than any perdurable alignment between Church and Crown. Prejudices inherited from the Civil War became crucial as other reasons for supporting Charles eroded. Even diehard Cavaliers, however, disliked popery and Louis XIV. The political balance depended largely on how issues were defined. Danby knew that most of the political nation remained committed to the Restoration, whatever their reservations about the court, and therefore insisted that the basic question remained that of loyalty to the established Church and State. Opposition politicians like Marvell and Shaftesbury tried to redefine the contest as one between a conspiratorial court clique of papists and venal politicians, and the great mass of honest, disinterested, Protestant Englishmen who represented the country. Each position gave meaning to contemporary events by drawing upon deep cultural memories. Neither was particularly accurate.

The Crisis of 1679–81 and the Hardening of Partisan Cultures

Titus Oates's bogus revelations of a popish plot against the King in August 1679 initiated a new period of political turmoil. Within a short time revelations of secret dealings of Charles and Danby with Louis XIV, and the publication of highly damaging documents confiscated from York's secretary, Edward Coleman, confirmed the reality of popish and ministerial conspiracies at Whitehall, irrespective of the authenticity of Oates's specific allegations.[258] The impeachment of Danby and dissolution of the Cavalier Parliament followed in due course, touching off a major political struggle.

That struggle used to be characterized as an 'Exclusion Crisis', centring around efforts led by the Earl of Shaftesbury to bar James II from the throne as a Roman Catholic, an issue over which Whig and Tory parties were thought to have coalesced. Jonathan Scott and Mark Knights have now demolished this view, revealing a more chaotic crisis that passed through several stages. Scott found that of 1450 pamphlets produced in these years now in the Cambridge University Library, only 60 dealt entirely or in large part with the succession. Knights has emphasized that Exclusion was, in any case, only one of several alternative proposals for dealing with the threat of a popish heir to the throne.[260] The image of an organized exclusionist party under Shaftesbury is mostly a product of hostile propaganda by writers like L'Estrange and Dryden, while the labels, Whig and Tory, came into general usage only in 1681, to describe polarities of belief rather than structured parties.[261] Nor is it accurate to see the *entire* crisis as a contest between a parliamentary opposition and the court, since the latter remained in disarray for much of the period.[262]

But if it was not a conflict of organized parties, the crisis certainly produced another explosion of print and cultural partisanship, approaching the levels of the early 1640s and 1659. This outpouring was aided by the fortuitous expiration of the Licensing Act in 1679. The number of titles published rose from 700 in 1677 to over 1300 in 1679 and peaked at about 1800 in 1680.[263] The monopoly of the official government *Gazette* collapsed with the appearance of *The Domestick Intelligence*, edited by the fiercely Protestant Benjamin Harris, in July 1679. This was almost immediately countered by another journal of the same name, sympathetic to the court. Several additional partisan newspapers sprouted up over the next two years. Knights has estimated that, in addition, between five and ten million copies of pamphlets were distributed between 1679 and 1681, many for prices as low as 1d. L'Estrange alone produced tracts that sold at least 64,000 copies. Since many pamphlets passed through several hands or were read aloud, the total audience was enormous.[264]

There was some organization behind the appeals to public sentiment. The Green Ribbon Club in London, which included at least thirty-seven MPs and prominent London activists, helped mobilize large-scale demonstrations and co-ordinate strategy.[265] Wealthy politicians subsidized some pamphlets, distributing them gratis and Shaftesbury may have employed a staff of stationers to mass-produce manuscript newsletters and tracts.[266] The introduction of a penny post in 1680 also facilitated the wide distribution of printed material. Some libels seem to have been released first in the provinces, to make it more difficult for the government to suppress them before damage had been done.[267]

For a time the stage also contributed to anti-popish agitation with plays like Nathaniel Lee's *Massacre of Paris* and Elkanah Settle's *The Female Prelate* (May, 1680).[268] More important were public demonstrations, especially huge pope-burning processions. The first pope-burning had occurred in 1673, as a protest against York and his unpopular marriage to Mary of Modena.[269] These rituals now became a central fixture of London street politics. The City's 'pope-maker', Stephen College, presided over the construction of ornate effigies with garments costing as much as £100; sometimes the great prelate's belly was filled with live cats which added excitement to the final bonfire. Audiences were reported to number as many as 200,000 people.[270] The two Lord Mayor's shows of 1679 and 1680 provided additional occasions for street theatre, while in the provinces, as well as London, the period's three elections witnessed some imposing demonstrations. The Duke of Buckingham reportedly brought 6000 followers with him to one poll, while elsewhere partisan voters marched in military formation, chanting slogans and holding banners aloft.[271] The carefully managed trials and executions of people implicated in the popish plot provided grimmer spectacles. Other vehicles of controversy included sermons – which became especially important in the rallying of support for the court in the latter stages of the crisis – and visual images, like a deck of playing cards decorated with pictures of 'all the Popish Plots that have been in England' from Elizabeth's reign until 1678.[272]

The content of this flood of controversial material has only recently begun to receive close attention. The main emphasis in 1679–80 was on the dangers to the lives, liberties and properties of Englishmen posed by popery and arbitrary government. It was assumed that Catholicism could only be imposed by force, by mercenary – and quite likely foreign – troops.[273] Marvell's *The Growth of Popery and Arbitrary Government* (1678) had foreshadowed this argument, which was now continually reiterated and embellished with stories of Catholic atrocities.[274] It was alleged that 'a secret universal Catholic league' had long been at work to destroy Protestantism throughout the world. Belief in the reality of the Catholic threat, more than any specific policy, bound together the disparate coalition mobilizing against Danby and the Duke of York.[275]

For a short period anti-popish arguments appealed across almost the full spectrum of English Protestant opinion. As Tim Harris was the first to show in detail, however, the anti-popish campaigns of 1679 were often particularly slanted toward dissenting audiences. The pope-burning processions took an untraditional route through the capital's northern suburbs, where the Nonconformist population was concentrated, while the Green Ribbon Club and other associations active in fomenting anti-popish feeling included disproportionate numbers of dissenters among their members.[276] Many of the leading activists, especially in London, had earlier links to radical movements of the 1650s.

These facts were quickly noted and skilfully exploited by publicists on the other side, to portray the campaign against popery at court as a revival of the 1641 rebellion, conducted by the same assortment of presbyterians, sectaries and republicans. Controversy quickly acquired a retrospective quality, defined by hallowed memories as much as by current events. By 1681 pope-burning processions were being countered by burnings of 'John Presbyter', a figure inherited from Civil War polemics. Conflict over popish plots had become thoroughly intertwined with memories of earlier crises, especially the Civil War and regicide.

This retrospective quality did not prevent highly original work from appearing. John Locke's *Two Treatises of Government*, Algernon Sidney's *Discourses* and Henry Neville's *Plato Redeviva* were all major pieces of political theory written in response to the issues of the early 1680s. On another plane of controversy, Dryden's *Absalom and Achitophel*, a savage account of Shaftesbury's relations with the Duke of Monmouth, is arguably the century's most brilliant satire.

Yet by 1681 it had become abundantly clear that convictions dividing Protestant Englishmen had once again triumphed over any shared values that might have united them. Although consensus remained an ideal, it could evidently only be achieved through the political proscription of a significant segment of the nation and the denigration of its cherished values. Between 1682 and Charles's death in 1685 the court and its Tory allies set about achieving these results, through public trials of Whig leaders, purges of county magistracies, the remodelling of fifty-one borough charters and a flood of sermons and printed literature refuting and denouncing Whig arguments. The parliamentary election following James's accession seemed to confirm the triumph of this reaction, the final political victory of conformist and Cavalier values over those stigmatized by association with the good old cause.

Within three years the provocations of James II's actions and the intervention of William of Orange and the Dutch army destroyed this resolution and again reshuffled the deck. Memories and symbols of seventeenth-century conflicts survived, becoming caught up in 'the rage of party' of William's and Anne's reigns, but politics had changed fundamentally. The year 1685 is therefore as good a place as any to end one long chapter in the history of English political culture and begin another.

In the period we have covered, culture exhibited a remarkable blend of fertility and pugnaciousness, qualities that were often deeply connected. It was because they disagreed so passionately over so many vital issues that people were driven not only to think deeply about affairs of state, but to fashion cultural weapons of political combat. A succession of controversies helped unify and integrate English culture both geographically – by drawing provincial audiences into national affairs – and intellectually – by stimulating efforts to search out connections between subjects that might otherwise have remained disjointed. The effects of political contention spread outwards to shape aesthetic ideas, literary forms and even attitudes towards the pleasures of gardening and fishing. At the same time politics, hitherto the preserve of a small elite, became a matter of vital interest to hundreds of thousands of people.

How can we ultimately explain this wonderfully creative combativeness? Part of the answer obviously lies in the legacy of civil war and regicide, a traumatic experience of bloody conflict that contemporaries sometimes described as a collective loss of innocence. As I have been arguing all along, however, this cannot be the *whole* explanation, for at least two reasons. The Civil War was itself ultimately related to a larger European experience of religious and civil conflict. Although precipitated by short-term and contingent events, it involved issues that can only be fully appreciated within wider and deeper contexts.

Secondly, cultural memories, even of civil wars, are never inexorable forces, imposing themselves without human agency. The meanings people give to the past always derive from complex processes of selection, transmission and construction, whether unconscious or deliberate in nature. The history we have traced provides an extended illustration of this point. In these years the English not only lived through the most bloody and turbulent period in their modern history. They also erected layer upon layer of political myth, legend and argument, much of it conveyed through seductive language and imagery that continues to beguile even today.

One of the enduring achievements of revisionist scepticism in the 1970s and 1980s has been to emphasize the need to treat such contemporary representations with extreme caution. There is a danger, however, that justified scepticism may give rise to a reductive positivism that treats raw events as the true stuff of history and political culture as a mere epiphenomenon. In the end it is every bit as misleading to underestimate the cultural dimensions of seventeenth-century politics as it is to take contemporary polemics at face value. The construction of political narratives and the analysis of cultural attitudes and representations need to be treated as complementary, rather than antagonistic modes of explanation. A number of recent books on the period, especially by younger historians, have been pointing the way towards such an approach. One hopes that this trend will soon produce a more complete and sophisticated understanding of an incomparably rich and important century.

NOTES AND REFERENCES

Summary citations are given for works appearing in the bibiliography and for all but the first reference in each chapter for other items. Place of publication is London when not otherwise noted.

1 Frames of Reference

1. For example, Sharpe and Zwicker (eds), *Politics of Discourse*; Peck (ed.), *Mental World*; Sharpe and Lake (eds), *Culture and Politics*; Smuts (ed.), *Stuart Court*.
2. The classic treatment, albeit for the eighteenth century, is Douglas Hay, 'Property, Authority and the Criminal Law' in *idem.*, ed., *Albion's Fatal Tree* (1975), pp. 17–64, which should be contrasted with Thomas W. Laquer, 'Crowds, carnival and the state in English executions, 1604–1868' in A. L. Beier, David Cannadine and James M. Rosenheim (eds), *The First Modern Society: Essays in English History in Honour of Lawrence Stone* (Cambridge, 1989), pp. 305–56. See also J. A. Sharpe, *Crime in Early Modern England 1550–1750* (1986); Cynthia Herrup, *The Common Peace: Participation and the Criminal Law in Seventeenth-Century England* (Cambridge, 1987) and Peter Lake, 'Deeds against Nature: Cheap Print, Protestantism and Murder in Early Seventeenth Century England' in Sharpe and Lake (eds), *Culture and Politics*, pp. 257–84.
3. See Susan Amussen, *An Ordered Society: Gender and Class in Early Modern England* (Oxford, 1988); David Underdown, 'The Taming of the Scold: the Enforcement of Patriarchal Authority in Early Modern England' in Fletcher and Stevenson (eds), *Order and Disorder*, pp. 116–36 and Martin Ingram, 'Ridings, Rough Music and "Reform of Popular Culture"', *Past and Present*, 105 (1984) 79–113.
4. Cf. Tuck, *Philosophy and Government*, ch.1, esp. p. 5.
5. For all these usages see *OED*. For literature see, in addition, MacLean, *Culture and Society*, Introduction.
6. Since words like 'culture' and 'politics' are anachronistic anyway, I have not tried to define them with any rigour, preferring to let meanings emerge from the context of discussion. In particular, 'culture' is deliberately employed in ways that elide the distinction between humanist and anthropological usages, since this has little real meaning in most seventeenth-century contexts.

7. Tillyard, *Elizabethan World Picture*. A recent work that remains embedded in this tradition is Stephen L. Collins, *From Divine Cosmos to Sovereign State: An Intellectual History of Consciousness and the Idea of Order in Renaissance England* (New York and Oxford, 1989).
8. See esp. Burgess, *Ancient Constitution*.
9. E.g. Perry Miller, *The New England Mind of the Seventeenth Century* (New York, 1939); William Haller, *The Rise of Puritanism* (New York, 1938).
10. I would not claim that my four categories necessarily form an exhaustive list. A book oriented towards culture at the village level would almost certainly need to add a fifth, involving concepts of patriarchy, family and gender relationships and household management, a topic on which I comment briefly below, pp. 27–8. Readers wishing to explore this subject should begin with Schochet, *Patriarchalism*; Amussen, *Ordered Society*; Anthony Fletcher, *Gender, Sex and Subordination in England, 1500–1800* (New Haven and London, 1995); and David Cressy, *Birth, marriage and death: ritual, religion and the life-cycle in Tudor and Stuart England* (Oxford, 1997).
11. A classic exposition is Mervyn James, 'English politics and the concept of honour, 1485–1640' in *Society, Politics and Culture*, pp. 308–416. See also 'At a crossroads of political culture: the Essex revolt, 1601', ibid., pp. 416–65.
12. For discussions see, esp., Amussen, *Ordered Society*, idem., '"The part of a Christian man": the cultural politics of manhood in early modern England' in Amussen and Kishlansky (eds), *Political Culture* and Ingram, *Church Courts*.
13. James, 'Honour', esp. pp. 310–12.
14. Edmund Spenser, *The Faerie Queene*, 6.3, stanzas 1–2.
15. See Todd, *Humanism*, ch. 6.
16. Peltonen, *Classical humanism*, pp. 19–53.
17. A. B. Grossart (ed.), *Lord Brooke's Works* (1870; rpt. New York, 1966) IV, pp. 7–8. Cf. Heal and Holmes, *Gentry*, pp. 24–34.
18. Cust, 'Honour, rhetoric and political culture'.
19. Folger Shakespeare Library Vb 5, pp. 23, 24, *passim*, a treatise of the 1590s.
20. D. C. Peck (ed.), *Leicester's Commonwealth* (Athens, Georgia, 1985).
21. For discussion see Flynn, 'Donne's *Ignatius His Conclave*', pp. 165–6.
22. James, 'Honour', pp. 312–14.
23. For the importance of the house see Lawrence Stone and Jeanne C. Fawtier Stone, *An Open Elite? England 1540–1880* (Oxford, 1984) and Heal and Holmes, *Gentry*, pp. 297–301.
24. Sidney Lee (ed.), *The Autobiography of Lord Herbert of Cherbury* (Westport, Connecticut, 1976).
25. British Library Cotton Mss., Julius CIII, fos. 204, 205.
26. James, 'Honour', pp. 312–14 and *passim*.
27. Heal, *Hospitality*, esp. pp. 7 and 10–13.
28. James, 'Honour', pp. 312–13.
29. *Historical Manuscripts Commission Salisbury Manuscripts*, XV, p. 26.
30. James, 'Honour', pp. 332–91; cf. Stone, *Crisis of the Aristocracy*, ch. 5; Frances Yates, 'Elizabethan Chivalry, the Romance of the Accession Day Tilts' in her *Astraea*, pp. 88–111; Ferguson, *English Chivalry*.

31. On the latter point see Caspari, *Humanism and the Social Order* and Ferguson, *English Chivalry*.
32. James, 'Honour', pp. 328–9; Heal and Holmes, *Gentry*, p. 7.
33. *The Schoolmaster*, ed. Lawrence Ryan (Ithaca, New York, 1967), e.g. p. 51.
34. Arlette Jouanna, *Le Devoir de Révolte: La noblesse française et la gestation de l'Etat moderne, 1559–1661* (Paris, 1989).
35. For an overview see Geoffrey Parker, *The Military Revolution* (Cambridge 1988). Jonathan Dewald, *Aristocratic Experience and the Origins of Modern Culture: France 1570–1715* (Berkeley and Los Angeles, 1993), ch. 2, surveys this development in France. For French political theory see Jouanna, *Devoir de Révolte*.
36. The differences have been rightly stressed by Wallace MacCaffrey, *Elizabeth I* (1993), p. 150.
37. Smuts, 'Court Centred Politics', in Sharpe and Lake, *Culture and Politics* p. 27; Hammer, 'Uses of Scholarship'.
38. Yale University Beineke Library Ms. 370, p. 5 from rear, speech of 15 February 1598 recorded in commonplace book of William Camden. This document is discussed and partly reprinted in William Huse Dunham, 'William Camden's commonplace book', *The Yale University Library Gazette*, 43 (1969).
39. See Linda Peck, 'The Mentality of a Jacobean Grandee' in *idem.*, (ed.), *Mental World*, pp. 148–68.
40. McCoy, *Rites of Knighthood*, pp. 2–3. The treatise survives as Folger Library Mss. Vb. 7, from which we have already quoted several times.
41. See, in particular, McCoy, *Rebellion in Arcadia* and *Rites of Knighthood*. Katherine Duncan Jones, *Sir Philip Sidney* (New Haven, 1991) stresses Sidney's ambitions and keen sense of family honour.
42. See, for example, Jones, *Sidney*.
43. McCoy, *Rebellion in Arcadia* and *Rites of Knighthood*.
44. Ellen Chirelstein, 'Emblem and Reckless Presence: The Drury Portrait at Yale' in Gent (ed.), *Albion's Classicism*.
45. William Cornwallis, *Essays*, p. 41.
46. Bedford Estates Office mss. vol. 240, 8v, 9, account of the Star Chamber case of Peter Apseley. Bedford marked the quoted passage in the margin.
47. George Chapman, *Bussy D'Ambois*, II, i, 197–9.
48. For a suggestive article developing these points see Hibbard, 'Theatre of dynasty'.
49. Adamson, 'Chivalry in Caroline England' for the first two points; Hibbard, 'Theatre of dynasty' for the third.
50. William Hunt, 'Spectral origins of the English Revolution: legitimation crisis in early Stuart England' in Geoff Eley and William Hunt (eds), *Reviving the English Revolution: Reflections and Elaborations on the Work of Christopher Hill* (1988), pp. 305–32, and below, pp. 62–5.
51. Elkin Calhoun Wilson, *England's Eliza* (Cambridge, Mass., 1939), p. 294; Ferguson, *English Chivalry*, ch. 5 provides useful historical background.
52. Marlowe, *Edward II*, I, iv, 385–400.
53. On the importance of steadfastness to the pledged word see James, 'Honour', p. 316.

Notes and References 159

54. Cf. the quarrel of Brutus and Cassius in *Julius Caesar*, IV, iii, which also centres on honour and reputation, but is conducted in far more restrained language.
55. Cust, 'Honour and Politics' p. 60.
56. McCoy, 'Old English Honour' in Smuts (ed.) *Stuart Court*, pp. 146–7; below, pp. 77–8.
57. Maija Jansson and William B. Bidwell (eds), *Proceedings in Parliament 1625* (New Haven and London, 1987), p. 450.
58. See Brooks, *Pettyfoggers*.
59. Pocock, *Ancient Constitution*, p. 31.
60. Ibid., p. 36.
61. Burgess, *Ancient Constitution* and *Absolute Monarchy*; Christianson, *John Selden*. For Pocock's own summary and assessment of the debate through the late 1980s, see the 'Retrospect' in the edition cited. An important exception to the consensus is Sommerville, 'The ancient constitution reassessed'.
62. See, e.g., J. S. Cockburn, *A History of English Assizes from 1550 to 1714* (Cambridge, 1972), pp. 219–21.
63. Sommerville, *Politics and Ideology*, esp. chs 3–5.
64. This position is developed throughout *Ancient Constitution* and is lent further support by *Absolute Monarchy*.
65. Burgess, *Ancient Constitution*, ch. 7.
66. Ibid., p. 17.
67. This is especially true of *Ancient Constitution*; *Absolute Monarchy* seems more inclined to see the Civil War as the decisive turning point.
68. Pocock, p. 279.
69. Prest, pp. 151–3, 221; Brooks, *Pettyfoggers*, ch. 8.
70. Heal and Holmes, *Gentry*, p. 272.
71. Sommerville, 'Ancient Constitution Reassessed', p. 46.
72. See *Ancient Constitution*, e.g. pp. 20, 21, 57, 65, 78. *Absolute Monarchy* ch. 6 provides a more cautious and nuanced treatment.
73. Cf. Sommerville, 'Ancient Constitution Reassessed', p. 47; Pocock, *Ancient Constitution*, p. 278.
74. See *The Reverse or Back Face of the English Janus*, trans. Redman Wescot (1682), esp. p. a4. The apparent inconsistency may reflect a change of emphasis rather than a real contradiction, since Selden's earlier position emphasized both change and continuity. For discussions, see Paul Christianson, 'Young John Selden and the Ancient Constitution', *Proceedings of the American Philosophical Society* 128 (1984); id., *John Selden*, ch. 1.
75. *Past and Present*, 72 (1996), pp. 262–304.
76. Parry, *English Antiquarians*; Levy, *Tudor Historians*; Arthur Ferguson, *Clio Unbound* (Durham, N. C., 1979).
77. Many of these are discussed below, pp. 41–9.
78. Alexander Grosart (ed.), *Complete Works in Prose and Verse* (1896; rpt. New York, 1963), IV, p. 47; Richard Helgerson, *Forms of Nationhood*, ch. 2 and *passim*.
79. Parry, *English Antiquarians*, pp. 7–8.
80. Sommerville, 'Ancient Constitution Reassessed', pp. 46–58. Cf. W. O. Hassell (ed.), *A catalogue of the library of Sir Edward Coke* (New Haven, 1950).

81. Christianson, *John Selden*.
82. See Brooks, *Pettyfoggers*, from which much of the argument in this paragraph derives.
83. Ibid., pp. 132–7. I derived the quotation from Folger Shakespeare Library Mss. Vb. 215 (n.p.). For the barristers and serjeants see Wilfred Prest, *The Rise of the Barristers* (Oxford, 1996).
84. The anxiety to establish the common law as an 'art of well ordering a civil society' grounded in philosophy is especially clear in Sir Henry Finch, *Law, a Discourse Thereof* (1627), pp. 1–24.
85. As Lake has shown for Hooker. See *Anglicans and Puritans?*.
86. Burgess, *Ancient Constitution*, p. 18.
87. Lake, *Anglicans and Puritans?*
88. Law French was the language in which legal pleadings were conducted before the 1650s – a bastardized French mixed with Latin and English. Hayward, *Norman Kings*, p. 100.
89. *Of Monarchy*, verse 195 (*Works* I, p. 76).
90. Alexander Grosart (ed.), *Works of Samuel Daniel* (1885; rpt. New York, 1963) V, pp. 268, 269. Although Greville and Daniel were not lawyers, their views still provide evidence for views of the law within the culture of the period.
91. The quotation is from the answer of the judges to a discussion of the status of *post nati*, quoted in J. Spedding (ed.), *Works of Bacon* 14 vols, (1858–74; rpt. Stuttgart-Bad, 1962), X, p. 331.
92. Sir Thomas Wilson, *The State of England*, *Camden Society Publications*, 3rd series, 52 (1936), pp. 24–5.
93. Helgerson, *Forms of Nationhood* ch. 3.
94. Burgess, *Absolute Monarchy*, p. 165.
95. See Sommerville, 'Ancient Constitution Reassessed', pp. 58–64.
96. For Cotton see Sharpe, *Sir Robert Cotton* (Oxford, 1979) and Parry, *English Antiquarians*, ch. 3.
97. E.g. BL Cotton Mss. Julius IV, a volume of precedents on 'courses used in military affairs'.
98. J. Spedding (ed.), *Works of Bacon*, XI, p. 49.
99. James O. Halliwell (ed.), *Autobiography and Correspondence of Sir Simonds D'Ewes* (1845) II, pp. 268–9.
100. Love, *Scribal Publication*, ch. 1; Woudhuysen, *Sidney and manuscripts*, ch. 2.
101. *Works*, X, pp. 383–4.
102. Hans S. Pawlisch, *Sir John Davies and the Conquest of Ireland: a Study in Legal Imperialism* (Cambridge, 1985).
103. Sir William Davies, *Ireland*, p. 271.
104. There were two main variants on this theme. One was that William and certain of his successors, like Henry I, had ratified the laws of Edward the Confessor as a way of appeasing the English. The other was John Hayward's view that William created new laws 'laid upon the English as fetters about their feet', which through long usage eventually became 'not only tolerable, but easy and sweet...by force of long grounded custom' (*Norman Kings*, pp. 100, 102). Cf. Christianson's comments on Selden's 'Machiavellian' view of the Conqueror's use of law, *John Selden*, pp. 26–7.
105. Spedding (ed.), *Works of Bacon*, XI, p. 90.

106. 'The Conflicting Loyalties of a "vulger counselor": The Third Earl of Southampton, 1597–1624', in *Public Duty and Private Conscience: Essays Presented to Gerald Aylmer* (Oxford, 1993), pp. 121–50.
107. Cf. Christianson, *John Selden*, p. 292.
108. Library of Congress microfilm 041/camb.793A, p. 711 of mss.
109. Sir Thomas Smith, *De Republica Anglorum* (1583), esp. pp. 7, 9, 17 and 22.
110. *Works*, X, pp. 371–2.
111. Knafla, *Egerton*, p. 297.
112. Ibid., p. 255.
113. PRO SP16/87 piece 11.
114. For an example see Margaret Spufford, *Contrasting Communities* (Cambridge, 1974), pp. 121–8.
115. For a superb discussion see C. W. Brooks, *Pettyfoggers*.
116. Sacks, 'Bristol's Little Business'.
117. On this see Herrup, *Common Peace*.
118. William Shakespeare, *Henry VI*, Part II, IV, ii, 76–82.
119. Cf. Patterson, *Reading Holinshed's Chronicles*, ch. 8.
120. Quoted from Arthur Kinney (ed.), *Elizabethan Backgrounds: Historical Documents of the Age of Elizabeth I*, (Hamden, Connecticut, 1975), p. 60; I have modernized spelling and punctuation.
121. See Schochet, *Patriarchalism*. This points out that fully developed patriarchal justifications of royal power were a relatively late phenomenon, although the basis for them had been implicit in Western thought since antiquity. Formal theories of patriarchalism should be distinguished from the more fluid and varied uses to which contemporaries put the metaphor of kings-as-fathers. For an interesting discussion of this latter topic in connection with James I and Lancelot Andrewes see Shuger, *Habits of Thought*, ch. 6.
122. Amussen, *Ordered Society*, *passim*.
123. Among many discussions of this by-now familiar point see Keith Wrightson and David Levine, *Poverty and Piety in an English Village: Terling, 1525–1700* (1979); Wrightson, *English Society*, ch. 6; Herrup, *Common Peace*; David Underdown, 'Taming of the Scold'; and Ingram, *Church Courts*.
124. E.g. R. H. Tawney, *Religion and the Rise of Capitalism* (1922); Hill, *Society and Puritanism*; Keith Thomas, *Religion and the Rise of Magic* (1972); Wrightson, *English Society*, chs 6 and 7.
125. Robert Bireley, *The Counter-Reformation Prince: Anti-Machiavellianism or Catholic Statecraft in Early Modern Europe* (Chapel Hill, N.C., 1990).
126. The classic exposition is Arthur Lovejoy, *The Great Chain of Being* (Cambridge, Mass., 1936).
127. J. G. A. Pocock, 'Time, History and Eschatology in the Thought of Thomas Hobbes' in *Politics, Language and Time* (New York, 1973), pp. 148–201; Ashcraft, *Revolutionary Politics*; Robert Iliffe, ' "Is he like other men?" The Meaning of the *Principia Mathematica*, and the author as idol' in McClean (ed.) *Stuart Restoration*, pp. 159–76.
128. For an interesting discussion see David Harris Sacks, *The Widening Gate: Bristol and the Atlantic Economy, 1450–1700* (Berkeley, 1991), esp. chs 3 and 10.

129. Smuts, 'The Court and its Neighborhood'; Sharpe, *Personal Rule*, pp. 403–12.
130. *Works*, VI, p. 757.
131. For this distinction see Collinson, 'Biblical rhetoric', p. 19, which argues that apocalyptic thought was less common than analogies to Old Testament prophets.
132. See especially Christianson, *Reformers and Babylon*. William Haller, *The Elect Nation: the Meaning and Relevance of Foxe's Book of Martyrs* (New York, 1963), a pioneering essay, is unreliable on some points.
133. Jesse Lander, ' "Foxe's" *Books of Martyrs*: printing and popularizing the *Acts and Monuments*' in *Religion and Culture*, pp. 69–92.
134. E.g. Michael Walzer, *Revolution of the Saints* (New York, 1969). For a corrective see Patrick Collinson, *Religion of the Protestants* (Oxford, 1984), ch. 4.
135. 'Biblical rhetoric', esp. pp. 23–36.
136. For the Tudors see King, *Tudor Royal Iconography* (Princeton, 1989), esp. chs 2 and 3. Stuart religious imagery has not yet received systematic treatment.
137. Shuger, *Habits of Thought*, p. 141 and chs 3–7.
138. The classic early statement is J. H. Hexter, 'The Education of the Aristocracy in the Renaissance' in *Reappraisals in History* (New York, 1963), pp. 45–70.
139. See esp. Caspari, *Humanism*; Ferguson, *Articulate Citizen*; James McConica, *English Humanists and Reformation Politics under Henry VIII and Edward VI* (Oxford, 1965); Stone, 'Educational Revolution'; Gordon Zeeveld, *Foundations of Tudor Policy* (Cambridge, Mass., 1948). A good recent study that often follows the trajectory of this earlier scholarship is Todd, *Christian Humanism*.
140. David Starkey, 'England'.
141. Anthony Grafton and Lisa Jardine, *From humanism to the humanities: education and the liberal arts in fifteenth- and sixteenth-century Europe* (1986).
142. O'Day, *Education and Society*, p. 42.
143. J. A. Sharpe, *Early Modern England: A Social History 1550–1770* (1987), p. 264.
144. For surveys see O'Day, *Education*, ch. 4 and Joan Simon, *Education and Society in Tudor England* (Cambridge, 1966).
145. *Autobiography* I, pp. 102–3.
146. Donna Hamilton, *Virgil and the Tempest: The Politics of Imitation* (Columbus, 1990). Cf. Charles and Michelle Martindale, *Shakespeare and the Uses of Antiquity* (1990).
147. Neil Rhodes, *The Power of Eloquence and English Renaissance Literature* (New York, 1992), p. 50.
148. O'Day, *Education*, pp. 31–8.
149. Ibid., p. 105.
150. Ibid., ch. 6; Holmes and Heal, *Gentry*, ch. 7; Mark Curtis, *Oxford and Cambridge in Transition, 1585–1642* (Oxford, 1959); Hugh Kearney, *Scholars and Gentlemen* (1970); Todd, *Christian Humanism*, ch. 3.
151. This argument of much of the older secondary literature has been deepened and reinforced by Todd, *Christian Humanism*.

152. Logan Pearsall Smith (ed.), *Life and Letters of Henry Wotton* (Oxford, 1907), II, p. 494, quoted in Lisa Jardine and William Sherman, 'Pragmatic readers: knowledge transactions and scholarly services in late Elizabethan England' in Anthony Fletcher and Peter Roberts (eds), *Religion, Culture and Society in early modern Britain* (Cambridge, 1994), p. 107.
153. Jardine and Grafton, 'Gabriel Harvey'; Jardine and Sherman, 'Pragmatic readers'; Sherman, *John Dee: the Politics of Writing and Reading in the English Renaissance* (Amherst, Mass., 1995).
154. Quoted by Vernon Snow, *Huntington Library Quarterly* 23 (1960), 372.
155. Now preserved in the Bedford Estate Office, London.
156. Library of Congress Microfilms 041/Camb.793A. Under heading 33 the writer refers to an event of 1608 as occurring 'en ceste année'; several other references to early seventeenth century events suggest a date of composition around this time.
157. *Letters of John Holles*, I, p. 55.
158. *Nugae Antiquae*, p. 77.
159. Holinshed, *Chronicles*, 6 vols (1807–8; rpt. New York, 1965), I, p. 330.
160. Winthrop S. Hudson, *The Cambridge Connection and the Elizabethan Settlement of 1559* (Durham, N.C., 1980).
161. Jardine and Sherman, 'Pragmatic readers'.
162. Jardine and Grafton, 'Harvey'.
163. Francis Bacon, *Works* IX, p. 17.
164. Jardine and Sherman, 'Pragmatic readers'.
165. Lipsius, *Six Books of Politics*, pp. 59–60.
166. Treatments of this tradition include Peter Donaldson, *Machiavelli and Mystery of State* (Cambridge, 1988); Kelly, *Beginning of Ideology*, ch. 5; Oestreich, *Neostoicism and the Early Modern State* (Cambridge, 1982); Richard Schelhase, *Tacitus in the Renaissance* (Chicago, 1976); and Tuck, *Philosophy and Government*.
167. For discussions see Schelhase, *Tacitus*; Salmon, 'Seneca and Tacitus'; Levy, 'Bacon and the Style of Politics'; *idem* 'Hayward, Daniel and Politic History'; and Smuts, 'Court Centred Politics'.
168. Tuck, *Philosophy and Government*, chs 2–3.
169. E.g. by Peltonen, *Republicanism*, p. 15.
170. Ascham, *The Schoolmaster*, p. 66. On Castiglione and his European influence see Peter Burke, *The Fortunes of the Courtier* (1995).
171. John Harington, *Nugae antiquae*, pp. 112–13.
172. Well discussed by Todd, *Christian Humanism*, pp. 27–30 and in 'Seneca and the Protestant Mind: The Influence of Stoicism on Puritan Ethics', *Archive für Reformationsgeschichte*, 74 (1983), 182–99.

2 Political Imagination, *c.* 1585–1640

1. See, for example, the range of approaches displayed in two recent collections, Sharpe and Lake, (eds), *Culture and Politics* and Amussen and Kishlansky (eds), *Political Culture*.

2. Kishlansky, *Parliamentary Selection*.
3. *Prose Works*, ed. Feuillart (Cambridge, 1912) III, p. 52.
4. Ian Archer, *The Pursuit of Stability: Social Relations in Elizabethan London* (Cambridge, 1991), pp. 210–11, 230.
5. For a general European treatment of this problem see Kelly, *Beginning of Ideology*. For political theory see Skinner, *Foundations of Modern Political Thought*, II.
6. See, in particular, J. S. Scarisbrick, *The English Reformation and the English People* (1984), Christopher Haigh, *English Reformations* (Oxford, 1993) and Eamon Duffy, *The Stripping of the Altars* (New Haven and London, 1992).
7. Collinson, *Birthpangs*, p. 55.
8. Natalie Zemon Davis, 'The Rites of Violence' in *Society and Culture in Early Modern France* (Stanford, 1975), pp. 152–88; Barbara Diefendorf, *Beneath the Cross* (New York and Oxford, 1991) and Philip Benedict, *Rouen during the Wars of Religion* (Cambridge, 1981).
9. Christopher Marlowe, *Massacre at Paris* (1592), v, 29 vii, 9–15.
10. White, *Theatre and Reformation*.
11. For what follows see King, *Spenser's Poetry*, ch. 1.
12. Ibid. and Andrew Hadfield, *Literature, Politics and National Identity: Reformation to Renaissance* (Cambridge, 1995), ch. 1.
13. Collinson, *Birthpangs*, pp. 99–120.
14. Watt, *Cheap Print*, pp. 41–50.
15. Ibid., ch. 4, esp. p. 135.
16. King, *Spenser's Poetry*; Norbrook, *Poetry and Politics*, pp. 63–4, 89 and ch. 8; Grundy, *Spenserian Poets*.
17. Spikes, 'Jacobean History Play'.
18. Margot Heinemann, 'Rebel Lords, Popular Playwrights and Political Culture: Notes on the Jacobean Patronage of the Earl of Southampton', in Cedric C. Brown (ed.) *Patronage, Politics and Literary Traditions in England 1558–1658* (Detroit, 1993) p. 149.
19. Spikes, 'Jacobean History Play', esp. p. 147.
20. Parmelee, 'Printers', p. 857 and *Newes from Fraunce*.
21. Parmelee, 'Printers', pp. 858–9; *Newes from Fraunce*, pp. 54–5; Peter Donaldson, *Machiavelli and Mystery of State* (Cambridge, 1988), p. 103.
22. Lake, 'Anti-popery', pp. 95–6. Cf. Collinson, *Birthpangs*, p. 148.
23. Worden, *Philip Sidney's Arcadia*, pp. 32–6.
24. Lake, *Anglicans and Puritans?* and 'Avant-garde Conformity'; Milton, *Catholic and Reformed*, Part I.
25. Collinson, 'Ecclesiastical Vitriol' and 'Ben Jonson's *Bartholomew Fair*: The Theatre constructs Puritanism' in David L. Smith, Richard Strier and David Bevington (eds), *The Theatrical City: Culture, Theatre and Politics in London, 1576–1649* (Cambridge, 1995).
26. *A Survey of the Pretended Holy Discipline* (1593), pp. 7–8.
27. Ibid., pp. 47–8.
28. R. Warwick Bond (ed.), *Complete Works of John Lyly* (Oxford, 1967) III, p. 420.
29. *Laws of Ecclesiastical Polity*, 2 vols. (London, 1907) II, p. 6.
30. Ibid., p. 4.
31. John Hayward, Folger Ms. Ga 12, fo. 13v.

32. *Pretended Discipline*, pp. 62–3.
33. See, e.g., *Laws of Ecclesiastical Polity*, I, p. 360. Collinson appears to share this view in *Birthpangs*, pp. 143–54.
34. Kristen Poole, 'Saints Alive! Falstaff, Marprelate and the Staging of Puritanism', *Shakespeare Quarterly* 46 (1995), pp. 47–75; Helgerson, *Forms of Nationhood*, pp. 252–3 and Patterson, 'Sir John Oldcastle'.
35. Poole, p. 49.
36. Milton, *Catholic and Reformed*, Part I.
37. *Britain, or a chorographical description of England, Scotland and Ireland*, trans. P. Holland (1610) p. 163.
38. 'A Panegyre, On the Happie Entrance of James, Our Soveraigne, To his First High Session of Parliament in this his Kingdome, The 19 of March, 1603', ll. 95–106.
39. Ibid., pp. 310–22. For Spelman and Dugdale see Graham Parry, *English Antiquarians*, chs 6 and 8.
40. *Political Works of James I*, ed. Charles Howard McIlwain (Cambridge, Mass., 1918), p. 126.
41. Julian Lock, 'How Many Tercios Has the Pope? The Spanish War and the Sublimation of Elizabethan Anti-Popery', *History* 81 (1996), 197–214.
42. On suspicion of Northampton see Lake, 'Anti-popery', p. 88.
43. Ibid., pp. 87–92.
44. Cogswell, 'England and the Spanish Match' in Cust and Hughes, *Conflict*, pp. 107–34; T. H. Howard-Hill, *Middleton's "Vulgar Pasquin"* (Newark, Delaware, 1995).
45. *Birthpangs*, p. 130.
46. Alexander Leighton, *Speculum Belli Sacri* (1629) p. 77. Cf. Collinson, *Birthpangs*, pp. 130–54.
47. Lake, 'Anti-popery'.
48. E.g. Howarth, *Images of Rule*. Cf. Peter Burke, *The Fabrication of Louis XIV* (New Haven and London, 1992).
49. Yates, *Astraea*; Strong, *The Cult of Elizabeth* (1977) and *Splendour at Court: Renaissance Spectacle and the Theatre of Power* (1973). Cf. King, *Tudor Royal Iconography*.
50. Yates, *Astraea*, particularly 'Queen Elizabeth I as Astraea', a *tour de force* for this kind of scholarship.
51. Strong, *Cult of Elizabeth*, ch. 4.
52. Cressy, *Bonfires and Bells*, ch. 4; Hutton, *Merry England*, pp. 146–51.
53. For an attempt to correct this problem see Hackett, *Virgin Mother*.
54. E.g. McCoy, *Rebellion in Arcadia* and *Rites of Knighthood*; Peterson, *Poems of Ben Jonson*; Sharpe, *Criticism and Compliment*.
55. Susan Doran, 'Juno vs. Diana: The Treatment of Elizabeth I's Marriage in Plays and Entertainments, 1561–1581', *Historical Journal* 38 (1995), 257–74.
56. See Jerzy Limon, *The Masque of Stuart Culture* (Newark, Delaware, 1990), ch. 1; R. Malcolm Smuts, 'Occasional Events, Literary Texts and Historical Interpretations: Some Comments on Methodological Issues' in Glenn Burgess, Robin Headlam Wells and Rowland Wymer, *Cultural Pluralism new essays in Renaissance Literature, History and Politics* (forthcoming).
57. Smuts, 'Art and Material Culture'.

58. Thomas Greene, 'Shakespeare's Richard II: The Sign in Bullingbroke's Window' in Gent (ed.), *Albion's Classicism*, pp. 313–24.
59. Diary of von Wedel, TRHS, 2, ix, p. 256.
60. Manley, *Early Modern London*, ch. 5; Tittler, *The Reformation and the Towns*, Part IV.
61. In London these had already appeared in the Middle Ages. I owe this point to an unpublished paper by Anne Lancashire.
62. I have benefited from a paper on this subject by James Robertson.
63. C. Munday, *The Triumphs of Re-united Britania* (1605). The pioneering study of the mayoral processions is David Bergeron, *English Civic Pageantry 1558–1642* (Columbia, SC, 1971).
64. Tittler, *Reformation and the Towns*, pp. 297–304.
65. A point that will be demonstrated by Mary Hill Cole, *The Portable Queen: Elizabeth I and the Politics of Ceremony* (Amherst, Mass., forthcoming, 2000).
66. Waldstein Diary, p. 73.
67. Starkey, 'Intimacy and Innovation: The Rise of the Privy Chamber 1485–1547' in *idem*, (ed.), *English Court*; Thurley, *The Palaces of Tudor England*, chs 7–8.
68. Tittler, *Architecture and Power: The Town Hall and the English Urban Community, c. 1500–1640* (Oxford, 1991); *idem*., 'Political culture and the built environment of the English country town, c. 1540–1620' in Hoak (ed.) *Tudor Culture*, pp. 133–56; Maurice Howard, 'Classicism and Civic Architecture in Renaissance England' in Gent (ed.), *Albion's Classicism*, pp. 29–50.
69. For Spain see J. H. Elliott, 'The Court of the Spanish Habsburgs: a Peculiar Institution?' in *Spain and its World, 1500–1700* (New Haven and London, 1989), pp. 142–61 and 'Philip IV of Spain: Prisoner of Ceremony' in A. G. Dickens (ed.), *The Courts of Europe: Politics, Patronage and Royalty, 1400–1800* (New York, 1977), pp. 169–90. The decline of the English royal entry is discussed in Smuts, 'Ceremony and Charisma', pp. 82–93.
70. King, *Tudor Iconography*; Hackett, ch. 1.
71. Hackett, *Virgin Mother*, p. 162.
72. King, *Tudor Iconography*; Hackett, *Virgin Mother*, esp. pp. 144–62.
73. Below, pp. 129–30.
74. Anne Barton, *Ben Jonson, dramatist* (Cambridge, 1984), ch. 14; Smuts, *Court Culture*, pp. 29–31.
75. Wilson, *England's Eliza* (Cambridge, Mass., 1939).
76. For example, Eleanor Rosenberg, *Leicester: Patron of Letters*; Javitch, *Poetry and Courtliness*; Peter Saccio, *The Court Comedies of John Lyly: A Study in Allegorical Dramaturgy* (Princeton, 1969), esp. ch. 1; Helgerson, *Forms of Nationhood*.
77. 'The Stigma of Print', p. 140.
78. E.g. Javitch, *Poetry and Courtliness*; May, *Elizabethan Courtier Poets*; Love, *Scribal Publication*; Marotti, *Manuscript, Print and Lyric*; Woudhuysen, *Sidney and manuscripts*.
79. See Jurgen Habermas, *The Structural Transformation of the Public Sphere: an Inquiry into a Category of Bourgeois Society* (Cambridge, Mass., 1989).
80. Riggs, *Ben Jonson*.

81. May, *Courtier Poets*, p. 52.
 82. The sonnet had earlier been introduced by Wyatt and Surrey but had since fallen out of fashion.
 83. May, *Courtier Poets*, pp. 104–13 and ch. 4 generally.
 84. Ibid., pp. 124–5.
 85. Bates, *Rhetoric of Courtship*, esp. ch. 2.
 86. Doran, 'Juno vs. Diana'.
 87. E.g. Wilson, *England's Eliza*, p. 297.
 88. See Marotti, '"Love is not Love": Elizabethan Sonnet Sequences and the Social Order', *ELH* 49 (1982) 396–427 and *John Donne*; Achsah Guibroy, '"Oh let mee not serve so": The Politics of Love in Donne's *Elegies*' in Arthur Marotti (ed.) *Critical Essays on John Donne* (New York, 1994), pp. 17–36.
 89. Norbrook, *Poetry and Politics*, pp. 109, 131.
 90. Hackett, *Virgin Mother*, p. 166 and ch. 6.
 91. Smuts, 'Occasional Events'.
 92. Love, *Scribal Publication*, ch. 1 is a good introduction.
 93. For the scriveners and other producers see Woudhuysen, *Sidney and manuscripts*, ch. 2.
 94. Helgerson, *Self-Crowned Laureates*; Peterson, *Imitation and Praise*.
 95. John Peacock, 'Court Masque'.
 96. Collinson, 'Ecclesiastical Vitriol'.
 97. *Manuscript and Lyric*, pp. 100–1 discusses the circulation of Ralegh materials.
 98. Hammer, 'Myth-Making', pp. 621–42.
 99. *Historical Manuscripts Commission De Lisle Dudley Manuscripts* II, p. 435; Collins, *Letters and Memorials of State* II p. 194.
100. Sp12/274, piece 138 (Essex to the Queen, 15 May 1600).
101. *Public Sphere*, p. 57.
102. Especially Patterson, *Censorship and Interpretation* and *Reading Between the Lines*.
103. Richard Rambuss, *Spenser's Secret Career* (Cambridge, 1993).
104. E.g. Norman McClure (ed.) *Letters of John Chamberlain* 2 vols. (Philadelphia, 1939); P. R. Seddon, (ed.), *Letters of John Holles 1587–1637*, Thornton Society Record Series, 31 (Nottingham, 1975).
105. Marotti, 'Love is not Love', p. 406. Woudhuysen, *Sidney and manuscripts*, pt 2 systematically examines the evidence on this point.
106. Jan van Dorsten, Dominic Baker-Smith and Arthur Kinney (eds), *Sidney and the Creation of a Legend*; J. F. R. Day, 'Death be very proud: Sidney, subversion, and Elizabethan heraldic funerals' in Hoak (ed.) *Tudor Political Culture*, pp. 179–203.
107. Marotti, *Manuscript, Print and Lyric*, pp. 28–30; *Sidney and the Creation of a Legend*, passim.
108. For Mary Sidney and her family see Brennan, *Literary Patronage*.
109. Roy Strong, *Prince Henry and England's Lost Renaissance* (1986) reviews the evidence while reinscribing the legend.
110. 'The spectral Origins of the English Civil War' in Eley and Hunt (eds), *Reviving the English Revolution: Reflections and Elaborations on the Work of Christopher Hill* (1988).

111. McCoy, 'Old English honour' in *Stuart Court and Europe*, pp. 133–55; Norbrook, *Poetry and Politics*, chs 8–9; Grundy, *Spenserian Poets*.
112. McCoy, 'Old English Honour'.
113. Kelly, *Beginning of Ideology*.
114. Adams, 'Favourites and Factions at the Elizabethan Court' in Ronald Asch and Adolf Birke (eds), *Princes, Patronage and the Nobility* (Oxford, 1991), pp. 265–84.
115. There is a modern edition with a full introduction, D. C. Peck (ed.), *Leicester's Commonwealth* (Athens, Georgia, 1985).
116. Adams, 'Factionalism', pp. 276–87. For the circulation and influence of the treatise see Peck, ed., *Leicester's Commonwealth*, Introduction.
117. Peck, pp. 93–4.
118. Ibid., pp. 95, 96.
119. Ibid., pp. 103–4, 107.
120. Ibid., pp. 185–6.
121. Ibid., pp. 25–32.
122. For attempts to lay the blame on Cuffe see Lacey Baldwin Smith, *Treason in Tudor England: Politics and Paranoia* (Princeton, 1986), pp. 249–55.
123. Jouanna, *Devoir de révolte*, ch. 4.
124. *Philotas*, III, iii, 1135–47.
125. Sc. xx, ll. 67–9. The manner of Guise's assassination – he was surrounded and stabbed to death by the King's bodyguard – made the allusion especially appropriate.
126. William Shakespeare, *Henry VI, Part II*, I, iv, 23–9.
127. Among many treatments see Goldberg, 'John Hayward'; Levy, 'Politic History', pp. 16–21; James, *Society, Politics and Culture*, pp. 418–23. A modern edition of Haywarde's work is J. J. Manning (ed.), *The First and Second Parts of John Hayward's The Life and Reigns of King Henri the IIII*, Camden Soc., 4th Ser., xlii (1991).
128. Lambeth Palace Ms. 923, p. 11.
129. Marlowe, *Edward II*, I, i, 50–60.
130. See, e.g., Robert Bireley, *The Counter-Reformation Prince: Anti-Machiavellianism or Catholic Statecraft in Early Modern Europe* (Chapel Hill, 1990) and J. A. Fernandez Satamarin, *Reason of State and Statecraft in Spanish Political Thought, 1585–1640* (Lanham and London, 1983), esp. ch. 4.
131. Richard Hooker, *Laws of Ecclesiastical Polity* II, pp. 4–5.
132. Henry Savile, *End of Galba*, p. 1.
133. *Works of Samuel Daniel*, ed. Grosart (1885; rpt. New York, 1965) V, p. 46. Cf. Bacon's comment, 'States, as great engines, move slowly, and are not so soon put out of frame' (J. Spedding (ed.) *Works of Francis Bacon*, 14 vols. [1858–74; rpt. Stuttgart-Bad, 1963], III, p. 445).
134. See *End of Galba*, p. 11.
135. Cf. David Womersley, 'Sir Henry Savile's Translation of Tacitus and the Political Interpretation of Elizabethan Texts', *Review of English Studies*, n.s. 42 (1991), 313–42.
136. Manning (ed.), *Hayward's Henri IIII*.
137. *Works* IX, p. 41.

138. Walter Devereux, ed., *Lives and Letters of the Devereux Earls of Essex, 1540–1646* (London, 1853) I, p. 409.
139. Jonson, *Sejanus*, I, i, 159–73.
140. See, esp., Shakespeare, *Richard II*, I, iv.
141. For recent surveys see Wallace MacCaffrey, *War and Politics, 1558–1603* (Princeton, 1992) and R. B. Wernham, *The Return of the Armadas* (Oxford, 1994).
142. Shakespeare, *Henry VI*, Part I, I, i, 72–80.
143. Helgerson, *Forms of Nationhood*, ch. 5, esp. pp. 206–14.
144. Even James VI argued that tyranny often led to successful rebellion. See McIlwain (ed.), *Political Works of James I*, p. 19.
145. Greene, 'Bullingbroke's Window', pp. 316–7.
146. Michelle O'Callaghan, ' "Talking Politics": Tyranny, Parliament, and Christopher Brooke's *The Ghost of Richard the Third* (1614)', *Historical Journal*, 41, (1998), 96–120, examines one interesting case.
147. Donald Kelly, 'Murd'rous Machiavel in France, *Political Science Quarterly*, 85, (1970), 545–59.
148. Worden, *Sidney*, ch. 6.
149. Marlowe, *The Jew of Malta*, lines 3, 15–21.
150. Ibid., line 4.
151. Smuts, 'Court-Centred Politics'; Worden, 'Ben Jonson among the Historians' in Sharpe and Lake (eds), *Culture and Politics*, pp. 67–90; Salmon, 'Seneca and Tacitus'; Levy, 'Politic History'.
152. Martin Butler, 'Romans in Britain, *The Roman Actor* and the Early Stuart classical play' in Douglas Howard (ed.), *Philip Massinger: A Critical Reassessment* (Cambridge, 1985), pp. 139–70.
153. *The Tragedy of Julia Agrippina* (1639), p. 8. This play was performed in 1628.
154. William Bidwell and Maija Jansson, (eds), *Proceedings in Parliament 1626* (New Haven and London, 1992), II, p. 343. The speaker was Sir Humphrey May, Chancellor of the Duchy.
155. Ibid., p. 222.
156. Richard Cust, *The Forced Loan and English Politics, 1626–1628* (Oxford, 1987), esp. pp. 21–39; Peck, *Patronage and Corruption*, esp. ch. 4.
157. Thomas Birch (ed.), *Court and Times of Charles I* (1849), p. 223.
158. Howarth, *Images of Rule*, pp. 180–3.
159. Manley, *Early Modern London*, pp. 394–5, concludes that the triad of court, country and town probably became established as a theme in English literature in the 1570s.
160. 'The Court and the Country'.
161. See, esp., Perez Zagorin, *The Court and the Country* (New York, 1969), Stone, *Causes of the English Revolution* (1972), pp. 91–117; P. W. Thomas, 'Two Cultures: Court and Country under Charles I', in Conrad Russell (ed.), *Origins of the English Civil War* (1973), pp. 168–93.
162. On this see esp., Derek Hirst, 'Court, Country and Politics before 1629' in Kevin Sharpe (ed.), *Faction and Parliament* (Oxford, 1978), pp. 102–38.

163. See Sharpe, *Criticism and Compliment*; Smuts, *Court Culture*, esp. ch. 3; Holmes, 'County Community'; Martin Butler, *Theatre and Crisis* (Cambridge, 1982), ch. 6. The groundwork for much of this analysis was laid by F. J. Fisher, 'The Development of London as a Centre for Conspicuous Consumption in the Sixteenth and Seventeenth Centuries', *Transactions of the Royal Historical Society*, 4th series, vol. 30, (1948), 37–50 and Stone, *Crisis*, pp. 384–98.
164. See Robertson, 'Bridging Court and Country?'; Cust, 'News and Politics in Early Seventeenth-Century England', *Past and Present* 112 (1986), pp. 60–90 and F. J. Levy, 'How Information Spread'.
165. Hirst, 'Court, country and politics'.
166. Geoffrey Parker, *The Military Revolution: Military Innovation and the Rise of the West, 1500–1800* (Cambridge, 1988), esp. pp. 45–6.
167. Croft, 'Libels', esp. 261–75.
168. Croft, 'Libels', 271 and 'Reputation of Cecil'.
169. *Essays and New Atlantis* (Roslyn, New York, 1942), p. 56 ('Of Seditions and Troubles').
170. Ibid., p. 35 ('On Envy').
171. SP12/273/35. Speech in Star Chamber.
172. For the Inns environment see Philip Finkelpearl, *John Marston of the Middle Temple* (Cambridge, Massachusetts, 1969), pp. 3–80; Wilfred Prest, *The Inns of Court under Elizabeth I and the Early Stuarts, 1590–1640* (London, 1972), esp. ch. 7. A recent discussion of satire emphasizing the London context is Manley, *Early Modern London*, ch. 7.
173. John Donne, 'Satire V', ll. 47–60.
174. Donne, 'Metempsychosis', verse 7. Cecil is not named but is plainly intended. An interesting commentary is Flynn, 'Donne's *Ignatius His Conclave*'.
175. Ibid., stanza 33.
176. Cf. the account of the vulture and the parrot in Michael Drayton's *The Owle* (William Hebel [ed.], *Works of Michael Drayton* (1941) II, p. 492).
177. The best treatment remains Peterson, *Poems of Ben Jonson*. Amidst an extensive literature see also Manley, *Early Modern London*, ch. 7.
178. Katherine Eisman Maus, *Ben Jonson and the Roman Frame of Mind* (Princeton, 1984); Oestreich, *Neostoicism*. See, however, the suggestive comments about Epicurean influence in Smith, 'French philosophy'.
179. *Works of Bacon*, ed. Spedding, III, p. 457.
180. For two discussions see Norbrook, *Poetry and Politics*, pp. 205–13 and McCoy, 'Old English Honour'.
181. Alastair Bellany, '"Raylinge rymes"'; Cogswell, 'Underground verse'; Croft, 'Libels'.
182. Marotti, *Manuscript, Print and Lyric*, pp. 94–107. A more systematic study of responses to the Overbury murder is Alastair Bellany, 'The Poisoning of Legitimacy? Court Scandal, News Culture and Politics in England, 1603–1660', unpublished Princeton Ph.D. thesis, 1995, pp. 12–438.
183. Cogswell, 'Underground verse', p. 294; Croft, 'Libels', 279.
184. Public Record Office SP16/172/10.
185. Maren Sophie Røstvig, *The Happy Man*, 2 vols. (Oslo and Oxford, 1954).

186. *Woodstock*, III, ii, 1288–1311; for early examples in Shakespeare see *Henry VI* Part 2, IV, x; *Henry VI* Part 3, II, v, 21–9 and 42–55.
187. E.g. Fulke Greville, 'Of Monarchy', verse 108 (Alexander Grosart [ed.], *Lord Brooke's Works*, I, pp. 44–5).
188. See, esp., Alan Everitt, *The Community of Kent and the Great Rebellion* (Leicester, 1966) and *The Local Community and the Great Rebellion* (Leicester, 1969).
189. Conrad Russell, *Parliaments and English Politics, 1621–1629* (Oxford, 1979), p. 8.
190. Holmes, 'County Community'.
191. Holmes and Heal, *Gentry*, provides the most up-to-date survey.
192. Herbert, *Autobiography*, p. 4.
193. Stone, *Crisis*, pp. 199–270 remains useful. An up-to-date summary, with references to the secondary literature, is Holmes and Heal, *Gentry*, pp. 190–8.
194. A case-study is A. H. Smith, *County and court: Government and Politics in Norfolk 1558–1603* (Oxford, 1974). But cf. Thomas Cogswell, *Home divisions: Aristocracy, the state and provincial conflict* (Manchester, 1988).
195. Kishlansky, *Parliamentary Selection*, Part I.
196. Heal and Holmes, *Gentry*, pp. 198–214.
197. Underdown, *Fire from Heaven*; William Hunt, *The Puritan Moment: The Coming of Revolution in an English County* (Cambridge, Mass., 1983); Wrightson and David Levine, *Poverty and Piety in an English Village: Terling, 1525–1700* (1979), chs 5–6.
198. Robert Greene, *The History of Friar Bacon and Friar Bungay* (c. 1589?), xvi, 44–63.
199. Rhodes Dunlap (ed.) *Poems of Thomas Carew* (Oxford, 1949), p. 77; cf. Smuts, *Court Culture*, ch. 9.
200. Strong, *Charles I on Horseback*, ch. 6; Palme, *Triumph of Peace*, pp. 245–7.
201. Bacon, *Essays*, p. 131 ('Of the True Greatness of Kingdoms and Estates')
202. Sir William Cornwallis, *Seneca the Tragedian* (1601).
203. Shakespeare, *Henry IV*, IV, iv, 444–5.
204. Alexander Grosart (ed.), *Complete Works of Samuel Daniel* (1885; rpt. New York, 1963) II, pp. 19–23.
205. E.g. William Camden, *Britannia*, p. 176
206. William Hebel (ed.), *Works of Michael Drayton* (1941) II, p. 512.
207. George Wither, *Britain's Remembrancer* (1880; rpt. New York, 1967), pp. 367–8.
208. Quoted by LeCoq, *Satire en Angleterre*, pp. 63–4.
209. E.g. Trevor Roper, 'The General Crisis of the Seventeenth Century' in Trevor Aston (ed.), *Crisis in Europe* (1965); Stone, *Crisis*, p. 385.
210. See Felicity Heal, 'The Crown, the gentry and London, 1596–1640' in *Law and Government under the Tudors*, ed. Claire Cross, David Loades and J. J. Scarisbrick and Smuts, 'The Court and its Neighborhood'.
211. Heal sees three periods of fairly vigorous enforcement: 1595–1601, 1622–4 and 1632–6 (ibid., p. 215). Smuts found that the population of the parish of St Martin-in-the-Fields stabilized in the latter years of James I, after tripling earlier in the reign, but resumed its growth in the late 1620s.

212. Stone, *Family and Fortune* (Oxford, 1973), pp. 28, 62–91.
213. *Letters of Peter Paul Rubens*, trans. and ed. Ruth Magurn (Cambridge, Mass., 1955), p. 314.
214. For the evidence see Smuts, 'Art and material culture'.
215. Ibid.
216. Stone, *Crisis of the Aristocracy*, p. 561.
217. Fisher, 'Development of London'; Stone, *Crisis*, pp. 384–98; Smuts, *Court Culture*, pp. 53–64.
218. Smuts, 'Court and its Neighborhood'; Heal, 'Crown, Gentry and London'; James Robertson, 'London 1580–1642: The View from Whitehall, the View from the Guildhall', unpublished Washington University Ph.D. thesis, 1993.
219. Fisher, 'Development of London'.
220. Westminster Public Library Mss. F 330–67.
221. The best survey is Stoye, *English Travellers*.
222. Above, pp. 57–8.
223. Friedman, *House and Household*, pp. 71–95 provides a good discussion.
224. P. R. Seddon, (ed.), *Letters of John Holles 1587–1637*, (Thornton Society Record Series, 31 (Nottingham, 1975) p. 53.
225. Stoye, *English Travellers*, ch. 12.
226. Dewald, *Aristocratic Experience and the Origins of Modern Culture* (Berkeley, 1993), pp. 81, 82–3.
227. Ronald Lightbown, 'Charles I and the tradition of European princely collecting' in Arthur MacGregor (ed.), *The Late King's Goods* (1989).
228. Smuts, 'Art and Material Culture', pp. 96–101; David Howarth, *Images of Rule*, ch. 7.
229. A. R. Braunmuller, 'Robert Carr, Earl of Somerset, as collector and patron' in Peck (ed.), *Mental World*, pp. 230–50. Carleton's role in the art world is described in Jonathan Brown, *Kings and Connoisseurs: Collecting Art in Seventeenth-Century Europe* (New Haven and London, 1995), pp. 18–19.
230. Strong, *Henry, Prince of Wales*, pp. 30–45.
231. The artists are surveyed in ibid., pp. 86–137.
232. D. J. Howarth, *Lord Arundel and his Circle* (New Haven and London, 1985) and Maria F. S. Hervey, *The Life, Correspondence and Collections of Thomas Howard, Earl of Arundel* (Cambridge, 1921).
233. Information derived from St Martin's overseers accounts, Westminster Public Library Mss. F 330–67.
234. Howarth, *Arundel*, pp. 15–18.
235. Oliver Millar, *Van Dyck in England* (1982).
236. See esp. 'Making a Fresh Start: Sixteenth-Century Agriculture and the Classical Inspiration' in Leslie and Raylor (eds), *Culture and Cultivation* (Leicester, 1992).
237. Ibid.; Lowe, *The Georgic Revolution*; MacRae, *God Speed the Plow*.
238. Winn, *Dryden*, pp. 29–33.
239. Andrew McRae, 'Husbandry Manuals and the Language of Agrarian Improvement' in Leslie and Raylor (eds), *Culture and Cultivation*; idem., *God Speed the Plow*.

240. Joan Thirsk, 'Farming Techniques, 1500–1640' in *idem*, (ed.), *Chapters from the Agrarian History of England and Wales, 1500–1700: Agricultural change: policy and practice 1500–1750* (Cambridge, 1990), pp. 15–53.
241. Heal, *Hospitality*, ch. 4.
242. Heal, *Hospitality*, pp. 1–24. Cf. Friedman, *House and Household*.
243. Heal, *Hospitality*, chs 3–4.
244. Hutton, *Merry England*, p. 174.
245. Stone, *Crisis*, chs 2 and 6 remains valuable on these readjustments.
246. The decline of the hall to a vestibule was in some cases delayed, however, until the eighteenth century. See Girouard, *English Country House*, p. 136.
247. Platt, *Great Rebuildings*, p. 77. Even yeomen houses were eventually affected (p. 152).
248. Heal, *Hospitality*, p. 114.
249. Brathwaite, *English Gentleman* (1630), p. 66.
250. For examples, McCoy, 'Old English Honour'; Richard F. Hardin, *Michael Drayton and the Passing of Elizabethan England* (Lawrence, Kansas, 1973).
251. Gent (ed.), *Albion's Classicism*, provides a stimulating discussion.
252. Anderson, 'Learning to Read Architecture'; David Cast, 'Speaking of Architecture: the Evolution of a Vocabulary in Vasari, Jones and Sir John Vanburgh', *Journal of the Society of Architectural Historians* 52 (1993): 179–88; J. Peacock, 'Inigo Jones and Renaissance Art', *Renaissance Studies* 4 (1990), 245–72; J. Newman, '"Inigo Jones and his Italian Treatises in Use": the Significance of Inigo Jones Annotations' in *Les Traités d'Architecture de la Renaissance* (Paris, 1988); Gordon Higgot, 'Varying with reason: Inigo Jones's theory of design', *Architectural History* 35 (1992), 51–77; *idem*, 'Inigo Jones, Italian Art, and the Practice of Drawing', *Art Bulletin* 74 (1992), 247–9. For studies of Jonson's uses of classical models see esp. Trimpi, *Ben Jonson's Poems: a Study in the Plain Style* (Stanford, 1962); Maus, *Jonson*, Peterson, *Imitation and Praise*; Manley, *Literature and Culture in London*, ch. 9.
253. J. Alfred Gotch, *Inigo Jones* (1928), pp. 81–2. I have modernized Jones's erratic spelling.
254. William J. Hebel (ed.), *Works of Drayton*, IV, p. 322.
255. Leah Marcus, *The Politics of Mirth* (Chicago, 1986).

3 From Civil War to Tory Reaction

1. Historical surveys include Robert Ashton, *Counter-Revolution*, Charles Carlton, *Going to the Wars: The Experience of the British Civil Wars, 1638–1651* (1992), Fletcher, *Outbreak*; Ian Gentles, *The New Model Army* (1992), Mark Kishlansky, *The Rise of the New Model Army* (Cambridge, 1979), J. S. Morrill, *The Revolt of the Provinces* (1976) and *English Revolution*; Russell, *Causes* and *British Monarchies*; Underdown, *Revel, Riot and Rebellion*. For literary surveys see, esp., Thomas N. Corns, *Uncloistered Virtue: English Political Literature, 1640–1660* (Oxford, 1992), Healy and Sawday (eds), *Literature and Civil War*; Potter, *Royalist Writings*; Smith, *Literature and Revolution*; and Michael Wilding, *Dragon's Teeth: Literature in the English Revolution* (Oxford, 1987).

2. See *Catalogue of the Pamphlets, Books, Newspapers, and Manuscripts Relating to the Civil War, the Commonwealth, and Restoration, Collected by George Thomason, 1640–1661* (British Library Catalogue, rpt. Liechtestein, 1969), p. xxi.
3. See, e.g., Hill, *Society and Puritanism*; Smuts, *Court Culture*; P. W. Thomas, 'Two Cultures? Court and Country under Charles I' in Conrad Russell (ed.), *The Origins of the English Civil War* (1973), pp. 168–93; Perez Zagorin, *The Court and the Country* (New York, 1971); Lawrence Stone, *Causes of the English Revolution* (1972), esp. pp. 79–117.
4. Among the more important, *Puritanism and Revolution* (1958); *Society and Puritanism*; *Intellectual Origins, World Turned Upside Down, Milton and Some Contemporaries*, (1984), *The Consequences of the English Revolution* (Madison, WI, 1980), *The Experience of Defeat, Change and Continuity in Seventeenth-Century England* (1975) and *English Bible*.
5. For an appreciative but tough-minded critique see Morrill, *English Revolution*, ch. 14.
6. Alastair MacLachlam, *The Rise and Fall of Revolutionary England: An Essay on the Fabrication of Seventeenth Century History* (1996)
7. Cf. Conrad Russell's comment in the Preface to *British Monarchies*: 'Ever since I was an undergraduate, it has worried me that so much work on the causes of the English Civil War was accompanied by so little investigation into the effects for which causes had to be found' (p. vii).
8. Russell, *Causes*, p. 5. The Lord Chamberlains were the Earls of Pembroke and Essex.
9. Morrill, *English Revolution*, p. 13.
10. J. S. Morrill, *Revolt of the Provinces*.
11. Underdown, *Revel, Riot and Rebellion*.
12. *British Monarchies*, p. vii.
13. E.g. Kevin Sharpe, *Personal Rule*; Fletcher, *Outbreak*; Russell, *Fall*; Ashton, *Counter Revolution*. The shift back towards detailed narrative was anticipated by two pre-revisionist works, Blair Worden, *The Rump Parliament* (Cambridge, 1974) and David Underdown, *Pride's Purge: Politics in the Puritan Revolution* (London, 1971).
14. 'England's Troubles 1603–1702' in Smuts (ed.), *Stuart Court*, pp. 20–38 at p. 22.
15. For some perceptive comments see Peter Lake's review article on Conrad Russell's *Causes* and *Britsh Monarchies* in *Huntington Library Quarterly* 57 (1994), 167–97.
16. See, e.g. Morrill, *English Revolution*, ch. 4.
17. Russell, *Causes*, ch. 4; Morrill, 'The Religious Context of the English Civil War' in *English Revolution*; Peter Lake, *Anglicans and Puritans?*; N. R. N. Tyacke, *Anti-Calvinists: the Rise of English Arminianism* (Oxford, 1987); Milton, *Catholic and Reformed*.
18. See, esp., Smith, *Constitutional Royalism*; Tuck, *Philosophy and Government*, chs 6 and 7; Michael Mendle, *Henry Parker*; David Wootton, 'From Rebellion to Revolution: the crisis of the winter of 1642/3 and the origins of civil war radicalism' in *English Historical Review* 105 (1990), 634–69.
19. In addition to the works cited above, n. 1, see C. John Sommerville, *News Revolution*; Friedman, *Pulp Press*; Love, *Scribal Publication*.

Notes and References

20. Russell, *Fall*, p. 1, a position shared by Kevin Sharpe, *Personal Rule*; David Underdown, *A Freeborn People: Politics and the Nation in Seventeenth-Century England* (Oxford, 1996).
21. Russell, *Causes*, ch. 1; *British Monarchies*, *passim*.
22. Hibbard, *Popish Plot*.
23. An exception – significantly produced by a literary scholar rather than an historian – is Erica Veevers, *Images of Love and Religion: Queen Henrietta Maria and Court Entertainments* (Cambridge, 1993).
24. Morrill, *English Revolution*, ch. 4; Smith, *Constitutional Royalism*, chs 3–4.
25. For the royalists a start has been made by Smith. For Selden see Richard Tuck, '"The Ancient Law of Freedom": John Selden and the Civil War' in Morrill (ed.), *Reactions to the Civil War* and Christianson, *John Selden*.
26. Keith Wrightson and David Levine, *Poverty and Piety in an English Village: Terling, 1525–1700* (1979); Underdown, *Revel, Riot and Rebellion* and *Fire from Heaven* (1992).
27. This summary attempts to recapitulate the main arguments of Wrightson and Levine, *Poverty and Piety*, ch. 1 and *passim*; Wrightson, *English Society*, esp. chs 2 and 5–7; Underdown, *Revel, Riot and Rebellion*, chs 2 and 3 and *Fire From Heaven*. See, in addition, William Hunt, *The Puritan Moment: the Coming of Revolution in an English County* (Cambridge, Mass., 1983), parts I and II.
28. Wrightson and Levine, *Poverty and Piety*; Underdown, *Fire from Heaven*.
29. *Revel, Riot and Rebellion*, p. 40; cf. p. 72.
30. Ibid., p. 5.
31. Ingram, *Church Courts*.
32. Ibid., pp. 101–7; J. S. Morrill, 'The Ecology of Allegiance in the English Civil Wars', *Journal of British Studies* 26 (1987), 451–67 (rpt. as *English Revolution*, ch. 11); Underdown, 'A Reply to John Morrill', ibid., pp. 468–79; Hughes, *Causes*, pp. 137–48; *idem*, *Politics, society and Civil War in Warwickshire, 1620–1660* (Cambridge, 1987), chs 1, 2 and 4.
33. Peter Burke, *Popular Culture in Early Modern Europe* (1979).
34. For a summary of the objections see Tim Harris, 'Problematising Popular Culture' in Harris (ed.), *Popular Culture in England, c. 1500–1850*, (1995), pp. 1–27.
35. Watt, *Cheap Print*; Peter Lake, 'Deeds Against Nature: Cheap Print, Protestantism and Murder in Early Seventeenth Century England' in Sharpe and Lake (eds), *Culture and Politics*; Hutton, *Merry England* and 'The English Reformation and the Evidence of Folklore', *Past and Present*, 148 (1996), 89–116.
36. Russell, *Causes*, p. 85.
37. A point emphasized by Collinson, *Birthpangs*, pp. 141–3.
38. A recent attempt to test Underdown's thesis is Mark Stoye, *Loyalty and Locality: Popular Allegiance in Devon during the English Civil War* (Exeter, 1994).
39. See Harris, 'Propaganda and Public Opinion' and Richard Cust and Anne Hughes, 'Introduction: after Revisionism' in *Conflict in Early Stuart England: Studies in Religion and Politics 1603–1642* (1989), p. 13.

40. Shagan, 'Constructing Discord'.
41. Fletcher, *Outbreak*, 'Introduction'.
42. Smith, *Literature and Revolution*, p. 24.
43. Ibid., p. 24; Friedman, *Pulp Press*, pp. 13–14.
44. Mendle, 'De Facto Freedom De Facto Authority: Press and Parliament, 1640–43', *Historical Journal* 38 (1995), esp. 313–18.
45. For speeches see A. D. T. Cromartie, 'The Printing of Parliamentary Speeches November 1640–July 1642' in *Historical Journal*, 33 (1990), 23–44; for sermons John F. Wilson, *Pulpit in Parliament: Puritanism during the English Civil Wars 1640–1648* (Princeton, 1969). Appendix Two of this work provides a complete list of printed sermons preached to the Long Parliament.
46. This and the following paragraph are based on the *Catalogue*. For discussion see Sommerville, *News Revolution*, esp. pp. 34–43; Smith, *Literature and Revolution*, ch. 1; Achtinstein, *Milton and the Revolutionary Reader* (Princeton, 1994) pp. 10–13.
47. Ibid., pp. 323–5.
48. Morrill, *English Revolution*, p. 61.
49. Mendle, 'De Facto Freedom', 307–32; Shagan, 'Constructing Discord'.
50. As recent work has exhaustively shown. See, in particular, Hibbard, *Popish Plot*; Morrill, *English Revolution*; Fletcher, *Outbreak* and, with a somewhat different emphasis, Russell, *British Monarchies*.
51. Fletcher, *Outbreak*, p. 60; *The Copy of a Letter of Father Philips, which was thought to be sent into France to Mr Montague* (1641). Fears of a French invasion had surfaced as early as April (ibid., p. 15).
52. For the remonstrance see John Kenyon, ed., *The Stuart Constitution* (Cambridge, 1966), pp. 228–40.
53. See, esp., R. Clifton, 'The Fear of Catholicism during the English Civil War', *Past and Present*, 52 (1971), 23–55.
54. A count based on the *Catalogue*.
55. Shagan, 'Constructing Discord'.
56. See, e.g., clause 28 of the Root and Branch Petition in Kenyon, *Stuart Constitution*, p. 175.
57. For the petition itself see Richard Strier, 'From Diagnosis to Operation', in David L. Smith, Richard Strier and David Bevington (eds), *The Theatrical City: Culture, Theatre and Politics in London, 1576–1649* (Cambridge, 1995), pp. 224–43. The divisiveness of the assault on episcopacy has again been stressed in recent accounts, for example Fletcher, *Outbreak*, esp. ch. 3; Morrill, *English Revolution*, esp. pp. 52–90, 149–175; Russell, *Causes*, ch. 5; Smith, *Constitutional Royalism*, ch. 4.
58. Fletcher, *Outbreak*, pp. 94–6, 110.
59. Valerie Pearl, *London and the Outbreak of the Puritan Revolution* (Oxford, 1961), pp. 210–36. For two recent analyses see David L. Smith, 'From Petition to Remonstrance' and Richard Strier, 'Diagnosis to Operation', both in *Theatrical City*, pp. 224–43.
60. Ibid., p. 97; Morrill, *English Revolution*, p. 71.
61. See, among many sources that might be cited, the opening clauses of the Root and Branch Petition (Kenyon, *Stuart Constitution*, pp. 172–4) and

Pym's speech of 17 April, 1640 (Ibid., p. 200). Cf. Strier, 'Diagnosis to Operation', pp. 226–33.
62. E.g. 'Of Reformation' in *Works*, ed. Frank Allen Patterson et al. (New York 1931), v. i, p. 67.
63. 'Of Reformation', ibid., pp. 24–5.
64. Ibid., pp. 37–8.
65. Capp, *Fifth Monarchy Men*, pp. 30–40; Wilson, *Pulpit in Parliament*.
66. Milton, *Works*, v. 4, p. 340.
67. Ibid., p. 339; cf. p. 342.
68. Among many examples see ibid., pp. 310–11, 348.
69. Thomas Edwards, *Gangraena* (1646), p. 4.
70. A point especially emphasized by Underdown, *Freeborn People*, ch. 5.
71. Above, p. 46.
72. Capp, *John Taylor*, p. 144. For two very different interpretations see Brian Manning, *The English People and the English Revolution* (1976) and Morrill, *English Revolution*, ch. 18. Both agree on the importance of *perceptions* of disorder in fuelling a backlash that benefited the King.
73. Fletcher, *Outbreak*, p. 89.
74. Ibid., p. 112; Capp, *John Taylor*, p. 164
75. Above, p. 46; Smith, *Literature and Revolution*, pp. 295–319; Potter, *Royalist Literature*, pp. 30–1.
76. 'The Rebel Scot', John Cleveland, *Poems*, ed. Morris and Withington (Oxford, 1967).
77. See Corns, *Uncloistered Virtue*, pp. 8–9.
78. Abraham Cowley, *The Civil War*, ed. Allan Pritchart (Toronto, 1973), p. 92. A good commentary is MacLean, *Time's Witness*, pp. 194–9.
79. Corns, *Uncloistered Virtue*, pp. 3–7.
80. Ashton, *Counter-Revolution*, pp. 199–200.
81. Cleveland, 'The Hue and Cry after Sir John Presbyter', *Poems*, p. 47.
82. Edward Symmons, *A Militarie Sermon... Preached at Shrewsbury... To His Majesty's Army* (1644), quoted in Carlton, *Going to the Wars*, p. 52. Chapter 3 of this book discusses the different cultures of royalist and parliamentary soldiers.
83. For examples see Ashton, *Counter-Revolution*, pp. 203–4.
84. For a good brief discussion see ibid., pp. 197–205.
85. Among the best analyses are Miner, *Cavalier Mode*; Marcus, *Politics of Mirth*; Potter, *Royalist Literature*; and Zwicker, *Lines of Authority*, chs 2–3,
86. The most thorough treatment is Smith, *Constitutional Royalism*.
87. Useful information can be gleaned from a number of specialized studies, including David Underdown, *Royalist Conspiracy in England, 1649–1660* (New Haven, 1960); Ronald Hutton, *The Royalist War Effort 1642–1646* (1982); Carlton, *Going to the Wars*, pp. 49–59; P. R. Newman, *The Old Service: Royalist regimental colonels and the Civil War, 1642–46* (Manchester, 1993); Ashton, *Counter-Revolution*, chs 6–8 and several county histories, e.g. David Underdown, *Somerset in the Civil War and Interregnum* (1973); Hughes, *Warwickshire*. There is no recent general treatment of the royalist gentry comparable to J. T. Cliffe, *Puritans in conflict: the Puritan gentry during and after the civil wars* (1988) and *The Puritan gentry besieged, 1650–1700*

(1993). For popular royalism Underdown, *Revel, Riot and Rebellion* is suggestive. The last book-length survey, Paul Hardacre, *The Royalists During the Puritan Revolution* (The Hague, 1956) badly needs updating.
88. P. W. Thomas, *Berkenhead*; Potter, *Royalist Literature*, ch. 1.
89. Smith, *Constitutional Royalism* is a thorough survey.
90. Mendle, *Parker*, esp. pp. 70–93; Smith, pp. 221–7.
91. This has been a major theme of several recent discussions, e.g. Morrill, *Revolt of the Provinces*; Robert Ashton, 'From Cavalier to Roundhead Tyranny, 1642–9' in Morrill (ed.), *Reactions to Civil War*; Ashton, *Counter-Revolution*, esp. chs 3, 5 and 6.
92. Hence the demand for indemnity from malicious prosecutions by the soldiers. For discussions see Kishlansky, *New Model Army*, pp. 156–7; Gentles, *New Model Army*, ch. 5; Ashton, *Counter-Revolution*, pp. 159–62 and 223–8.
93. Ibid., pp. 203–12. For the popularity of Robin Hood ballads in the seventeenth century as a vehicle for popular protest see Christopher Hill, *Liberty Against Law* (1996) chs 5 and 6.
94. Smith, *Literature and Revolution*, pp. 134–42; Ashton, *Counter-Revolution*, pp. 109–16.
95. Smith, *Literature and Revolution*, pp. 59–61; Potter, *Royalist Literature*, pp. 7–13; Thomas, *Berkenhead*.
96. Sommerville, *News Revolution*, pp. 38–40 and 51–2. Cromwell's nose and Speaker Lenthall's stammer were among the frequent targets.
97. Timothy Raylor, *Cavaliers, Clubs and Literary Culture: Sir John Mennes, James Smith and the Order of the Fancy* (Newark, Delaware, 1994).
98. For two particularly good examples see Potter, *Royalist Literature* and Miner, *Cavalier Mode*.
99. Potter, *Secret Rites*, ch. 1 and Manley, *Early Modern London*, pp. 516–30 discuss royalist printing.
100. Marotti, *Manuscript, Print and the Lyric*, pp. 259–61.
101. For a discussion of this point with respect to a specific poem see Graham Parry, 'A Troubled Arcadia' in Healy and Sawday (eds), *Literature and the Civil War*.
102. Miner, *Cavalier Mode*; Manley, *Early Modern London*, pp. 516–30.
103. Miner, *Cavalier Mode* is an appreciative survey. More recent treatments include Marcus, *Politics of Mirth*, esp. ch. 7; Corns, *Uncloistered Virtue*, pp. 76–129; Potter, *Royalist Literature*.
104. Marcus, *Politics of Mirth*, pp. 151–68.
105. Marotti, *Manuscript, Print and the Lyric*, pp. 76–8.
106. Jonathan Dewald, *Aristocratic Experience and the Origins of Modern Culture: France, 1570–1750* (Berkeley, 1973); Veevers, *Henrietta Maria*, ch. 1.
107. Dudley, Lord North, *The Promiscuous Forest* (1659).
108. Cowley, *Essays, Plays and Sundry Verses*, ed. A. R. Waller (Cambridge, 1906), p. 381.
109. Ibid.
110. Jonathan Sawday, '"Mysteriously divided": Civil War, madness and the divided self' in Healy and Sawday (eds), *Literature and Civil War*; Smuts, *Court Culture*, pp. 253–62.

111. Hobbes, *Leviathan*, ed. C. B. MacPherson (1968), p. 168.
112. Amidst the vast bibliography see Richard Tuck, *Thomas Hobbes* (Oxford, 1989) and *Philosophy and Government*, esp. ch. 7, and the essays in *The Cambridge Companion to Hobbes* (Cambridge, 1996).
113. See Smith, 'Interregnum Poetry'.
114. David F. Gladish (ed.), *Sir William Davenant's Gondibert* (Oxford, 1971), p. 22.
115. Ibid., p. 18.
116. Smith, 'Interregnum Poetry'. Cf. Reid Barbour, 'The Early Stuart Epicure' in *English Literary Renaissance*, 23 (1993), pp. 170–200 and *English Epicures and Stoics: Ancient Legacies in Early Stuart Culture* (Amherst, Ma., 1998).
117. Røstvig, *Happy Man*, pp. 48–9, 122–51.
118. See Zwicker, *Lines of Authority*, ch. 3. Smith has argued convincingly that evidence commonly used to demonstrate an attraction to Epicureanism by puritans and supporters of the Commonwealth actually suggests the opposite ('English Epicureanism', pp. 200–9).
119. See, for example, David Norbrook, 'Marvell's 'Horatian Ode and the politics of genre' in Healy and Sawday (eds), *Literature and Civil War*; Blair Worden, 'Andrew Marvell, Oliver Cromwell, and the Horatian Ode' in Kevin Sharpe and Steven Zwicker (eds), *The Politics of Discourse: The Literature and History of Seventeenth-Century England* (Berkeley, 1987); Annabel Patterson, *Andrew Marvel and the Civic Crown* (Princeton, 1978), pp. 60–9. One effect of this reinterpretation is to bring Marvell's views much closer to those of his friend, John Milton.
120. For discussions see Ashton, *Counter Revolution*; Kishlansky, *New Model Army* and 'Ideology and Politics in the Parliamentary Armies' in Morrill (ed.), *Reactions to Civil War*; Morrill, *English Revolution*, ch. 17; Underdown, *Pride's Purge*; Gentles, *New Model Army*, chs 7–10 and Blair Worden, *Rump Parliament*. Sean Kelsey, *Inventing a Republic: the Political Culture of the English Commonwealth, 1649–1653* (Manchester, 1997) reached me too late to be taken into account here.
121. The evidence is reviewed in the introduction to the standard modern edition, Philip Knachel (ed.), *Eikon Basilike: The Portraiture of His Sacred Majesty in His Solitudes and Sufferings* (Ithaca, 1966).
122. Potter, *Royalist Literature*, p. 170. Potter rightly describes these figures as 'one of the most important facts of the period'.
123. Friedman, *Pulp Press*, p. 36.
124. Capp, *Fifth Monarchy Men*.
125. William Lamont, *Richard Baxter and the Millennium: Protestant Imperialism and the English Revolution* (1979).
126. Friedman, *Pulp Press* ch. 4; Keith Thomas, *Religion and the Decline of Magic*, chs 11–13; B. S. Capp, *English Almanacs, 1500–1800: Astrology and the Popular Press* (Ithaca, 1979).
127. Bernard Capp, 'The Fifth Monarchists and Popular Millenarianism' in MacGregor and Burns (eds), *Radical Religion*, p. 178.
128. See, for example, Worden, 'Providence and Politics'.
129. Three recent studies are Patsy Griffin, *The Modest Ambition of Andrew Marvell: A Study of Marvell and His Relation to Lovelace, Fairfax, Cromwell and Milton*

(Newark, Delaware, 1995); David Norbrook, 'Marvell's "Horatian Ode" and the Politics of Genre' in Healy and Sawday (eds), *Literature and Civil War*, pp. 147–69; and Blair Worden, 'Andrew Marvell, Oliver Cromwell, and the Horatian Ode' in Sharpe and Zwicker (eds), *Politics of Discourse*, pp. 147–80.
130. Worden, 'Andrew Marvell', p. 151.
131. Worden, 'Andrew Marvell', Norbrook, 'Horatian Ode'; Griffin *Modest Ambition*, esp. p. 42.
132. Andrew Marvell, 'An Horatian Ode upon Cromwell's Return from Ireland', 11. 101–4.
133. Worden, 'Andrew Marvell', comments ' "An Hannibal to Italy" would do everything but win' (p. 171).
134. Cf. Parry, *Seventeenth-Century Poetry*, pp. 227–42.
135. Hirst and Zwicker, 'High Summer at Nun Appleton'.
136. For the Hermetic strains see Røstvig, *Happy Man* I, p. 154.
137. This is the conclusion of Hirst and Zwicker as well as Griffin, who arrived at it by a different route. See *Ambition of Andrew Marvell*, pp. 56–61.
138. Quentin Skinner, 'Conquest and Consent: Thomas Hobbes and the Engagement Controversy' in Gerald Aylmer (ed.), *The Interregnum: The Quest for Settlement 1646–1660* (1972), pp. 79–98.
139. Christopher Hill, 'The Norman Yoke' in *Intellectual Origins*, pp. 361–66.
140. Ferdinand Tonnies (ed.), *Behemoth, or the Long Parliament* (1969), p. 3.
141. Worden, 'English Republicanism', pp. 444–6; Peltonen, *Republicanism*.
142. Worden, 'Classical Republicanism and the Puritan Revolution' in *History and Imagination: Essays in Honour of H. R. Trevor-Roper* (1981), pp. 181–200.
143. Smuts, 'Court-Centred Politics', pp. 41–2.
144. David Norbrook, 'Lucan, Thomas May, and the Creation of a Republican Literary Culture' in Sharpe and Lake (eds), *Culture and Politics*, pp. 45–66.
145. Cf. Morrill, *English Revolution*, p. 50 and ch. 3 generally.
146. Mendle, *Parker*; Wootton, 'Rebellion to Revolution', esp. 666–9 for exceptions.
147. David Wootton. 'Leveller democracy', pp. 418–19.
148. Above, pp. 12–13, 71–3; McCoy, 'Old English Honour'.
149. See Scott, *Sidney and the Restoration Crisis*.
150. Blair Worden, ' "Wit in a Roundhead": the dilemma of Marchamont Nedham' in *Political culture and cultural politics in early modern England: Essays presented to David Underdown* (Manchester, 1995).
151. Blair Worden, 'Marchamont Nedham and the Beginnings of English Republicanism' in David Wootton (ed.), *Republicanism, Liberty and Commercial Society, 1649–1776*, pp. 45–81; Pocock and Schochet, 'Interregnum and Restoration', pp. 157–61.
152. Marchamont Nedham, *The Case of the Commonwealth Truly Stated*, ed. Philip Knachel (Charlottesville, 1969).
153. Martin Dzelzainis, 'Milton's classical republicanism'; Thomas N. Corns, 'Milton and the characteristics of a free commonwealth'; Cedric Brown, 'Great senates and godly education: politics and cultural renewal in some pre- and post-revolutionary texts of Milton'; and Blair Worden, 'Milton and Marchamont Nedham' all in David Armitage, Armand Himy and Quentin Skinner (eds), *Milton and Republicanism* (Cambridge, 1995).

154. Ibid., p. 112.
155. Dzelzainis, 'Milton's republicanism', p. 22.
156. Scott, *Sidney and the Republic* is perceptive on this point, e.g. pp. 15–16, 21–3, 29.
157. *Protestantism*, p. 19.
158. Ibid., p. 79 and, more generally, pp. 1–187.
159. *Calendar of State Papers Venetian* vol. 30, p. 136, Sagredo dispatch of 12 November 1655.
160. Ibid., pp. 72–3
161. Ibid., p. 197.
162. Worden, 'Cromwell and the Sin of Achan'; David Armitage, 'The Cromwellian Protectorate and the Languages of Empire', *Historical Journal*, 35 (1992), 531–55.
163. Worden, 'Nedham and Republicanism', p. 77 and Ruth E. Mayers, 'Real and Practicable, not Imaginary and Notional: Sir Henry Vane, *A Healing Question*, and the Problems of the Protectorate', *Albion*, 28 (1986), 37–72.
164. Blair Worden, 'James Harrington and "the Commonwealth of Oceana"', in Wootton (ed.), *Republicanism*, pp. 89–91.
165. James Harrington, *The Commonwealth of Oceana*, ed. J. G. A. Pocock (Cambridge, 1992), p. 8.
166. Ibid., p. 8 for the quoted passages and pp. 1–68 for Harrington's elaboration and explication of his argument.
167. Ibid., p. 53.
168. On this see, esp., the various essays of John Pocock, particularly the introductions to Harrington, *Oceana* and *Works of Harrington* and, for a broad contextualization, *The Machiavellian Moment* (Princeton, 1975), chs 10–12.
169. Oceana, ed. Pocock, pp. 13–14.
170. Ibid., p. 55. Harrington describes the yeomanry as 'middle people'.
171. Ibid., p. 54.
172. Ibid., p. 56.
173. Pocock and Schochet, 'Interregnum and Restoration', p. 168.
174. Worden, 'James Harrington', p. 102; Pocock, 'Introduction' to *Oceana*, pp. xxi–xxiv.
175. Wootton, *Republicanism* surveys this tradition.
176. The best treatment is Hutton, *Restoration*, Parts 1–2.
177. Ibid., p. 47. See also Weber, *Paper Bullets*, pp. 4–5.
178. Reay, *Quakers*, p. 83.
179. Ibid., ch. 5.
180. Hutton, *Restoration*, p. 61.
181. Ibid., pp. 53–61.
182. Ibid., p. 100.
183. For brief treatments see Hume, *English Drama*, pp. 111–15 and Backscheider, *Spectacular Politics*, pp. 23–8.
184. John Tatham, *The Rump; or the Mirrour of the late Times* (1660), p. 46.
185. Ibid., p. 27.
186. Ibid., pp. 66–8.
187. Hutton, *Restoration*, p. 216.

188. Ibid., pp. 125–7.
189. Underdown, *Revel, Riot, Rebellion*, pp. 273–83.
190. Ibid., pp. 271–2.
191. MacLean (ed.) *Stuart Restoration*, p. 4; Weber, *Paper Bullets*, ch. 1; Backscheider, *Spectacular Politics*, ch. 1.
192. Bruce Yardley, 'George Villiers, Second Duke of Buckingham and the Politics of Toleration', *Huntington Library Quarterly*, 55 (1992), 317–38, esp. 323–4.
193. Ronald Hutton, 'The Religion of Charles II' in Smuts (ed.), *Stuart Court*, pp. 228–46.
194. Harris, *London Crowds*, p. 55.
195. A point emphasized in much recent work. See, for example, Paul Seward, *The Cavalier Parliament and the Reconstruction of the Old Regime, 1661–1667* (Cambridge, 1989); Spurr, *Restoration Church*.
196. Harris, *London Crowds*, pp. 70–1; Spurr, pp. 51–61; Greaves, *Radicals and Nonconformists*. John Spurr, 'Religion in Restoration England' in Lionel Glassey (ed.), *The Reigns of Charles II and James VII & II* (1997), pp. 90–124. discusses the ambiguities of the 1660 settlement at the parish level.
197. Spurr, *Restoration Church* pp. 48–9. For a detailed analysis of Samuel Parker's *Discourse of Ecclesiastical Policy* (1669) see Ashcraft, *Revolutionary Politics*, pp. 22–74.
198. Scott, 'England's Troubles' in Smuts (ed.) *Stuart Court*.
199. Zwicker, *Lines of Authority*, pp. 7–8.
200. Steven Shapin, *Leviathan and the air-pump: Hobbes, Boyle and the experimental life* (Princeton, 1984).
201. Lamont, *Baxter and the Millennium*.
202. E.g. Harris, *London Crowds*; Ashcraft, *Locke*; Scott, *Sidney and Restoration Crisis*; Greaves, *Nonconformists*; Knights, *Politics and Opinion*.
203. On the sale of the royal collection see Brown, *Kings and Connoisseurs: Collecting Art in Seventeenth Century Europe* (Princeton and London, 1995), ch. 2.
204. Hutton, *Restoration*, p. 186.
205. Ibid., pp. 146–7. The situation in post-Restoration neighbourhoods has yet to be closely investigated.
206. Smuts, *Court Culture*, ch. 3.
207. On this subject see Michael Hunter, *Science and Society in Restoration England* (Cambridge, 1981).
208. Maguire, *Regicide and Restoration*, pp. 3–28. For Dryden's connections to the Howards, see Winn, *Dryden*, ch. 5.
209. Maguire, pp. 84–7; Frank Kernik, *British Drama, 1660–1779* (New York, 1995), pp. 5–8. The standard survey remains Hume, *English Drama*.
210. Maguire, *Regicide*, pp. 102–4, summarizes recent research on this topic.
211. Andrew Gurr, *The Shakespearean Stage, 1544–1642* (Cambridge, 3rd ed., 1992).
212. Maguire, *Regicide*, p. 127; Winn, *Dryden*, pp. 189–90.
213. O'Neill, *Buckingham*, pp. 62–4; Hume, p. 262.
214. Yardley, 'Buckingham'.
215. Sutherland, *Restoration Newspaper*, pp. 6–12; Sommerville, *News Revolution*, pp. 61–2.

216. Greaves, *Nonconformists*, p. 170; Keeble, *Literary Culture of Nonconformity*, pp. 102–8.
217. Greaves, p. 184; Keeble, p. 108.
218. Ibid., pp. 167–92.
219. Greaves, *passim*; Keeble, pp. 136–44; Cliffe, pp. 109–12 and *passim*.
220. Love, *Scribal Publication*.
221. Ibid., p. 189.
222. Ibid., p. 18.
223. Pincus, 'Coffee houses'.
224. Love, *Scribal Publication*, pp. 210 and 194–5.
225. The reactions of some of these have been ably retold by Christopher Hill, *The Experience of Defeat*. For many radicals, the experience of defeat began in 1649 or 1653 rather than 1660, although the Restoration compounded the humiliation.
226. Blair Worden, 'Milton, Samson Agonistes and the Restoration' in MacClean (ed.), *Stuart Restoration*, pp. 111–36.
227. Greaves, *Nonconformists*, p. 137.
228. Scott, *Sidney and the English Republic*; *Sidney and the Restoration Crisis*.
229. Greaves, *Nonconformists*, is the best survey.
230. Cliffe, *Puritan Gentry Besieged*, pp. 136–41, 170–4.
231. Ibid., pp. 147–50.
232. Keeble, *Literary Culture of Nonconformity*, pp. 140–4.
233. Ibid., p. 22.
234. Ibid., pp. 78–81.
235. Ibid., p. 5.
236. Ibid., pp. 50–4.
237. Ibid., pp. 82–5, 142–53, 211–13.
238. For a systematic discussion of Restoration arguments against concepts of inspiration and spiritually imparted knowledge, and in favour of materialist epistemologies, see Richard W. F. Kroll, *The Material World: Literate Culture in the Restoration and Early Eighteenth Century* (Baltimore, 1991).
239. On this point see, esp. Achinstein, *Milton*.
240. Milton, *Paradise Lost*, Book II, ll. 250–62.
241. See Aschraft, *Locke*, pp. 44–61.
242. Ibid., p. 72.
243. For a recent attempt to sort through the thicket of argument see Gary DeKrey, 'Rethinking the Restoration: Dissenting Cases for Conscience 1667–1672' in *Historical Journal*, 38 (1995), 53–83.
244. 'Astraea Redux' in John Dryden, *Works* (New York, 1961) I, p. 25.
245. See, esp., Pincus, *Protestantism and Patriotism*.
246. Ibid., pp. 198–248.
247. Ibid., pp. 256–65.
248. Ibid., pp. 259–66, 276–88, 302–10. For Dryden, see Annabel Patterson, '"Crouching at home and cruel while abroad": Restoration constructions of national and international character' in Smuts (ed.), *Stuart Court*, esp. pp. 213–16.
249. Ibid.
250. Spurr, *Restoration Church*, pp. 222–3.

251. Nancy Maguire, 'The duchess of Portsmouth: English royal consort and French politician, 1670–85', ibid., pp. 247–73.
252. Ibid., pp. 250–6.
253. Pincus, *Protestantism and Patriotism*, p. 393.
254. Schwoerer, *No Standing Armies!*.
255. An example is discussed in Anne Barbeau Gardiner, 'Swift on the Dutch East India Merchants: The Context of 1672–73 War Literature' in *Huntington Library Quarterly*, 54 (1991), 236.
256. Pincus, *Protestantism*, pp. 351–9 and 'Butterboxes to Wooden Shoes'.
257. J. F. Bosher, 'The Franco-Catholic Danger, 1660–1715' in *Historical Journal*, 37 (1994), 1–28.
258. The fullest and most up-to-date treatment is Knights, *Politics and Opinion*.
259. J. R. Jones, *The First Whigs* (1961).
260. Jones, *First Whigs*; Scott, *Sidney and the Restoration Crisis*, p. 21; Knights, *Politics*, pp. 33–43.
261. Ibid., pp. 110–11.
262. Ibid., pp. 106, 259–91, 314–16.
263. Ibid., p. 157.
264. Ibid., pp. 157, 168–72.
265. Ibid., p. 129. Cf. Tim Harris, 'The Parties and the People: the Press, the Crowd and Politics "Out-of-doors" in Restoration England' in Glassey (ed.), *Charles II and James VII & II* pp. 125–51.
266. Harris, *London Crowds*, p. 101.
267. Sommerville, *News Revolution*, p. 88; Knights, *Politics*, p. 173.
268. Hume, *English Drama*, pp. 223, 336.
269. Harris, *London Crowds*, p. 93.
270. Ibid., pp. 104–6. For College see B. J. Rahn, 'A Ra-ree Show – a Rare Cartoon: Revolutionary Propaganda in the Treason Trial of Stephen College' in Paul Korshin (ed.), *Studies in Change and Revolution* (1972).
271. Ashcraft, *Locke*, p. 167.
272. Harris, *London Crowds*, p. 110.
273. See, in particular, Ashcraft, *Locke*, pp. 195–206.
274. Harris, *London Crowds*, p. 111. Cf. Ashcraft, *Locke*, pp. 195–6.
275. Ibid., p. 139–41.
276. Harris, *London Crowds*, pp. 119–20.

SELECT BIBLIOGRAPHY

What follows is a very partial listing of relevant secondary works; additional references are contained in the notes. Place of publication is London unless otherwise noted

J. S. A. Adamson, 'Chivalry and Political Culture in Caroline England' in Sharpe and Lake (eds), *Culture and Politics*, pp. 161–89
Susan Amussen and Mark Kishlansky (eds), *Political culture and cultural politics in early modern England. Essays presented to David Underdown* (Manchester, 1995)
Christy Anderson, 'Learning to Read Architecture' in Gent (ed.) *Albion's Classicism*
David Armitage, Armand Himy and Quentin Skinner (eds) *Milton and Republicanism* (Cambridge 1995)
Richard Ashcraft, *Revolutionary Politics and Locke's Two Treatises of Government* (Princeton, 1986)
Robert Ashton, *Counter-Revolution: The Second Civil War and its Origins, 1646–8* (New Haven and London, 1994)
Paula Backscheider, *Spectacular Politics: Theatrical Power and Mass Culture in Early Modern England* (Baltimore, 1993)
Reid Barbour, 'The Early Stuart Epicure', *English Literary Renaissance*, 23 (1993) 170–200
Catherine Bates, *The Rhetoric of Courtship* (Cambridge, 1992)
Alastair Bellamy, ' "Raylinge rymes and vaunting verse": libellous politics in early Stuart England, 1603–1628' in Lake and Sharpe (eds), *Culture and Politics*
Michael Brennan, *Literary Patronage in the English Renaissance: the Pembroke Family* (1988)
C. W. Brooks, *Pettyfoggers and Vipers of the Commonwealth* (Cambridge, 1986)
Glenn Burgess, *The Politics of the Ancient Constitution: An Introduction to English Political Thought, 1603–1642* (1992)
—, *Absolute Monarchy and the Stuart Constitution* (New Haven and London, 1996). Important reconsiderations of the role of legal thought in early Stuart political culture.
B. S. Capp, *The English Fifth Monarchy Men: A Study in Seventeenth Century English Millenarianism* (1972)
—, *The World of John Taylor the Water Poet* (Oxford, 1994)
Fritz Caspari, *Humanism and the Social Order in Tudor England* (Chicago, 1954)
Paul Christianson, *Discourse on History, Law and Governance in the Public Career of John Selden, 1610–1635* (Toronto, 1996). Compare to the studies of Glenn Burgess.

—, *Reformers in Babylon* (Toronto, 1978)
Thomas Cogswell, 'Underground verse and the transformation of early Stuart political culture' in Amussen and Kishlansky (eds), *Political Culture*
Patrick Collinson, *The Religion of the Protestants* (1982)
—, *The Birthpangs of Protestant England* (1988)
—, 'Biblical rhetoric: the English nation and national sentiment in the prophetic mode' in McEachern and Shuger (eds), *Religion and Culture*
—, 'Ecclesiastical Vitriol: Religious Satire in the 1590s and the Invention of Puritanism' in John Guy (ed.), *The Reign of Elizabeth I* (Cambridge, 1995), pp. 150–70
David Cressy, *Bonfires and Bells: National Memory and the Protestant Calendar in Elizabethan and Stuart England* (1989)
Pauline Croft, 'Libels, Popular Literacy and Public Opinion in Early Modern England', *Bulletin of the Institute of Historical Research* 68 (1995), 265–285
—, 'The Reputation of Robert Cecil: Libels, Political Opinion and Popular Awareness in the Early Seventeenth Century', *Transactions of the Royal Historical Society*, 6th series, 1 (1991), 43–69
Richard Cust, 'Honour, rhetoric and political culture: the Earl of Huntingdon and his enemies' in Amussen and Kishlansky (eds), *Political Culture*, pp. 84–111
—, 'Honour and Politics in Early Stuart England: the Case of Beaumont v. Hastings', *Past and Present*, 149 (1995), 57–94
Jan van Dorsten, Dominic Baker-Smith and Arthur Kinney (eds), *Sir Philip Sidney: 1586 and the Creation of a Legend* (Leiden, 1986)
Arthur Ferguson, *The Indian Summer of English Chivalry* (Durham, N. C., 1960)
—, *The Articulate Citizen and the English Renaissance* (Durham, N. C., 1965)
Katherine Firth, *The Apocalyptic Tradition in Reformation Britain* (Cambridge, 1979)
Anthony Fletcher, *The Outbreak of the English Civil War* (1981)
— and John Stevenson (eds), *Order and Disorder in Early Modern England* (1985)
Dennis Flynn, 'Donne's *Ignatius His Conclave* and Other Libels on Robert Cecil' in *John Donne Journal*, 6 (1987), 163–83
Alice Friedman, *House and Household in Elizabethan England: Wollaton Hall and the Willoughby Family* (1989)
Jerome Friedman, *Miracles and the Pulp Press During the English Revolution* (1993)
Lucy Gent (ed.), *Albion's Classicism* (New Haven and London, 1995). A useful collection of essays on architecture and the visual arts.
Mark Girouard, *Life in the English Country House: A Social and Architectural History* (New Haven and London, 1978)
S. L. Goldberg, 'Sir John Hyward, "Politic" Historian', *Review of English Studies*, n.s. 6 (1951), pp. 233–44
Richard Greaves, *Enemies under His Feet: Radicals and Nonconformists in Britain, 1664–1677* (Stanford, 1990)
Joan Grundy, *The Spenserian Poets: A Study in Elizabethan and Jacobean Poetry* (1969)
Helen Hackett, *Virgin Mother, Maiden Queen* (1995). A good survey of literary panegyrics to Elizabeth I.
Donna Hamilton and Richard Strier (eds), *Religion, Literature and Politics in Post-Reformation England, 1540–1688* (Cambridge, 1996)

Paul Hammer, 'Myth-Making: Politics, Propaganda and the Capture of Cadiz in 1596', *Historical Jounal*, 40 (1997), 621–42
—, 'The Uses of Scholarship: the Secretariat of Robert Devereux, Second Earl of Essex, c. 1585–1601', *English Historical Review*, 109 (1994), 26–51
Tim Harris, *London Crowds in the Reign of Charles II: Propaganda and politics from the Restoration until the exclusion crisis* (Cambridge, 1987)
—, 'Propaganda and Public Opinion in Seventeenth Century England' in Jeremy Popkin (ed.), *Media and Revolution: Comparative Perspectives* (Lexington, Kentucky, 1995)
Felicity Heal, *Hospitality in Early Modern England* (Oxford, 1990)
Felicity Heal and Clive Holmes, *The Gentry in England and Wales, 1500–1700* (1994). A good survey.
Thomas Healy and Jonathan Sawday (eds), *Literature and the English Civil War* (Cambridge, 1990)
Richard Helgerson, *Self-Crowned Laureates: Spenser, Jonson, Milton and the Literary System* (Berkeley, 1983)
—, *Forms of Nationhood: the Elizabethan Writing of England* (Chicago, 1992)
Caroline Hibbard, *Charles I and the Popish Plot* (Chapel Hill, 1983)
—, The theatre of dynasty' in Smuts (ed.), *Stuart Court*, pp. 156–76
Christopher Hill, *Society and Puritanism in Pre-Revolutionary England* (1964)
—, *Intellectual Origins of the English Revolution*, 2nd ed. (Oxford, 1997)
—, *The World Turned Upside Down* (1972)
—, *The Experience of Defeat* (1984)
—, *The English Bible and the Seventeenth Century* (Harmondsworth, 1993)
Derek Hirst and Steven Zwicker, 'High Summer at Nun Appleton, 1651: Andrew Marvell and Lord Fairfax's Occasions', *Historical Journal*, 36 (1993), 247–69
Dale Hoak (ed.), *Tudor Political Culture* (Cambridge, 1995)
Clive Holmes, 'The County Community in Stuart Historiography', *Journal of British Studies*, 19 (1980), 54–73
T. H. Howard-Hill, *Middleton's 'Vulgar Pasquin'* (Newark, Delaware, 1995)
David Howarth, *Images of Rule: Art and Politics in the English Renaissance, 1485–1649* (1997)
Anne Hughes, *Causes of the English Civil War* (1991)
Robert Hume, *The Development of English Drama in the Late Seventeenth Century* (Oxford, 1976)
Ronald Hutton, *The Restoration: A Political and Religious History of England and Wales 1658–1667* (Oxford, 1985)
—, *The Rise and Fall of Merry England: the Ritual Year 1400–1700* (Oxford, 1994)
Martin Ingram, *The Church Courts, Marriage and Sex in England* (Cambridge, 1987)
Mervyn James, *Society, Politics and Culture: Studies in Early Modern England* (Cambridge, 1986). An important collection of essays, especially 'English Politics and the Concept of Honour, 1485–1642'
Lisa Jardine and Anthony Grafton, 'How Gabriel Harvey read his Livy', *Past and Present*, 129 (1990), 30–78. Important on humanist methods of reading.
Daniel Javitch, *Poetry and Courtliness in Renaissance England* (Princeton, 1978)
N. H. Keeble, *The Literary Culture of Nonconformity in Later Seventeenth Century England* (Leicester, 1987)
Donald Kelly, *The Beginning of Ideology* (Cambridge, 1981)

John King, *Tudor Royal Iconography* (Princeton, 1989)
—, *Spenser's Poetry and the Reformation Tradition* (Princeton, 1990)
Mark Kishlansky, *Parliamentary Selection: Social and Political Choice in Early Modern England* (Cambridge, 1986)
Mark Knights, *Politics and Opinion in Crisis, 1678–81* (Cambridge, 1994). Important.
Peter Lake, *Anglicans and Puritans? Presbyterianism and English Conformist Thought from Whitgift to Hooker* (1988)
—, 'Anti-Popery: the Structure of a Prejudice' in Cust and Hughes (eds), *Conflict in Early Stuart England*, pp. 72–105
—, 'Lancelot Andrewes, John Buckeridge and Avant-garde Conformity at the Court of James I' in Peck (ed.), *Mental World*, pp. 113–33
William Lamont, *Richard Baxter and the Millennium: Protestant Imperialism and the English Revolution* (1979)
Michael Leslie and Timothy Raylor (eds), *Culture and Cultivation in Early Modern England* (Leicester, 1992)
F. J. Levy, *Tudor Historians* (San Marino, 1967)
—, 'How Information Spread Among the Gentry, 1550–1640', *Journal of British Studies*, 21 (1982), 11–34
—, 'Francis Bacon and the Style of Politics' in Arthur Kinney and Dan S. Collins (eds), *Renaissance Historicism: Selections from English Literary Renaissance* (Amherst, 1987), pp. 146–67
—, 'Hayward, Daniel and the Beginnings of Politic History in England', *Huntingdon Library Quarterly*, 50 (1987), 1–34
Harold Love, *Scribal Publication in England* (Oxford, 1993). An important study of manuscript culture.
Anthony Lowe, *The Georgic Revolution* (Princeton, 1985)
Wallace MacCaffrey, *Elizabeth I: War and Politics, 1588–1603* (Princeton, 1992)
Richard McCoy, *Sir Philip Sidney. Rebellion in Arcadia* (New Brunswick, 1979)
—, *The Rites of Knighthood. The Literature and Politics of Elizabethan Chivalry* (Berkeley, 1989)
—, 'Old English honour in an evil time: aristocratic principle in the 1620s' in Smuts (ed.) *Stuart Court and Europe*
Claire McEachern and Deborah Shuger (eds), *Religion and Culture in Renaissance England* (Cambridge, 1997)
Gerald MacLean, *Time's Witness: Historical Representation in English Poetry, 1603–1660* (Madison, 1990)
—, (ed.), *Culture and Society in the Stuart Restoration: Literature, Drama, History* (Cambridge, 1995)
Andrew MacRae, *God Speed the Plow* (Cambridge, 1996)
Nancy Maguire, *Regicide and Restoration: English Tragicomedy, 1660–1671* (Cambridge, 1992)
—, 'The Theatrical Mask/Masque of Politics: the Case of Charles I', *Journal of British Studies*, 28 (1989), 1–22
Lawrence Manley, *Literature and Culture in Early Modern London* (Cambridge, 1995)
Leah Marcus, *The Politics of Mirth: Jonson, Herrick, Milton, Marvell and the Defense of Old Holiday Pastimes* (Chicago, 1986)

Select Bibliography

Arthur Marotti, *John Donne, Coterie Poet* (Madison, 1986)
—, *Manuscript, Print and the Renaissance Lyric* (Ithaca and London, 1995)
Steven May, *Elizabethan Courtier Poets: the Poems in their Contexts* (Columbia, Missouri, 1991)
Michael Mendle, *Henry Parker and the English Civil War* (Cambridge, 1995)
Anthony Milton, *Catholic and Reformed: The Roman and Protestant Churches in English Protestant Thought, 1600–1640* (Cambridge, 1993)
Earl Miner, *The Cavalier Mode from Jonson to Cotton* (Princeton, 1971)
J. S. Morrill, *The Nature of the English Revolution* (1993). An important collection of essays.
David Norbrook, *Poetry and Politics* (1984)
Rosemary O'Day, *Education and Society: 1500–1800: the Social Foundations of Education in Early Modern Britain* (1982). Good concise synthesis.
Per Palme, *The Triumph of Peace: A Study of the Whitehall Banqueting House* (Oslo, 1956). Still the most broadly focused treatment of this important building.
Lisa Ferraro Parmelee, *Good Newes from Fraunce: French Anti-League Propaganda in Late Elizabethan England* (Rochester, 1996)
—, 'Printers, Patrons, Readers and Spies: Importation of French Propaganda in Late Elizabethan England', *Sixteenth Century Journal*, 25 (1994)
Graham Parry, *Seventeenth Century Poetry: the Social Context* (1985)
—, *The Trophies of Time: English Antiquarians of the Seventeenth Century* (Oxford, 1995)
Annabel Patterson, *Censorship and Interpretation: The Conditions of Writing and Reading in Early Modern England* (Madison, 1984)
—, *Reading Between the Lines* (Madison, 1993)
—, *Reading Holinshed's Chronicles* (Chicago, 1994)
—, 'Sir John Oldcastle as symbol of Reformation historiography' in Hamilton, (ed.), *Religion, Literature and Politics in Post-Reformation England, 1540–1688* (Cambridge, 1996)
John Peacock, 'The Stuart Court Masque and the Theatre of the Greeks', *Journal of the Warburg and Courtauld Institute*, 56 (1993), 183–208
Linda Peck, *Court Patronage and Corruption in Early Stuart England* (Boston and London, 1990). Includes a discussion of cultural discourses on patronage and corruption.
—, (ed.), *The Mental World of the Jacobean Court* (Cambridge, 1991)
Makku Peltonen, *Classical humanism and republicanism in English political thought 1570–1640* (Cambridge, 1995). An important reconsideration of its topic.
Richard Peterson, *Imitation and Praise in the Poems of Ben Jonson* (New Haven and London, 1981)
Steven Pincus, *Protestantism and Patriotism: Ideologies and the making of English foreign policy, 1650–1668* (Cambridge, 1996)
—, '"Coffee Politicians Does Create": Coffeehouses and Restoration Political Culture', *Journal of Modern History*, 67 (1995), 807–34
Colin Platt, *The Great Rebuildings of Tudor and Stuart England* (London, 1994)
J. G. A. Pocock, *The Ancient Constitution and the Feudal Law: A Study of English Historical Thought in the Seventeenth Century. A Reissue with a Retrospect* (Cambridge, 1987). A classic discussion of common law thought.
—, (ed.), *The Political Works of James Harrington* (Cambridge, 1977). Includes an important introductory essay.

Lois Potter, *Secret Rites and Secret Writings: Royalist Literature, 1641–1660* (Cambridge, 1989)
Barry Reay, *The Quakers and the English Revolution* (1985)
David Riggs, *Ben Jonson: a Life* (Cambridge, Massachusetts, 1989)
James Robertson, 'Caroline Culture: Bridging Court and Country?', *History*, 75 (1990), 388–416
Maren Sophie Røstvig, *The Happy Man*, 2 vols (Oslo and Oxford, 1954)
Conrad Russell, *Causes of the English Civil War* (Oxford, 1991)
—, *The Fall of the British Monarchies, 1637–1642* (Oxford, 1991).
David Sacks, 'Bristol's Little Business 1625–1641', *Past and Present* 110 (1996) 69–105
J. H. M. Salmon, 'Seneca and Tacitus in Jacobean England' in Peck (ed.) *Mental World*, pp. 169–90
J. W. Sanders, 'The Stigma of Print. A Note on the Social Bases of Tudor Poetry', *Essays in Criticism*, 1 (1951). A much debated pioneering essay.
Gordon Schochet, *Patriarchalism in Political Thought* (New York, 1975)
Jonathan Scott, *Algernon Sidney and the English Republic: 1623–1677* (Cambridge, 1988)
—, *Algernon Sidney and the Restoration Crisis, 1677–1683* (Cambridge, 1991)
Lois Schwoerer, *No Standing Armies!: the Antiarmy Ideology in Seventeenth Century England* (Baltimore, 1974)
Ethan Howard Shagan, 'Constructing Discord: Ideology, Propaganda and English Responses to the Irish Rebellion of 1641', *Journal of British Studies*, 36 (1997), 4–34
Kevin Sharpe, *Criticism and Compliment: the Politics of Literature in the England of Charles I* (Cambridge, 1987), a revisionist study of court culture.
—, *The Personal Rule of Charles I* (New Haven and London, 1992)
Kevin Sharpe and Peter Lake (eds), *Culture and Politics in Early Stuart England* (1993). A good introduction to its topic.
Kevin Sharpe and Steven Zwicker (eds), *The Politics of Discourse* (Berkeley, 1987)
Deborah Shuger, *Habits of Thought in the English Renaissance: Religion, Politics and the Dominant Culture* (Berkeley, 1990). An intelligent study of Elizabethan and Jacobean religious thought.
Quentin Skinner, *The Foundations of Modern Political Thought*, 2 vols (Cambridge, 1978)
Charles Kay Smith, 'French Philosophy and English politics in interregnum poetry' in Smuts (ed.), *Stuart Court*
David Smith, *Constitutional Royalism and the Search for Settlement, c. 1640–49* (Cambridge, 1994)
Nigel Smith, *Literature and the English Civil War* (Cambridge, 1990)
R. Malcolm Smuts, *Court Culture and the Origins of a Royalist Tradition in Early Stuart England* (Philadelphia, 1987)
—, (ed.), *The Stuart Court and Europe: Essays in Politics and Political Culture* (Cambridge, 1996)
—, 'Public ceremony and royal charisma: the English royal entry in London, 1495–1642' in A. L. Beier, David Cannadine and James M. Rosenheim (eds), *The First Modern Society: Essays in English History in Honour of Lawrence Stone* (Cambridge, 1989), pp. 65–94

—, 'The Court and its Neighborhood: Royal Policy and Urban Growth in the Early Stuart West End', *Journal of British Studies*, 30 (1991), 117–49
C. John Sommerville, *The News Revolution in England: Cultural Dynamics of Daily Information* (Oxford, 1996)
Johann Sommerville, *Politics and Ideology in England 1603–1640* (1986)
—, 'The ancient constitution reassessed: the common law, the court and the languages of politics in early modern England' in Smuts (ed.), *Stuart Court and Europe*. Disagrees with Glenn Burgess and J. G. A. Pocock
Judith Dovlin Spikes, 'The Jacobean History Play and the Elect Nation', *Renaissance Drama*, 3 (1977), pp. 117–49
John Spurr, *The Restoration Church of England, 1646–1689* (New Haven and London, 1991)
David Starkey et al., *The English Court from the Wars of the Roses to the Civil War* (1987). A significant collection of essays
—, 'England' in Roy Porter and Milaus Teich (eds), *The Renaissance in National Context* (Cambridge, 1992)
Lawrence Stone, *The Crisis of the Aristocracy, 1558–1641* (Oxford, 1965)
—, 'The Educational Revolution, 1540–1640', *Past and Present*, 28 (1964), 41–80.
John Stoye, *English Travellers Abroad, 1604–1667* 2nd ed. (New Haven and London, 1989)
Roy Strong, *Charles I on Horseback* (1972)
—, *The Cult of Elizabeth: Elizabethan Portraiture and Pageantry* (1977). A collection of pioneering essays.
James Sutherland, *The Restoration Newspaper and its Development* (Cambridge, 1986)
Joan Thirsk, 'Making a Fresh Start: Sixteenth-Century Agriculture and the Classical Inspiration' in Leslie and Raylor (eds) *Cultivation in Early Modern England*
P. W. Thomas, *Sir John Berkenhead* (Oxford, 1969)
Simon Thurley, *The Royal Palaces of Tudor England: Architecture and Court Life, 1460–1547* (New Haven and London, 1993)
E. M. Tillyard, *The Elizabethan World Picture* (1943)
Robert Tittler, *The Reformation and the Towns in England c. 1540–1640: Politics and Political Culture*, (Oxford, 1998)
Margo Todd, *Christian Humanism and the Puritan Social Order* (Cambridge, 1987). Especially good on university education.
Richard Tuck, *Philosophy and Government 1572–1651* (Cambridge, 1995). Sets British political thought within a European context.
David Underdown, *Revel, Riot, Rebellion: Popular Politics and Culture in England 1603–1660* (Oxford, 1985). An ambitious and important, if controversial book.
—, *Fire from Heaven: Life in an English Town in the Seventeenth Century* (New Haven and London, 1992)
Tessa Watt, *Cheap Print and Popular Piety, 1550–1640* (Cambridge, 1991)
Harold Weber, *Paper Bullets: Print and Kingship under Charles II* (Lexington, Kentucky, 1996)
Paul Whitfield White, *Theatre and Reformation: Protestantism, Patronage and Playing in Tudor England* (Cambridge, 1993)
Michael Wilding, *Dragons' Teeth: Literature in the English Revolution* (Oxford, 1987)

James Anderson Winn, *John Dryden and his World* (New Haven, 1987)
David Wootton (ed.), *Republicanism, Liberty and Commercial Society, 1649–1776* (Stanford, 1994)
—, 'Leveller democracy and the Puritan Revolution' in J. H. Burns (ed.), *Cambridge History of Political Thought, 1450–1700* (Cambridge, 1995)
Blair Worden, *The Sound of Virtue: Philip Sidney's Arcadia and Elizabethan Politics* (New Haven and London, 1997)
—, 'Providence and Politics in Cromwellian England', *Past and Present*, 109 (1985), 55–99
—, 'English Republicanism' in J. H. Burns (ed.), *The Cambridge History of Political Thought, 1450–1700* (Cambridge, 1991), pp. 443–75
—, 'Oliver Cromwell and the Sin of Achan' in Derek Beales and Geoffrey Best (eds), *History, Society and the Churches* (Cambridge, 1985), pp. 125–46
H. R. Woudhuysen, *Sir Philip Sidney and the Circulation of Manuscripts* (Oxford, 1996)
Keith Wrightson, *English Society, 1580–1680* (1982)
Frances Yates, *Astraea: the Imperial Theme in the Sixteenth Century* (1975). A collection of classic essays on Elizabethan and sixteenth-century European court culture.
Perez Zagorin, 'The Court and the Country: a note on political terminology in the earlier seventeenth century', *English Historical Review*, 77 (1962), 306–11
Steven Zwicker, *Lines of Authority: Politics and English Literary Culture, 1646–1689* (Ithaca, 1993).

INDEX

Numbers in bold type indicate illustrations

Abbot, George, Archbishop of
    Canterbury, 48
Acuna, Don Diego Sarmiento de (Count
    of Gondomar), 48, **49**, 77
agricultural improvement, 92
agricultural manuals, 93
Andrewes, Lancelot, 45
Anjou match, 58, 77
antiquarianism, 20–1, 23–4, 26, 47
architecture
    domestic, 93–5
    Elizabethan, 95
    European influences on, 90
    fosters social separation and
        exclusivity, 54, 94
    in London, 140
Aristotle, 29, 129
armies, in the Civil War, 101
    The New Model Army, 124, 134
    unpopularity of, 135
Army Plot (1641), 116
art collecting, 90–2
    gentry attitudes toward, 92
Arundel, Earl of, *see* Howard, Thomas
Ascham, Roger, 39
astrology, 124

Bacon, Anthony, 13, 37
Bacon, Francis, 13, 22, 23, 24, 26, 82, 132
    educational ideas of, 35, 37
    mistrusts peace, 86
    philosophical views of, 30
    sees libels as threat to the state, 80
    warns Essex to beware of Elizabeth's
        jealousy, 72–3
Bagg, James, 26
Bale, John, 31

ballads
    anti-puritan, 137
    as Protestant propaganda, 43, 44
    relating to Elizabeth I, 56, 58
    satirizing the court, 87
Bancroft, Richard, 46, 111
Baxter, Richard, 123, 139, 145
Bedford, Earl of, *see* Russell
Berkenhead, John, 118
Botero, Giovanni, 38
Boyle, Roger, Earl of Orrery, 141
Brathwaite, George, 94
Buchanan, George, 127
Buckingham, Dukes of, *see* Villiers
Bunyan, John, 146
Burghley, Lord, *see* Cecil, William
Burgess, Glenn, 18–19, 21
Butler, Samuel, 138
Byrd, William, 57

Cade's rebellion, 74, 109, 111
Caesar, Julius, 67, 68, 125
Calvinism, 65, 106
Camden, William, 33, 34, 47, 66
Carew, Thomas, 86, 118
    Coelum Britannicum, 82
Carleton, Dudley, 37, 91
Carr, Robert, Earl of Somerset, 82, 91
Casaubon, Isaac, 37
Castiglione, 39, 81–2
Castlemaine, Barbara, 149
Catherine de Medici, Queen Mother of
    France, 44, 77
Catholicism
    alleged plots of, 109, 150–1, 152
    and atrocities, 43, 153
    and the Civil War, 103, 108
    depicted as clerical conspiracy, 43
    infiltration of court by, 48, 77, 108–9, 150
    political propaganda of, 66–7

Catholicism (*continued*)
  and rebellion, 66
  and the throne, 151–4
Catullus, 118
Caus, Saloman de, 91
Cavalier
  image 113–17, **114**
  sentiment, after 1660, 136–9
Cavalier Parliament (1661–78), 138
Cavalier verse, 118–19
Cavendish, Margaret, Duchess of Newcastle, 122
Cecil, Robert, first Earl of Salisbury, 25, 59, 91
  expenditures of, at court, 88
  reputation of, 10
  satires and attacks on, 80, 81, 82
Cecil, William, Lord Burghley, 36, 37, 44, 45, 59
Cecil, William, Lord Cranbourne and second Earl of Salisbury, 91
censorship
  after the Restoration, 143
  collapses, 1642, 107
  expires, 1679, 151
Chapman, George
  Bussy d'Ambois, 15, 68
  Tragedy of Byron, 68
Charles I, 2, 15, 48
  his *Answer to the Nineteen Propositions*, 111
  and *Eikon Basilike*, 123
  and English law, 17
  panegyrics of, 119
  Scottish journey of (1641), 106
  treated as a religious symbol, 55
Charles II, 123, 124
  coronation entry of, 54, 136
  decline in prestige of, after 1660, 148–50
  improves St James's Park, 140
  mistresses of, 141, 149
  restoration of, 136
  and the Restoration theatre, 141
Chaucer, Geoffrey, 43
chivalry, 8, 11, 13–15, 72; *see also* honour
Cheke, John, 37
Cicero, 35, 40, 129
civic culture and ritual, 53
Civil War, the
  constitutional issues in, 101, 117, 125, 126
  divisions leading to, 102–6
  historiography of, 99–102
  impact of, upon culture, 99
classicism, 95–8
Cleveland, John, 113
coffee houses, 133, 139, 144
Coke, Sir Edward, 19, 20, 21, 22–3, 24, 26
Coleman, Edward, 151
College, Stephen, 152
Collinson, Patrick, 31, 44, 48
Columella, 92
common law mind, the, 7, 17–27
  antiquarianism and, 20–1, 23–4
  Charles I and, 17, 20
  consistency of, 19–20
  constitutional theories and, 17, 18, 20
  custom and the, 17, 18, 20, 21, 24, 26
  dissemination of, 19
  historical obscurantism of, 18
  insularity of, 17, 20
  royal prerogatives and, 24, 26
  scholarly methods and tools of, 23–4, 26
  see also law *and names of individual jurists*
Commonwealth, the (1649–53), 123, 124
Cooper, Anthony Ashley, Earl of Shaftesbury, 150, 151, 153
Cornwallis, Sir William, 13, 86
Cosin, John, 46
costume, and displays of rank, 11, 52
Cottington, Francis, 48
Cotton, Sir Robert, 11, 23, 69, 91
country, cultural concepts of the, 79–98 *passim*
  among the gentry, 84–5
  morally purer than the court, 82–4
  peace within, 85–6
  royalist depictions of, 122
country house poetry, 97–8
court, the, 2
  cultural patronage of, 140–2
  cultural representations of, 79, 80–2, 85, 108
  disarray within, in 1679–80, 151
  escapes royal control, 88
  expenditure at, 88
  intellectual culture of, 36–7
  of Oliver Cromwell, 139
  relationship of, to country, 79–80
  relationship of, to London, 140–2
  revived, at Restoration, 140
  service at, 12
Coventry, Sir William, 142

Index

Cowley, Abraham, 113, 118, 120, 122, 139
Crashaw, Richard, 118
Cromwell, Oliver, 123, 124, 131
   depicted as Machiavellian hero, 125
   hanged in effigy, 135
   religious demonstrations by, 130
Cromwell, Richard, 133, 134
Cuffe, Henry, 13, 68
Culpepper, Sir John, 117
culture, definitions of, 2, 3
custom, *see* common law mind
Cust, Richard, 17

Dallington, Robert, 91
Danby, Earl of, *see* Osborne
Daniel, Samuel, 20, 22, 63, 65, 71, 86
   Philotas, 61, 68
Davenant, Sir William, 121, 122, 139, 141, 142
Davies, Sir William, 24
Declaration of Breda (1660), 136
Declaration of Indulgence (1672), 138, 147
Dekker, Thomas, 44
Devereux, Robert, second Earl of Essex, 12, 36, 37, 69, 74, 96
   inherits Sir Philip Sidney's legacy, 63
   intellectual outlook of, 13, 72–3
   poetry of, 57–8, 59, 83
   publicity concerning, 61
   rebellion and execution of, 61
   reputation of, 68
Devereux, Robert, third Earl of Essex, 69
D'Ewes, Sir Simonds, 23, 33
dissenters (in Restoration religion), 143, 144–7
   and anti-popery, 153
Donne, John, 58, 118
   depicts the court, 81
   Ignatius his Conclave, 77
   'Metempsychosis', 81
Drake, Sir Francis, 15
drama, *see* plays, history plays, theatres *and individual playwrights*
Drayton, Michael, 63, 65, 87, 97
   The Owle, 82
Drury, Sir William, 13, **14**
Dryden, John, 92, 142, 151
   Absalom and Achitophel, 153
   Annus Mirabilis, 148
Du Bartas, *see* Saluste, Guillaume de

Dudley, Robert, first Earl of Leicester, 36, 63, 74
   reputation of, 10, 66–7
duels, 8, 11, 13–15, 120
Dugdale, William, 47
Dyck, Anthony Van, 86
Dyer, Edmund, 58

Edward II, 67, 70
Edward VI, 43
Edwards, Thomas, 111, 128
Egerton, Thomas, Baron Ellesmere, 21, 22, 23, 24, 26
   denounces libellers, 80
Eikon Basilike, 65, 120, 121, 123
Eliot, Sir John, 78
Elizabeth I, 2, 21, 36, 43
   criticized for insufficient vigilance against popery, 45
   dislikes printed publicity concerning Essex, 61
   images of, 42
   public behaviour of, 53–4
   the succession to, 42
Elizabethan cult, 50–61
   Accession Day celebrations and jousts, 50–1, 53, 96
   classical influences on, 50, 60
   early historiography concerning, 50–1
   literary dimensions of, 55–61
   love poetry and, 57
   material paraphernalia of, 52
   and posthumous elegies, 63
   religious dimensions of, 54–5
   and royal progresses, 52, 53
   the virginity topos in, 58
Elizabethan nostalgia, 65, 95
Elizabethan world picture, 4, 5
Epicureanism, 82, 96, 122
Erasmus, Desiderius, 35
Essex, Earls of, *see* Devereux

Fairfax, Sir Thomas, 124, 126, 142
Fanshawe, Thomas, 118
favourites, at court, 69–70
Fifth Monarchists, 123, 131, 136, 138
Foxe, John, 31, 109, 110, 146
Frobisher, Martin, 15

gardens, 91, 92, 94, 154
   in royalist literature, 122
Gassendi, Pierre, 122

Gauden, John, 123
Gentillet, Alberico, *Anti-Machiavell*, 77
Gondomar, *see* Acuna, Don Diego Sarmiento de
Gorges, Arthur, 57
grand tour, *see* travel abroad
Grand Remonstrance (1641), 109
Green Ribbon Club, 152, 153
Greene, Robert
  Friar Bacon and Friar Bungay, 85–6
Greville, Fulke, Lord Brooke, 10, 22, 58
Guise family and faction, 66, 67, 77
Guise, Henry Duke of, 44, 68, 77
Gunpowder Plot (1605), 42

halcyon reign (of Charles I), 86
Harington, John, 36, 40, 72
Harrington, James, 128
  and the Rota Club, 133
  Oceana, 131–3
Hartlib, Samuel, 93
Harvey, Gabriel, 37
Haselrig, Arthur, 134
Hatton, Sir Christopher, 74
Hay, James, Earl of Carlisle, 89
Hayward, John, 22, 69, 76
Helgerson, Richard, 20, 23, 74
Henrietta Maria, Queen of Charles I, 82, 103, 109
  poetic tributes to, 119
Henry, Prince of Wales, eldest son of James I, 63–5, 91
Henry III, King of France, 43
Henry IV, King of France (Henry of Navarre), 45
Henry VIII, 43
Herbert, Edward Lord of Cherbury, 11, 84–5
Herrick, Thomas, 117, 118
Hesiod, 92
Heylyn, Peter, 118, 128
Hibbard, Caroline, 15, 103
Hill, Christopher, 100
historical narratives, 70–2, 132–3
history plays, 15–16, 20
  decline of, 76
  as religious propaganda, 44, 47
  see also under individual authors and titles
Hobbes, Thomas, 30, 138
  attacks religious enthusiasm, 120–1
  blames universities for republicanism, 127

Leviathan, 126
  preface to Thucydides, *History of the Peloponnesian War*, 128
Holinshed, Gabriel, 27, 70
Holland, Earl of, *see* Rich
Holles, John, first Earl of Clare, 90
Holmes, Clive, 84
honour, 8–17
  and Civil War royalism, 116, 120
  in Elizabethan drama, 15–16
  fosters competition, 11
  and humanism, 10, 12–15
  as a language of resistance, 12
  and lineage, 8–11, 75
  purported degeneration of, after 1603, 65
  and republicanism, 129
  and violence, 11, 13
  see also chivalry, duels
Hooker, Richard, 21–2, 45, 46, 70, 147
Horace, 60, 81, 96, 118
houses, of peers and gentry, 8, **9**, 11
  seventeenth-century evolution of, 93–4
hospitality, 11, 85, 89, 94–5, 98
Hotham, Sir John, **115**
Howard, Frances, Countess of Somerset, 82
Howard, Henry, Earl of Northampton, 10, 13, 25, 48
Howard, Robert, 142
Howard, Thomas, Earl of Arundel, 11, 77, 91, 96
humanism, 32–40
  and applications of knowledge, 35–6
  at court, 36–7, 39–40, 80
  education in, 32, 33–6
  and honour values, 10, 12–15
  and intelligence gathering, 37–8
  and legal scholarship, 20
  and moral instruction, 35
  and political careers, 2, 37–40
  relationship of, to medieval culture, 32–3
  and royal cults, 60
  stimulates interest in court documents, 59–60
  Tudor development of, 32–3
  in universities, 34–6
  varieties of, 39
Hyde, Edward, Earl of Clarendon, 103, 117, 149
  History of the Great Rebellion, 120

Inns of Court, 19, 21, 26, 60
Ireland, 24–5, 37
   rebellion of, in 1642, 106, 109

James I, 2, 37
   attitude of, towards superstitious ritual, 55
   compared to biblical figures, 55
   compares puritans to Jesuits, 48
   coronation entry of, 11, 52–3
   criticized for relations with Spain, 48
   and English law, 25
   publishes poetry, 56–7
James, Duke of York (James II), 141, 151
   Catholicism of, 150, 153
Jones, Inigo, 34, 91
   classicism of, 95–6
Jonson, Ben, 21, 33, 34, 60, 63, 83, 118
   classicism of, 95–7
   as court poet, 57, 81–2
   criticizes Henry VIII's break with Rome, 47
   'To Penshurst', 65, 97
   Bartholomew Fair, 135
   Sejanus, 73
Junius, Francis, 91
Juvenal, 60, 80, 81

Keroualle, Louise de, Duchess of Portsmouth, 149
Killigrew, Thomas, 141
Kynaston, Sir Francis, 90

Lake, Thomas, 91
Lambert, John, 135
Laud, William, 46, 109
law, 13, 17–27
   and the ancient constitution, 17, 20
   and Celtic regions, 24
   and Civil War royalism, 117–18, 123
   demands for reforms of, 22–4, 134
   historical views of, 17–18, 20
   as language of consensus, 18, 21, 24
   and liberty, 25–6
   and litigation, 22, 27
   research on, 23
   and royal authority, 24–5, 26–7
   in society, 26–7
   as source of stability, 21
   training in the, 19, 21
   unitary nature of, 25
   see also common law mind
Law French, 22

lawyers, reputations of, 21–2
Lee, Nathaniel, 152
Leicester's Commonwealth (pamphlet), 10, 66–7
Leicester, Earls of, *see* Dudley (first); Sidney (second)
L'Estrange, Roger, 139, 143, 151
Leveller movement, 123, 126, 128, 131
   see also Lillburne, John
libels, 80, 142
   Restoration manuscript, 143–4
   see also satire
Lillburne, John, 118
Lilly, William, 124
Lipsius, Justus, 38
Locke, John, 29, 153
Lollardy, 47
London
   artistic sophistication in, 91
   a centre for printed controversy, 108
   Charles II welcomed to (1660), 136
   Covent Garden, 30, 89, 90, 140
   culture in, 15
   the 'exclusion crisis' in (1679–82), 152
   fire of (1666), 148–9
   gentry resort to, 79, 84, 86, 89
   greets Elizabeth (1585), 52
   Lord Mayor's Pageants in, 53, 136, 152
   migration to, 104
   Plague in (1665), 148
   recovers from Civil War, 139
   regulation of buildings in, 30, 88
   religious radicalism in, 111
   royal hostility toward, 88
   St James's Square, 140
   turbulence in, before Restoration, 134, 135
   West End of, 140
Long Parliament, the, 107, 109, 123
   petitions to, 109–10
   printed attacks on, 108
Louis XIV, King of France, 149, 150, 151
Lovelace, Richard, 82, 117, 118
Lyly, John, 46

Machiavelli, 127
   and Interregnum republicanism, 125, 129
   cultural representations of, 77
   The Prince, 71
   Discourses on Livy, 129
Magna Carta, 26

malcontents (representations of), 67–9
manuscript texts, 62, 107
   and the Civil War, 102
   contrasted with print, 56, 57
   and libels, 82, 143–4
Markham, Gervase, 93
Marlowe, Christopher, 2, 15–16, 34, 70
   Edward II, 15, 69
   The Jew of Malta, 77
   Massacre at Paris, 43, 44, 68
Martial, 60, 80, 96
Martin Marprelate, 45, 46, 47, 60, 113
Marvell, Andrew, 122, 131, 150
   'An Horatian Ode on Oliver
      Cromwell's Return from Ireland',
      124–6
   'Upon Appleton House', 126
   *The Growth of Popery and Arbitrary
      Government*, 152
Marxist historiography, 4, 5, 100, 103
Mary Stuart, Queen of Scotland, 42, 44
masques (at court), 53, 55, 60, 78
   images of peace in, 86
   as tools of evil favourites, 69
   Salmacida Spolia (1640), 120
material culture, 52, 90
May festivities, 98, 105
May, Thomas, 77, 128
Mayerne, Theodore, 91
Mead, Joseph, 34
Middleton, Thomas, 34
   A Game at Chess, 48, 77
Mildmay, Sir Walter, 74
Milton, John, 44, 55, 92, 131
   anti-episcopal pamphlets of, 110
   republicanism of, 127, 129
   Areopagitica, 110, 147
   Eikonoklastes, 123
   Paradise Lost, 119, 146–7
   Samson Agonistes, 145
Monck, George, 134, 135
Montagu, Richard, 46
Montagu, Walter, 109
Moseley, Henry, 118
Moulin, Pierre de, 150

Nashe, Thomas, 60
natural philosophy, 30, 92, 138
   and agriculture, 92
   at the Restoration, 141
Nedham, Marchamont, 124, 125, 148
   career summarized, 129
   Machiavellianism of, 129
   republicanism of, 127, 128
   The Excellency of a Free State, 131
Neville, Henry, 153
newsbooks, 102, 107
   disseminate information about sects,
      111
   in the 'exclusion crisis' (1679–82), 151
   parliamentarian, 129
   royalist, 118
New Criticism, 1
New Model Army, *see* armies
Newton, Isaac, 29
Norman Conquest, 25
North, Dudley Lord, 120
Northampton, Earl of, *see* Howard,
   Henry
Northern Rebellion (1569), 43

Oates, Titus, 150
Osborne, Thomas, Earl of Danby, 150,
   151
Overbury, Thomas, 82
Ovid, 60, 118
Oxford (city), royalist presses in, 108,
   117, 118
Oxford, Earl of, *see* Vere, Edward

paintings, 11, **9**, **14**
   discussed, 13
Parker, Henry, 117, 128
parliamentary speeches printed, 107
party and faction
   at court, 62, 80, 142
   perceptions and representations of,
      by contemporaries, 42, 47, 65–7,
      74, 78
   Whig and Tory, 151, 153–4
peace, as a cultural theme, 85–7
Peacham, Henry, 91
Peter, Hugh, 144
Petrarchanism, 57–9
Plato, 29, 36
plays, as Protestant propaganda, 43, 44
Pocock, J. G. A., 5
   concept of common law mind, 17–18,
      19, 20
poetry
   amateur vs. 'professional', 56
   and the Elizabethan cult, 55–61
   by James I, 56
   printed versus manuscript circulation
      of, 56–7
pope burning processions, 152, 153

popery, *see* Catholicism
popular culture (concept), 105
population growth and cultural change, 104–5
Portsmouth, Duchess of, *see* Keroualle, Louise de
presbyterians, 137, 138
Preston, John, 34
Pride's Purge, 123
print culture
　almanacs, 124
　anti-puritan, 137
　in the Civil War, 106–9
　and the dissemination of rumour, 108–9
　in the 'exclusion crisis' (1679–82), 151
　and oral culture, 108
　and panegyrics of Elizabeth, 56
　and religious dissent, 145
　and the Restoration, 134–5, 136, 143
　see also newsbooks
Privy Chamber (at court), 54
prophecies, 124
progresses, by royalty, 52, 53
Protestant Reformation, 42
　views of, 47, 50
Protestantism
　breaks with cultural tradition, 42
　cultural propaganda for, 42–5
　see also puritanism, religious ideas and culture
prudential thought, 38–9
public sphere (concept), 56, 62
puritanism, 85
　aids the Earl of Leicester, 67
　and attacks on bishops, 45
　caricatures and criticisms of, 45–7, 108, 111–13, **112**, 138
　as cause of the Civil War, 101, 106
　and court ceremony, 55
　enthusiasm, criticized, 120–1
　historiographical interpretations of, 7, 100
　and radical sects, 110–11
　reactions against, after Restoration, 137
　relationship of, to republicanism, 46, 128, 129–30
　as religion of social discipline, 104–5
　in Restoration literature, 145, 146–7
　see also Dissenters, Martin Marprelate, religious ideas and culture, roots and branches agitation

Puttenham, George, 55
Pym, John, 109, 111

Quakers, 134–5, 145
　response to persecution, 146
　riots against, 136

Ralegh, Sir Walter, 12, 55, 96
　literary remains of, 61
　poems to Elizabeth of, 57
　posthumous popularity of, 65
　reason of state, 38, 70, 77
Reformation, *see* Protestant Reformation
regicide, the, 123
　trials and executions resulting from, after 1660, 136, 144
religious ideas and culture
　in the Civil War, 101, 107–8
　concepts of order, 27–31
　the divine right and sanctity of kings, 31, 54–5, 75
　eschatological, 31–2, 110, 123–6
　national election, 44, 110
　and natural philosophy 29–31
　and political radicalism, 128, 129–30
　predicts allegiance in Civil War, 103
　providence, 27–32
　redefined, after the Reformation, 43–5
　sectarian radicalism, 110–11
　social influences on, 103–6
　verse, 119
　see also Catholicism, puritanism, Reformation
republicanism, 72
　apocalyptic varieties of, 130
　Civil War, 127, 128–33
　in early Stuart period, 127
　in *Paradise Lost*, 146–7
Restoration, the
　character of, 136
　origins of, 133–7
revisionism, in historical studies, 1, 19, 99–103, 155
Rich, Henry, Earl of Holland, 15, 118
Richard III, 66
Rochester, Earl of, *see* Wilmot, John
Roe, Thomas, 83, 91
Roman history, as source of cultural paradigms, 71–2, 86
　and Oliver Cromwell, 125
　and military tactics, 12
　see also Tacitus

roots and branches agitation (1641–2), 109
Roundhead (stereotype), 113
Royal Society, 140–1
royalism, 100, 102
 and Anglicanism, 137–9
 antagonistic towards towns, 113
 caricatured, 113–16, **114**
 and defences of social hierarchy, 119–20
 demoralization of, in 1659, 134
 Epicureanism and, 121–2
 hostility of, toward puritans and sectaries, 111–13, 119, 120–1
 identified with honour, 116, 119
 and the law, 117–18, 123
 poetic expressions of, 118–19
 printed propaganda of, 117–20
 reaction to King's execution of, 123
 and the Restoration, 137–9
 romance traditions in, 121–2
 and sensuality, 119
 social values of, 119–20
 varieties of, 117
Rubens, Peter Paul, 86, 88
Rump parliament, 134, 135
Russell, Conrad, 101, 102
Russell, Francis, fourth Earl of Bedford, 36

St Bartholomew's Day Massacre (1572), 43
Salisbury, Earl of, see Cecil, Robert
Saluste, Guillaume de, Sieur du Bartas, 92
Savile, Henry, 13, 37, 76
 translations of Tacitus by, 70–2
satires, 60, 80, 81, 87
 in the Civil War, 108, 113–16
 dramatic, 142
 of Dutch, 150
 on eve of Restoration, 135
 of parliamentarians, 113
 of royalists, 113–16, **114**
 of Scots, 113
 see also libels, Martin Marprelate
schools and schooling, 33–5
science, see natural philosophy, Royal Society
Scotland
 rebellions in, 138
Scott, Thomas, the Jacobean pamphleteer, 48, **49**, 77

scribal publication, see manuscript texts
Selden, John, 19, 20, 21
 in the Civil War, 103
Settle, Elkanah, 152
Seymour, Sir Francis, 17
Shakespeare, William, 33, 34, 50, 63, 70, 83, 86
 depicts honour values, 16
 Coriolanus, 16, 61
 Henry IV, Part I, 16, 47
 Henry VI, Part I, 73–4
 Henry VI, Part II, 27, 68, 74
 Henry VI, Part III, 16
 Julius Caesar, 16, 127
 Richard II, 16, 27, 69, 73, 75–6
 Richard III, 68
 Troilus and Cressida, 16
Shaftesbury, Earl of, see Cooper, Anthony Ashley
Sheldon, Gilbert, Archbishop of Canterbury, 138
Shrewsbury, Earl of, see Talbot, Gilbert
Sidney, Algernon, 129, 145, 153
Sidney, Mary, Countess of Pembroke, sister of Sir Philip, 63
Sidney, Sir Philip, 37, 39, 45, 58, 98
 comments on religious factions, 42
 funeral of, 63, **64**
 and honour values, 12, 13
 posthumous cult of, 62–3, 65
 publication of his literary works, 63
 warns against a French marriage for Elizabeth, 77
 Arcadia, 65
 Astrophil and Stella, 58
Sidney, Robert, second Earl of Leicester, 25, 36, 37, 97
Skelton, John, 43, 44
Skinner, Quentin, 5
Smith, Sir Thomas, 26
Society of Antiquaries, 23, 24
Somer, Paul Van, 91
Sommerville, J. P., 18, 19
Southampton, Earl of, see Wriothesley, Henry
Spain, attitudes towards, 48
Spelman, Henry, 47
Spenser, Edmund, 24, 44, 60, 63, 95
 The Faerie Queene, 50, 56, 58, 62
 Mother Hubberd's Tale, 59
Stanley, Thomas, 118
Star Chamber Court, 15, 107
Stoicism, 81, 82, 96

Stone, Lawrence, 32, 79, 100
Strong, Roy, 50
Stubbes, Philip, 77, 108
Suckling, Sir John, 82, **114**, 117, 118, 119
Sylvester, Joshua, 92

Tacitus, 39, 70–2, 77, 80, 86
Talbot, Gilbert, Earl of Shrewsbury, 92
Taylor, John, 111
teleology in cultural history 4–5
Thatham, John, *The Rump*, 135
theatres
　closed in 1642, 99
　in the 'exclusion crisis' (1679–82), 152
　during the Interregnum, 139–40
　at the Restoration, 135, 141–2
　see also history plays, *individual playwrights*
Thomason Tracts, 99
town (cultural concept), 79, 87–8
town halls, 54
travel abroad, 38, 90
trial narratives, 117–18, 146

Underdown, David, 102, 104–5
Union of England and Scotland, the, 25
universities, 34–6
　blamed by Hobbes for spreading republicanism, 127
　links to the court of, 37

Vaughan, Henry, 118
Valois, Francis de, Duke of Alencon and Anjou, 58
Vane, Henry, 127, 144
　A Healing Question, 131
Varro, 92
Vere, Edward, Earl of Oxford, 57
Villiers, George, first Duke of Buckingham, 26, 48, 77
　iconographical representations of, 78
　libels of, 82
　parliamentary attacks on, 17, 70, 77–8
　reputation of, 10
Villiers, George, second Duke of Buckingham, 137, 141, 142, 152

Virgil, 60, 96
　The Georgics, 92

Wales, 24
Waller, Edmund, 118, 139
Walsingham, Sir Francis, 37, 44, 63, 74
Walton, Isaac, 117, 122
war
　cultural attitudes towards, 12, 48, 84, 85, **114**, **115**
　Dutch (first) 130; (second) 148–9; (third) 150
　Spanish (1586–1604), 59, 65, 74
　stimulates publication of cultural propaganda, 59
wars of religion in Europe, 12, 42, 68
　printed accounts of, 44, 66
　English participation in, 45
Webster, John, 34
　The Famous History of Thomas Wyatt, 44
Wentworth, Thomas, Earl of Strafford, 82, 107
Weston, Sir Richard, 93
Whitgift, John, 45
Whiteway, William, 92
Wildman, John, 142
Wilmot, John, Earl of Rochester, 119, 142
Windebanke, Sir Francis, Secretary of State, 13
Wither, George, 65, 87
　Abuses Stript and Whipped, 82
Wolfe, John, 44
Wollaton Hall (Northamptonshire), **9**
Wotton, Henry, 35, 37, 38, 91
Wrightson, Keith, 104–5
Wriothesley, Henry, Earl of Southampton, 25
Wyatt, Thomas, 83
Wycliffe, John, 43

Xenophon, 92

Yates, Frances, 50

Zagorin, Perez, 79